PRAISE FOR
Cancer Culture

I have had the honor of witnessing the transformative potential of a cancer diagnosis in thousands of people...many view death as the end, a failure, and yet my experience reveals another reality—that cancer is an opportunity, a messenger, and can heal people even into their dying. Fewer, however, take that opportunity and turn it into something that will leave a legacy for generations to come. Jackie was one of those people. Though our paths intersected briefly, her words kept me clinging to her essence. Her writing and rawness and ability to tell a story, not an easy one, has been a healing balm, a life raft in the storm, and a call to action for so many...one thing is for sure, Jackie sucked the marrow out of every morsel of life, and death, and left us all hungry for more.

—**Dr. Nasha Winters**, ND, FABNO, Executive Director and Co-Founder, Metabolic Terrain Institute of Health

The world is a better place due to Dr. Jackie Acho's contributions. She was a loving daughter, impeccable wife, nurturing mother, brilliant entrepreneur, a valued friend, and an expert on the power of empathy...She accurately and concisely details her heroic will to survive the empathy gap in current cancer care propagated by corporatism and big pharma. The future of cancer care undoubtedly will be closer to Dr. Acho's vision than the current failing models. This, her second book, is an enlightening read for patients, nurses, doctors, cancer clinic navigators, hospital administrators, and anyone associated with big pharma.

—**Mark Dabagia**, MD, FACS

Cancer Culture: Fixing the Landscape by Infusing Empathy should be required reading for anyone beginning cancer treatment. Jackie's collection of essays demonstrates the current state of cancer care in the United States, illustrating the problems and solutions. As a father who lost a child who battled cancer, I highly recommend Chapter 34, "Dear Aspiring Oncologist," for any person entering the medical profession. Jackie's conclusions bring us back to one word: Empathy. Every action must start with this ideal to change the cancer care paradigm.

—**Brandt Butze**, Founder, Jacob Butze Memorial Foundation

To my family:
John, Sophie, and Grant LeMay
without whom I would not have lived life fully.

With love and respect for all those who have
lived with cancer and the people who love them.

Cancer Culture
Fixing the Landscape by **Infusing Empathy**

A Memoir by Jacqueline Acho, PhD

HOUNDSTOOTH
PRESS

Cancer Culture
Fixing the Landscape by Infusing Empathy

Copyright © by Jacqueline A. Acho Trust U/A/D January 7, 2023

Notice of Rights
All rights reserved. No part of this publication may be reproduced, distributed, or transmitted in any form or by any means, including photocopying, recording, or other electronic or mechanical methods, without the prior written permission of the publisher, except in the case of brief quotations embodied in critical reviews and certain other noncommercial uses permitted by copyright law. For permission requests, please contact: jlemay@bluepointcapital.com.

For information about special discounts for bulk purchases, please contact: jlemay@bluepointcapital.com.

Editor: Andrea C. Turner
Book Production: Giraffe, Inc.

Note from Author: I am not a medical doctor, and this book is not a substitute for medical advice. It is a companion for you or your loved one's cancer journey, unencumbered by the motivations of the cancer industrial complex, from the perspective of a scientist/businesswoman/entrepreneur/wife/mom/patient with empathy for those affected by cancer.

Also available by Jacqueline Acho, PhD
Currency of Empathy: The Secret to Thriving in Business and Life
For further information about the author: www.jackieacho.com

v

Table of Contents

Preface	1
Introduction: How This Book Came To Be	3

PART 1: Empathy as a Window Into Cancer

1. Why Empathy Matters	9
2. Diagnosis 　　Empathy in the Time of Coronavirus and Cancer	13

PART 2: If You Have Been Diagnosed With Cancer, You Are in Good Company and Empowered

3. We Are Losing the War on Cancer	17
4. Worn-Out Genes 　　Why So Many of Us Get Cancer	19
5. Warning Signs 　　How Empathy for Your Body Can Help You 　　Understand and Unwind the Cancering Process	23
6. A Recovering Chemist Learns to 　　Empathize With Chemotherapy	29
7. Better Living Through Chemistry?	33
8. Hair Today, Gone Tomorrow	37
9. Cancer and the Fire-Breathing Dragon	41
10. The Healing Power of Music Is Empathy	47
11. What Does Freedom Mean to You? 　　A Taste of Music Therapy	53
12. Nontoxic Cancer Therapies That Work	59
13. The Adventure of a Lifetime	65
14. Learning From Other Cultures 　　What I Could Get In Istanbul That I Could Not Get 　　at "World-Class" US Healthcare Institutions	69
15. Reasons to Be Positive in Istanbul	77

**PART 3: Harvesting the Profound Emotional and
Spiritual Lessons of Cancer To Grow Your Soul**

16. Resilience 83

17. Keeping Company With Cancer –
aka Entering Sacred Spaces 89

18. Eat
Food Is Medicine 97

19. Pray
Faith, Science, and Healing 101

20. Love
The Best Medicine 105

21. Lost and Found
Reflections on Two Years of a Cancer Journey 111

22. Appreciating the Simple Things 115

23. Divine Inspiration 121

24. Keeping the Faith…In Science 127

25. Dreams Instead of Resolutions 131

26. Treat Yourself Well 135

27. Chronic Illness
A Master Class in Appreciating the Gift of the Present 141

28. I Am Still That Girl…Integrating Our Lives 145

29. The Healing Power of Good Friends Is Empathy –
Getting Your Own Triggers Out of the Way 151

30. Home With a Capital H 155

PART 4: More Empathetic Cancer Care

31. Is It Empathetic To Treat
Cancer as a Chronic Condition? 161

32. Will Western Medicine Change and How? 167

33. If Only Cancer Science Were as Brave as Cancer Patients 173

34. Dear Aspiring Oncologist 181

35. Looking Cancer in the Face, We Find Hope 185

36. Choosing Life Over Fear 191

37. Working Towards Checkmate –
A More Empathetic and Strategic View
of the Cancer Long Game 197

38. The Rhythm of Home	201
39. We Shouldn't Have to Choose Between Living and a Life	205
40. Immunotherapy Is the Answer	209

PART 5: Finding Peace at the End of the Journey

41. I Am Done	213
42. The Biggest Trip	217

PART 6

Acknowledgments	223
Afterword	227
About the Author	234
Appendix One: Cancer Treatment Information and Resources	236
Appendix Two: Eulogies from Jackie's Memorial Service, January 7, 2023	241

Preface

The story of this book begins with a horrible day in our lives back in February 2020. My wife, Jackie Acho, had been through a series of unremarkable medical appointments after experiencing a very small amount of post-menopausal bleeding. On that day, we received the results of a blood test for a marker for ovarian cancer (a CA-125 test). The "normal" range for that test is below 30 and Jackie tested at 4,466. This despite virtually no symptoms. At the time, of course, we didn't fully comprehend the meaning of that result but knew we had a very difficult road ahead of us. Jackie was 51 at the time and our kids Sophie and Grant were 17 and 16, respectively—one a senior and the other a sophomore in high school.

This book is many things at once. It is a guide to avoiding cancer. It is a guide to managing side effects and thriving during cancer treatment. It is a guide to complementary treatments that can supplement and make traditional Western treatments more effective. It is guide to staying sane and alive and positive during the journey. It is a guide to facing the end of life with an open, positive frame of mind. It is a manifesto on rethinking cancer care to make it more effective and empathetic. It is a reframing of our life experience through observing our time here in the context of limits, both in terms of time and physical capabilities.

Jackie had a remarkable life and career before being diagnosed with high grade serous ovarian cancer. She had enjoyed success as a scientist, consultant, entrepreneur, writer, and speaker. We had always known she was a great communicator, but we were not prepared for the extraordinary insight, wisdom, and soul she conveyed while blogging about her cancer journey from the time of her diagnosis until her passing in December 2022. This book is a compendium of those writings and is presented in mostly chronological order, providing you the ability to travel the journey with her.

While she drew a particularly difficult cancer card, she made the most of her time. Many of the insights and ideas in this book can help others that want to prevent, live with, and treat cancer more effectively—as well as help those that need to support a loved one through a cancer journey. It provides an inside-out view for those who devote their professional time to the world of cancer—researchers, doctors, health care administrators, and investors. Even those untouched by cancer today might want to read this remarkable story of a woman who found deep meaning in her journey and used that journey to teach, inspire and try to rethink the world of cancer care.

In the acknowledgments, Jackie has shared her deep gratitude for the amazing support she, and our family, received during her cancer journey. Sophie, Grant and I also want to thank you from the bottom of our hearts. Family, friends, and colleagues provided a powerful, loving, thoughtful counterweight to all the sadness, grief, and pain that this journey entailed. They were all the good in the world on those days when all we could see was the bad—allowing us to know we were cared for and loved in the moments we needed it most. We can never thank you enough.

John, Sophie, and Grant LeMay

INTRODUCTION • SEPTEMBER 2022

How This Book Came To Be

I *was supposed to die years ago, but I did not.* I never wanted to write a book like this. I wish I didn't have the experience. I wish it weren't needed. But it is.

I don't have "cancer genes." I have lived a "very healthy lifestyle," including eating clean, healthy, homemade food (at least as an adult), swimming, running, lifting weights, and becoming a certified yoga teacher at the age of 49. I was a happy wife, mom, and entrepreneur with work I loved, a peaceful home, and supportive community. I had just published a book: *Currency of Empathy—The Secret to Thriving in Business and Life*, and loved talking about it with people whether in large gatherings or just one-on-one. From a PhD in Chemistry at MIT, to partnership in the global management consulting firm of McKinsey, to successfully running my own consulting business while raising kids, I worked hard and was starting to reap the rewards of all of that experience. I had the powerfully good but elusive feeling that my work was making the world a better place. Our daughter was getting ready to go to college. Our son was living his best life in high school. My beloved husband of more than 20 years and I were looking forward to the freedom and travel that empty nesting and eventual "retirement" might bring, even as we knew we would miss all the day-to-day bustle of family life. I was looking forward to so much.

I struggled with some health issues, but looked healthy from the outside. After our daughter started suffering from hemiplegic migraines, we cleaned up our home, food, and water to eliminate toxins and other harmful substances, benefiting the whole family. Once she was well (thank goodness), I turned my attention to my own body, resolving some mold toxicity and its resulting problems (e.g., hives) as well as difficult menopausal symptoms. I had managed through some unusual work stress, but was on the other side of it. Emotionally and physically, things were clicking into place. Unfortunately, those triggers had already taken their toll.

In February 2020, I had just returned from a luncheon featuring a discussion of my book when I noticed the slightest bit of post-menopausal bleeding. It was the kind of thing you might ignore. I have a fabulous functional doctor who happens to also be trained as an OB/GYN and she knew better. Just in case, we tested my CA125, the marker for ovarian cancer. It came back high (4,466, on a scale of 1–30), but there are many false positives with this marker. She recommended an intravaginal ultrasound. Nothing too out of the ordinary. But, just in case, I went to see a gynecological oncologist who did a more sensitive CT scan as well as a biopsy. The results were definitive. High-grade serous carcinoma, ovarian cancer. Most often, as is true in my case, this cancer is caught late. Doctors do not routinely measure CA125, and most women are diagnosed at stage 3 or 4. The long-term survival rate is approximately 20%. We were devastated, to say the least.

Getting diagnosed with cancer is a surreal experience, especially when it's nothing that entered your consciousness prior to that moment. This can't be real. They must be wrong. How did this happen? What will become of our kids? They were teenagers, which is not young, but not old enough to lose a parent. What about the dreams my husband and I had for our future? One of the doctors we consulted asked, "I don't want to presume but is he your friend, boyfriend, or husband?" I replied, "Yes, all of that." We weren't finished living, together.

I hadn't taken so much as an aspirin in 10 years, focusing on natural and functional healing. I was working hard to avoid being one of those older people who end up going from doctor to doctor, taking pill after pill, only to slowly but surely decline. So you can imagine how surreal it was to accept invasive surgery (optimal debulking), removing everything in my abdomen touched by cancer (reproductive organs, omentum, and appendix), as well as undergoing chemotherapy.

Our lab at MIT had done research on the mechanism of cisplatin, one of the oldest chemotherapeutic agents, so I already knew too much about what chemo does to a human body. I tried hard to get out of these harsh treatments, but in the end I had to accept them. There is precious little evidence that anyone can survive high-grade serous carcinoma without surgery and chemo. And we did all of this in the midst of a global pandemic. Thus, I walked into chemo alone.

Jacqueline Acho, PhD

The good side of going into chemo alone is that I didn't have to worry about anyone worrying about me. I could just rest in the knowledge that, although I hated it, I was doing the best I could.

That didn't mean I didn't try like hell to augment these harsh treatments with natural supports. And it worked pretty well. A rock star nutritionist helped me feel uncommonly well, especially throughout chemo. I looked and felt relatively healthy, continued cooking and eating, running (slowly but surely), practicing and even teaching yoga occasionally, parenting, and working. In short, life went on. The fact that I started the process "so healthy" probably benefited my body as well. I finished the onslaught with none of the usual side effects (e.g., neuropathy, tinnitus, rashes). But, the treatment didn't really work. My cancer marker remained outside of normal (52, on the scale of 1–30), although my scans were clear. Treating a number with chemo didn't make sense to even the Western doctors, so we began our journey in naturopathic cancer care. It's a good thing my husband and I love to learn because there was much to learn.

Natural therapies bought me some more time, from May 2021 through the end of our son's soccer season (October 2021). He was a high school senior, co-captain, and loved the game, so that was meaningful. We were in the stands, rain or shine, huddled together, cheering him on. What did I do to treat what was left of the cancer? A lot. To be honest, it was exhausting. Working with a naturopathic doctor in the network of Nasha Winters, ND, I focused on a clean and plant-strong ketogenic diet, mistletoe and helleborus injections, hyperbaric oxygen therapy (HBOT), a novel hyperthermia treatment that heats and filters the blood, coffee enemas, supplements, intermittent fasting, rectal ozone, acupuncture, emotional support therapies (especially EMDR—eye movement desensitization and reprocessing—for recovering from trauma) and more.

This was all while continuing with yoga, running, weight lifting, parenting, and working. I was well enough to give a special talk outdoors at the Chautauqua Institution Amphitheater in August 2021, despite the fact that the pandemic morphed and lingered. We saw signs that things were working in my "terrain marker" measurements. Until they weren't. Despite all of that effort, spots returned on my scans. Pain emerged. Eating and digesting became a struggle. I lost too much weight, something in the cancer world known as cachexia. Fluid collected in my abdomen.

What could be done? Nothing, according to my traditional oncologist. He assigned me to hospice and gave me three months to live. At that rate, I wouldn't make it to our son's 18th birthday. I would die during his senior year. It was time to seek other options.

Talking to our kids about our options was another discerning time in this journey of profound moments with them. At that point, my options were down to either trying to die peacefully or seeking integrative cancer care across the globe in Istanbul, Turkey.

There are a couple of other centers in the US, but 1. we had a friend with stage 4 metastatic breast cancer who achieved remission in Istanbul, and 2. their philosophies (e.g., ketogenic diet, giving antioxidants, HBOT and hyperthermia along with targeted, fractionated insulin potentiated chemo) aligned with what we thought would give me the best chance at living. Both of our kids supported seeking treatment abroad. Keep in mind that even though we "had one of the best hospitals in the country" nearby, they had given up on me. There was no life for me, staying there. I didn't want to go so far away, but it was better than being dead. As our son put it, "My mom dying now is not part of my story." Within a couple of weeks, my husband and I were on a plane to Istanbul, me wheelchair-bound for much of the journey by then. It's amazing how quickly cancer and its treatments can take a toll on a human body that's been lovingly cared for, over decades.

In Istanbul, I came back to life. My family heritage can be traced to northern Iraq on my father's side, so in a way, it even felt like coming home. Much more on that in the chapters ahead.

This book is not a prescription for what you should do if you or a loved one is diagnosed with cancer. There are lots of books like that, and I've read most of them! That too, is exhausting, and there is a lot of conflicting advice and crazy, miraculous anecdotes that most of us dream about but can't seem to achieve. The only one who can determine your path is you—the patient—really. Even the doctors don't know, especially for difficult cancers.

This book is a view into the cancer journey focusing through the lens of empathy. It's been part of my professional focus for years and what I have to offer. The benefits are many, because empathy clarifies so much, particularly combined with my expertise in science and business and my husband's breadth and depth of research.

What I hope this book offers you is a compass, something to bring some calm to the storm of cancer and keep you connected to your true north. Your best chance at a vibrant life before/during/after a cancer diagnosis depends on that, more than any particular surgery, medicine, diet, supplement, or alternative therapy. How you cobble together your plan is your business, your right, and your best shot. Empathy can help steady your ship as you move through these relatively uncharted waters. *The cancer journey is an invitation to see your empathy as a superpower*—a strength that will get you through while the world is still in flux, with cancer treatments still a toxic assault on the human body.

I hope chemo becomes obsolete. I hope cancer prevention becomes more prevalent than cancer treatment. I hope there is no need for a book like this someday, but I have no illusions it will happen in my lifetime. So, here you go. Although it's focused on one of the worst diseases that strike our bodies—cancer—these ideas apply to any chronic disease that Western medicine names but does not cure.

I hope you and your loved ones find some clarity and peace in these pages. I know I did, writing them. ◉

Part 1
Empathy as a Window Into Cancer

CHAPTERS
1. Why Empathy Matters 9

2. Diagnosis
   Empathy in the Time of Coronavirus and Cancer 13

CHAPTER ONE • OCTOBER 5, 2022

Why Empathy Matters

What is empathy? The ability to understand the feelings of another *and* have an appropriate emotional response. That last part is really important and often omitted. To sit with someone in their pain, joy, etc. (empathy is not just about suffering!) requires that we recognize and move beyond our own emotional triggers. If not, we are just taking our own trip down memory lane or reacting based on how that person's emotions affect us, which is very common. To truly sit with someone in their truth, whatever it may be, is a gift like few others. Empathy is a human superpower.

Empathy is in short supply because we have personal and systematic barriers to practicing it—to developing our empathy muscles. Let's start in early childhood because that's the time when our empathy circuits are growing most quickly, given the right environment and attention. We first learn empathy affectively or emotionally, in body-to-body communication before we have words. If we are given what we need when we need it as babies (food, warmth, affection, etc.), empathy flows freely and develops. We grow our capacity for empathy in loving relationships. What gets in the way is lack of time, especially in the US, where we rank last in parental leave among the developed world and near the bottom in work/life balance. The second major chance most people have to remember empathy is as a parent because empathy is a two-way street. Of course, you don't have to parent to become empathetic, but hands-on caring is one of the best ways to practice. The other side of empathy is cognitive or

imaginative. Cognitive empathy develops later, as we have words to describe and connect to the situations others face. Again, this takes time, and we learn via modeling. Most people do not listen simply and sit with others. They skip to offering solutions or telling their own stories. None of that is empathetic. Work environments that force competition rather than collaboration exacerbate empathy deficits, and the political divides in recent years have been very emotionally triggering for people, which also gets in the way of empathy.

So many human-made problems stem from our empathy deficits, individually and societally. Individually, we are all built for connection. Lack of the opportunity to give and receive empathy creates a void that is unnatural and capable of contributing to loneliness, depression, anxiety, and more. Severe lack of empathy leaves people capable of great harm to others, physically and emotionally. Interestingly, the synergy between cognitive and affective empathy matters. Psychopaths have excellent cognitive empathy but lack the ability to feel—the affective or emotional piece—leaving them capable of manipulation and atrocities. Many of our inhumane policies and business practices stem from a lack of empathy for people, especially those most vulnerable. Would we really produce Pepsi and Jacked Doritos and market them to kids if we cared about their health? Political divides are made deeper by lack of empathy because judgment replaces curiosity, assumptions overwhelm conversations, and true communication stops. This dynamic affects democracy negatively overall because debate and dialogue lead to some of our best answers. |Many of our biggest worries about the future, such as climate change and the concurrent increase in environmental disasters, as well as human-made disasters like war, can be seen as a lack of empathy for others, future generations, and the planet.

We should be saving the earth for everyone rather than building spaceships for a rich few to escape.

We can rebuild our capacity for empathy in the here and now—both as individuals and across society at large. We need to change the way we live and work in order to steward empathy—our vital currency. The first step is to recognize empathy's economic value. It's a force driving elusive inclusion and organic innovation, which require trust, open communication, and mutual understanding. We've focused exclusively on competition and short-term profits for too long, at great human cost. Gallup has told us for years that approximately 65–70% of people are disengaged at work. We have lost their hearts and minds. To grow empathy at work, people need meaning, a chance to grow, and the ability to live whole lives. It's simple but not easy because we have to change how we've worked for a very long time. Most of the changes are about working differently and don't cost much. We don't need "empathy training" so much as a chance to live whole lives and practice affective empathy at work and at home. A great start would be parental leave on par with the developed world and work/life balance that acknowledges we are humans rather than cogs in a machine! Empathy is the secret sauce of great leaders; we would do better to give them time to practice hands-on caring on their path to leadership than sending them to Harvard for an MBA. Leaders would make decisions differently, affecting so many others. If we valued time for caring, understood how to mitigate our own emotional triggers, and were able to practice unencumbered empathy as individuals, our daily interactions and decisions would be much more generative, especially with our young children, when their capacity for developing empathy is enormous. We don't so much learn empathy as we mirror and absorb it. Empathy begets empathy. It's as contagious as a yawn.

One of the best examples of increasing empathy where it matters is the Cleveland Police. Detective Chris Gibbons in the Cleveland Division of Police (CDP) Employee Assistance Unit saw my 2014 TEDx talk, "A Good Day's Work Requires Empathy," and called me. He said, "I'm with the Cleveland Police, and I think we have a problem with empathy. Can you help us?" I just about dropped the phone! Instead, we got to work. Our focus was both individual and systemic. We supported the development of individual empathy through practices (e.g., yoga, mindfulness, meditation, equine therapy) that mitigate the emotional triggers police face every day. We also worked on systemic changes. Most organizations sap empathy. It's more immediately fatal when employees carry guns. We did an employee survey and engaged a CDP innovation team to make changes that helped the police recover the meaning they found in their jobs, grow as individuals and teams, and be whole at work. It was simple but not easy. Remarkably, because police led the work, the union was on board.

So was the Chief. A successful pilot in the most dangerous district proved the model, and we expanded from there.

It's working. In just two years, we saw a 45% reduction in citizen complaints, 29% reduction in use of force, and more than half of the transfer requests across the entire city were into the district where we started—the most violent one in the city. Going to work there is dangerous, so that kind of influx was unprecedented. Across the same two-year period, use of force was reduced by 55% for the police officers who participated in yoga/mindfulness/meditation programs. These kinds of changes work and create the results that matter in any organization, including the police.

The potential for the "currency of empathy" is unlimited in its ability to help resolve the modern issues of our day, like polarization, because empathy compounds. Empathy solves polarization every day in big and small ways. I see examples in real life and virtually, whether we are connecting to the story of mothers and children fleeing Ukraine or just reconnecting with an old friend on social media. One caveat—we connect more through our vulnerabilities and honesty rather than perfect pictures on Facebook.

Ovarian cancer has been a profound window into empathy, how it flows and how triggers get in the way. Cancer is brutal, requiring more strength than I imagined. I've written extensively about the lack of empathy in cancer research and medicine, holding back true cures and prevention. I earned my PhD working in a lab that focused on cancer drugs. I know this truth all too well, from inside and out, both systemically and personally. Yet I've experienced a great flow of empathy from family and friends. My own vulnerability has opened up new channels of honesty and enabled me to humbly accept help. I've also seen how fear about my situation and how it might affect someone else triggers a more narcissistic response. People often tell cancer patients to "be brave, strong, and positive!" That kind of advice is a way of separating yourself from the fear our situation triggers. What we really need is people who are just willing to be with us in what is.

Empathy is our secret sauce as human beings. It's what kept us alive as babies and what has underpinned our best innovations and true, inclusive progress. Stewarding this currency individually, organizationally, and societally is required for us to flourish. We've tried the other way—stewarding currency and economics without empathy and humanity—for long enough to see it's not working. It's past time to focus on empathy. We can and should demand it. Looking at our kids, I'm hopeful. ◉

CHAPTER TWO • APRIL 13, 2020

Diagnosis
Empathy in the Time of Coronavirus and Cancer

I've had a front-row seat to empathy these days, and not only in the context of a global pandemic.

On February 20, 2020, I was diagnosed with ovarian cancer. On March 2, of that year, I had extensive surgery. By the time I came home from the hospital, the country had begun going into Covid-related lockdown. Travel became impossible. Non-essential services, like cold caps to help preserve hair during chemotherapy, were discontinued. Visitors were not allowed in hospitals. On March 30, I walked into chemo completely alone. You might think this experience would breed lots of fear, and its companion, anger. It did, at first.

Then came the outpouring of love.

Deeply empathic and varied responses from family, friends, neighbors, colleagues—even strangers who are friends now—were swift and overwhelming. Not just for me, but for my husband and children. How do people help someone who is fighting a serious illness in the middle of a global pandemic?

Like this:
- Friends and family who already knew too much about ovarian and other cancers understood the journey I was about to take. They gently but swiftly guided me in big and small ways...

    - Helping discern a team of doctors and alternative healers.

- Choosing super-soft cozy nightgowns that would hug me in the difficult weeks after surgery...cute hats, scarves, and halo wigs that helped me adjust to losing my hair.

- Sharing their survival stories, as well as empathizing with the hard parts.

- Healthy broths and fresh-pressed juices arrived just in time to sustain me when eating really wasn't an option.

- Healthy food arrived after that and before lockdown, and people were so careful to ensure that it was clean, safe, and delicious. They fed me. They fed my family. We don't all eat the same food; this is like a "Chopped" challenge! So many winners.

- Beautiful flowers. So many.

- Cards—heartfelt and touching. And then there are friends who send funny cards because laughter is great medicine. I can still laugh. I have a stack of homemade cards with carefully curated sayings. I shuffle through them to get new inspiration.

- Shawls and blankets arrived because people have heard their friends talk about how cold they get when they receive chemo. So you see, I was not actually alone as I walked into chemo. I was enveloped in virtual embraces.

- Cookbooks! Does anyone else out there read them for fun? My friends know I do.

- Books! About the evolution of the soul, radical remission, and a woman who delivers books throughout the mountains of Kentucky (because distraction is good too).

- Meditation/positive visualization tips, tricks, and apps. I'm a certified yoga teacher who has tried in earnest to meditate through the years. Serious illness has a way of solidifying resolution.

- Open-minded, curious doctor friends who check in to help me safely navigate the world of Western medicine, while finding the best of what alternative medicine has to offer.

- Calls, texts, virtual healing sessions...people have offered everything they could with patience, understanding, and unusual talent.

- One generous neighbor even shared her ration of toilet paper!

These are just some of the ways I have felt held, even when I can't be hugged because my diagnosis and treatments make me immune compromised.

The epicenter of empathy now is the same as always: here at home. This pandemic is awful in so many ways, especially for people who live in economic insecurity or in homes that are not peaceful or functional. In some ways though, we are benefitting from the fact that empathy is a contact sport.

Going through a major illness is a strangely intimate experience for a couple. My husband of 20 years has been a rock and a soft landing place all at the same time. Our kids have turned the tables and are cooking healthy, yummy food. They provide me with all the inspiration I need to stick around into old age. I'm grateful for this time we have together as a family—especially with young adults, who would rather be with friends but are enjoying playing euchre, doing puzzles, watching movies, and sitting by the fire with Mom and Dad anyway.

While I don't recommend anyone paying such a high price for this front-row seat, I am watching a show of humanity that is leaving me richer and better than I was before. I have seen the way friends have been transformed by their own cancer journeys. Too many of us share this experience. For now, I'm swimming in currents of empathy, and the water is beautiful. ●

Part 2

If You Have Been Diagnosed With Cancer, You Are in Good Company and Empowered

CHAPTERS

3. We Are Losing the War on Cancer	17
4. Worn-Out Genes Why So Many of Us Get Cancer	19
5. Warning Signs How Empathy for Your Body Can Help You Understand and Unwind the Cancering Process	23
6. A Recovering Chemist Learns to Empathize With Chemotherapy	29
7. Better Living Through Chemistry?	33
8. Hair Today, Gone Tomorrow	37
9. Cancer and the Fire-Breathing Dragon	41
10. The Healing Power of Music Is Empathy	47
11. What Does Freedom Mean to You? A Taste of Music Therapy	53
12. Nontoxic Cancer Therapies That Work	59
13. The Adventure of a Lifetime	65
14. Learning From Other Cultures What I Could Get In Istanbul That I Could Not Get at "World-Class" US Healthcare Institutions	69
15. Reasons to Be Positive in Istanbul	77

CHAPTER THREE • JUNE 5, 2021

We Are Losing the War on Cancer

Many others have written on this subject, so I will not belabor the point. For those of you new to this realization, here is what you need to know.

Cancer is a big, profitable business without much progress on cures
In 2020, total spending for oncology worldwide was $167 billion (global research+treatment). It's an enormous business with growing markets, unfortunately. Of that, $6.1 billion went to research funding through the US National Cancer Institute alone.

Despite this spending, the rise in cancer and cancer-related deaths continues to be steep. "In 2022, there will be an estimated 1.9 million new cancer cases diagnosed and 609,360 cancer deaths in the United States." Source: American Cancer Society. *Cancer Facts & Figures 2022*. Atlanta: American Cancer Society; 2022.

Why the "Moonshot" on Cancer is not working
We first declared a "war on cancer" in 1971. It has been more than 50 years. The United States upped the ante with the "Cancer Moonshot" initiative in 2016, with Congress authorizing $1.8 billion in funding over seven years. We are closing in on that time frame without significant progress in avoiding cancer and cancer-related deaths.

You know what's interesting to contemplate? *How quickly we developed a vaccine for Covid, which is an opposite situation to cancer in a couple of ways:* the Covid disease pandemic had a big economic downside (shutting down economies, high cost to governments) but the market for the jab was **huge** and growing fast. So, of course, we mobilized quickly and got to an answer.

Cancer is different: the diseases are not (yet) recognized as an economic cost (most of us continue to work while being treated, and it's not infectious so it doesn't shut down economies the way Covid did) and the research and treatments are **huge** and growing market opportunities. Chemotherapy is a big business as is cancer research. A lot of people depend on the continuation of the disease for their livelihoods. None of this has anything to do with "putting the patient first" or even "doing no harm."

Many people taking chemotherapy end up suffering from a variety of issues not listed in the oncologist's "accounting books," so to speak, such as a cousin who now needs heart surgery to deal with an issue directly caused by her treatment for breast cancer 15 years ago (a known side effect).

As a cancer patient, I've been a tremendous profit center for two years, both in "gold standard of care" (not golden at all for me) and alternative treatments (out of pocket expenses which insurance does not cover, most likely for the rest of my life). There has been a lot of GDP flowing through my body (hundreds of thousands of dollars) which didn't happen before I had cancer. That's pretty egregious, no matter who is paying.

Unfortunately, the research spending is often not focused on the most powerful levers. It is generally drawn to patentable solutions that typically offer very incremental improvements. The technologies may be part of the solution, but suffer from a lack of holistic perspective.

Another part of the problem is that the paradigm of "cancer genes" is not working, yet we have not moved on. Ninety-five percent of people who get cancer these days, including me, do not have the genes identified in the Human Genome Project as "cancer genes," yet this is driving a lot of the research. It is good news for the 5% of people with cancer-gene driven mutations, but leaves many patients without effective treatments.

Certainly some of us are luckier than others, gene-wise, but it has more to do with our ability to weather a toxic modern world. Our dirty genes and immune systems get overwhelmed. (See Chapter 4). We are not mutants. We are canaries in the coalmine. What we do to the planet and put in and on our bodies has much more to do with the rise in cancer than the identified "cancer genes." The problem with this realization is that it's much harder to patent and profit from the solutions. In this way, curing cancer is less of a scientific challenge and more of an economic and moral challenge than we have considered. ◉

CHAPTER FOUR • MAY 28, 2021

 Worn-Out Genes
Why So Many of Us Get Cancer

We wonder why cancer is a raging epidemic. It's not because of "cancer genes" or living longer. Cancer is the leading cause of death world-wide because our bodies are worn out.

I've learned this the hard way, inside-out, fighting ovarian cancer without any of the approximately 650 known cancer genes around which Western medical treatments are designed. My story is not unusual. Amazingly, 90–95% of people with cancer do not have identified, inherited cancer genes, and many cancers are striking younger people than ever before. So, what's going on? How can we fight if we don't understand what we are fighting?

Here's what I've learned, looking at the science differently.

The amazing thing about the Human Genome Project is our ability to overlay our own human blueprint on average human DNA. In so doing, we see where and how our DNA base pairs (the two parts which make up each rung of the DNA ladder) vary from "normal." Differences are not all bad, of course. Variety is the spice of life, and some of these variants confer characteristics that serve us well. Certain flavors of intelligence. Humor. Even empathy! Yes, there is a gene associated with empathy (OXTR rs53576), and yes, I have a double variant there (GG). There we have it.

But functional genomic analysis shows that my body is also clearly vulnerable in three ways:

1. Detoxing molds and the mycotoxins they release
2. Detoxing heavy metals
3. Clearing environmental toxins and pharmaceutical metabolites

I was not surprised; the results were validating. Also, these are predispositions, not inevitabilities. As they say, genetics loads the gun; the environment pulls the trigger. If I lived in a Blue Zone, where many people live to be 100 without disease, would I have gotten cancer? Probably not. Knowing as much as I did for the last several years, I worked to clear a lifetime (conception to age 45) of accumulated toxins from my body. I didn't have extraordinary exposure. Just that of a normal, modern American. I was functional, but I didn't always feel well. I was getting to healthy…just not fast enough. I had learned a lot about how to protect our family from physical and emotional toxicity…just not in time to avoid a cancer journey myself. The best thing I can do now is to make some meaning out of it all. So, here goes…

First of all, even if your body can clear molds/metals/toxins better than mine, do we think human bodies should be processing all that s**t?! That would be a big, "Hell No!" At the very least, fighting toxins takes time and energy away from all the work our bodies need to do to thrive in the natural world. Even the trillions (seriously, they outnumber our own cells) of microbes who hitch a synergistic ride with us are choking on our trash. The good ones at least. The more opportunistic microbes thrive, leaving us unable to digest nutritious food without discomfort, bloating, and malabsorption. Diets consisting of Low FODMAP, Paleo, and Gluten-free are just some of the many ways we work around our worn-out bodies now.

Worn-out jeans are comfortable. Worn-out genes are not.

Heavy metal exposure exacerbates toxicity from molds, so mold is more anchored in us than before and benefits from us being surrounded by artificially sealed and wet environments in many homes and buildings. If we took a longer, broader view of human health, we'd design differently. At least we can breathe easily outside, right? Well, not when the air quality shows high levels of pollution, including smaller particulate matter (PM2.5). These inhalable particles from soot and industrial activities can pass into the bloodstream, entering multiple organs including the skin. The pandemic may be waning, but hang onto those N95 masks. For people like me, it pays to actively avoid toxins. Another seemingly innocuous example is pharmaceuticals which are supposed to heal us, but their toxic metabolites linger and do more damage than good in bodies like mine. This would be why the list of side-effects in commercials has long been a subject of parody. I'm sure you could use some comic relief at this point, so check out the skit of comedian Dana Carvey eavesdropping at the pharmacy.

What if other people are vulnerable in similar ways? The body is beautifully designed to address toxins and disease but our environment/diet/stress load can overwhelm that amazing system and open the door to diseases, including but not limited to cancers. The key is managing all those loads on our bodies rather than addressing them after the fact with chemicals and surgeries that can further damage our natural systems. The good news is everyone can take active, incremental steps to improve the health of our bodies, our families, our communities, and future generations.

We should be fighting against toxicity rather than compounding the problem. Western medicine aims to treat our conditions with yet more (patentable and profitable) chemicals our bodies aren't designed to process.

> *Doesn't this feel like the point in the horror movie where the young kids head out into the woods while we hear the chainsaw starting up?*

To me, it does. Chemo is the king of poisonous toxins, yet it was the "best option" and "urgently needed" when I was diagnosed with ovarian cancer. Is it any wonder that mold and bad microbes had a heyday when I finished, like most people with low white blood counts? Knowing all this empowers me to recover, heal, and protect my body going forward. What if I didn't know? What does oncology have for us? Toxic scans. Take home drugs. "Maintenance chemo." Sadly, that's a thing. How can a body get ahead of that onslaught? It's hard to imagine. Is it highly profitable for the cancer industrial complex? You betcha.

There is nothing empathetic about any of this. Take it from me. I'm an empathy expert. I also have scientific training, limitless curiosity, and now, unfortunately, too much personal experience in the oncological belly of the beast of the Western medical system.

How will this degenerative situation change? I'm not holding my breath for people who have made their careers in Western medicine, pharma, and chemical companies to wake up. That would be nice, but that will also be the very last thing to happen. People's livelihoods, mortgages...and most importantly, their **identities** are wrapped up in that system.

But we are not powerless. We can wake up. We, the patients. We, the consumers of healthcare. We, our bodies' longest allies and closest friends. When we do look around with eyes wide-open, we find there are alternative ways to heal our bodies. We find there are discerning and experienced people who can help us understand and defend ourselves against human-made toxins. We can learn how to buttress our immune systems rather than destroy them.

We can take small incremental steps to proactively protect our bodies from physical and emotional toxicity by:

- Meditating
- Drinking clean water
- Cooking at home with whole foods
- Buying organic and unprocessed food whenever possible
- Being mindful about protecting ourselves from emotional toxicity
- Clearing your home environment of molds and other toxins
- Patronizing restaurants with high quality, noninflammatory ingredients when eating out

More broadly, we can join like-minded others to support cleaning up the mess in our food system, water, environment, and buildings so that we fulfill our responsibility to leave the world better than we found it, rather than count on the next generation to make these changes. More and more people are waking up to these issues and doing something about them. To support your own health, you may need help. Look for people who work with the body's natural systems across a range of issues, not individuals who may have healed themselves (temporarily) with one dogma or another. Once you see what's going on, there is a lot you can do at the personal and societal levels. It feels good to do that work because it's aligned with the design of our bodies and the natural world. It's empathetic.

The more we move in the right direction, the more the broken elements of the Western medical system will be left to change...or die of their own weight.

Better them than us.

That would be real progress. ●

CHAPTER FIVE • JUNE 30, 2020

Warning Signs
How Empathy For Your Body Can Help You Understand and Unwind the Cancering Process

My body knows why I have ovarian cancer. I'm finally listening, so now I do too. I didn't get the answers from Western medicine, functional medicine, or even the scores of holistic healers who have shared wisdom through the years. I got the answers from empathizing with my body, which should be the most normal thing in the world. It's not. Our culture and medical practices too often dissociate us from our embodied experience. In doing so, they sometimes hinder us from healing. Reconnecting with my body has been an unexpected blessing of this cancer journey.

> *How are you today?* "*I am well in all the ways that really matter.*"
> *— Akua (aka Mary Alice) Saunders MEd, MSN, CNS*

A heartbreaking and heartwarming thing about being open with a cancer diagnosis is the countless people who write/call/text to share their stories. It's always inspiring but also sad to know I'm not alone. Not by a long shot. Cancer remains an epidemic, despite so much time and money spent on research. In reproductive cancers especially, people I've known for years have only recently revealed their heroic journeys. I understand why. We don't want to be written off, which is a strong temptation in a culture that struggles so mightily with mortality. We don't want you to see us as less of a woman or a man. We're not. We're still here, with as much to say as ever. More, even. I don't know anyone who has walked the cancer journey or empathetically accompanied a loved one with the diagnosis who isn't forever changed. As my fierce

23

two-time cancer-beating cousin Rhonda has said, "It's a cool club." The coolest club you never want to join.

When I was first diagnosed, I wondered, "Why me?" I'm only human. People who know me were shocked too because I diligently work at practicing a healthy lifestyle. I woke up to environmental toxicity years ago and cleaned up our family act. I cook and eat clean and thoughtfully. I teach yoga for goodness sake! In people's responses, I also detected a combination of faint worry (if you, then me?) and unspoken hope that what happened to me was the result of a difference that would be reassuringly unique. Do I have one of the typical cancer-causing genetic mutations? No. But, it's ok.

"Why me?" turned into "Why not me?!"

I have an unusual and powerful arsenal of tools and experiences. Although nobody handed over the Holy Grail, there were a lot of puzzle pieces to pick up and put together. I've been practicing that kind of work for decades, and this is the project of a lifetime for two strategists like my husband and me. It's amazing what you can sort out these days with a headful of science, a ton of experience in healing, great support, and the wisdom of online crowds, accessible as never before. Still, none of this could happen without the unusual blessing of feeling well most of the time *even in chemotherapy*. Another blessing these days is unfettered access to intuition and discernment, fueled by love, encouragement, virtual healing treatments...and so many prayers. There is no way to repay it all, but maybe this is something. Maybe what I'm learning could help someone, somewhere...so here goes.

I got cancer because my immune system failed.

My immune system was distracted off and on for approximately six years and then acutely challenged prior to my cancer diagnosis. Random cancer cells grew unchecked. Here's the logic:

1. **My body struggled with environmental toxins** like heavy metals, other chemicals, and molds that don't belong in a human body. It's a common modern challenge, and I was making good progress.

2. **Combining environmental triggers with unusual stress puts the immune system on high alert.** That's a double whammy. In hindsight, I can see that combination initiated Mast Cell Activation Syndrome (MCAS). MCAS is a condition in which our mast cells are overactive, beyond what's helpful for our immune system but instead leads to a variety of uncomfortable allergy symptoms (e.g., hives, swelling, itching, respiratory difficulty, brain fog, and pain).

3. **"Are Mast Cells Masters in Cancer?"** My body says yes! Maybe not all the time, but sometimes. Although there isn't much published yet in the medical literature, an article in "Frontiers in Immunology" from 2017 was prophetic, connecting cancer to a failure of the immune system. Medicine too often operates in silos, but the oncologists and immunologists should work together.

I have data on my own body through the years to support all of this logic. I reviewed countless scientific articles, putting my chemistry PhD to good use once again. If anyone, including me, at any time in the months prior to my diagnosis had understood all of this, I would not have cancer now. I know it. My body has told me so. How?

I felt better after chemotherapy than I did before I was diagnosed. Oh, not always. Chemo is brutal on the human body. However, in the low moments...when my husband holds me physically and emotionally without words...answers slip through the haze. It's helpful that my personal adaptation to stress is to solve problems. After the side effects were under control, I was thankful for the life-saving growth factor drugs (Neupogen and Neulasta) that are typically required to jack up white blood cell counts to protect chemo patients from infections. And yes, it's an especially good idea to use them in the middle of a pandemic that has ended socially before it's physically over. But the side effects? In my case, a constant headache. Hives and itching all over. Bone pain. Waking up every two hours at night. The scariest one? Brain fog. Better hurry with that Googling!!!!!

Then, it happened. The pieces fell into place because the most revealing thing about this new discomfort was that it was *familiar*. For years, rather than empathize with my body, I carried on. Sometimes, I numbed, but mostly, I just carried on. Environmental toxins? Not such a big deal; we don't have cancer in our family (yet). Couldn't sleep? Get up early and use that time to get work done. Increasing food sensitivities? Use all that creativity to cook around them. Dealing with emotional toxicity that made my stomach tight? Do what it takes to finish the job because "this too shall pass." Meanwhile, my immune system went on high alert. You can only live there for so long before your body really screams to get your attention.

Immune dysfunction manifests differently for different people, but the hives were particularly familiar to me. Naturopath Beth O'Hara lays out MCAS basics clearly, generously, and virtually, because there are more people suffering than she can personally help. If any of this applies to you, please don't worry. MCAS does not ever have to tilt into cancer. There's a lot of comfort in knowing that this may be one more way cancer won't seem as if it comes out of nowhere, not to mention how well a healthy immune system defends us naturally during pandemics. There is so much you can do now that doesn't cost a thing. Best of all, if any of these mysterious symptoms apply to you, it's possible to feel better.

To look into MCAS and healing, start here:

1. Read this article, "What Is MCAS? Mast Cell Activation Syndrome Basics" by Beth O'Hara, in "Functional Naturopath:" https://mastcell360.com/what-is-mcas/

2. Read "Mast Cell Activation Syndrome 101: The Beginner's Guide to Healing." Get the free report online. Check out the common stress triggers listed (#1 is important). https://mastcell360.com/mast-cell-activation-syndrome-101-the-beginners-guide-to-healing/

3. Nutrition/diet

When I shared the online article, "Low and High Histamine Foods Lists" from *Mast Cell 360*, (https://mastcell360.com/low-histamine-foods-list/) with rock star integrative oncological nutritionist Michelle Gerencser from Nutritional Solutions, she said the MCAS-cancer connection makes sense for many, perhaps all, of her ovarian cancer clients. She has decades of clinical experience. So, this was empowering! We adjusted my supplements to help metabolize excess histamine and treat MCAS naturally, even now. *With natural support, the symptoms dissipated almost immediately and ultimately, completely.* The clouds parted. The angels sang. For the first time in months, years really, I felt an intimate knowledge about what my body needed.

Not only did I continue to feel surprisingly well, but we also supported and rebuilt my immune system even in the midst of the chemo assault. This way my body will continue to kill cancer cells, naturally. I knew I was on the right track because I felt good most of the time even *after extensive abdominal surgery and while going through chemotherapy*. What?! True story.

What does "feeling good" mean?

- Running 30 minutes around the track or elliptical with interval training every day

- Sleeping six to eight hours without interruption per night

- Having a clear head

- Comfortable skin—some have used the kind word "radiant"… no doubt, I am benefiting from low expectations during chemo!

- Hopeful and peaceful, much of the time

- Fully enjoying cooking and eating a plethora of healthy food

- Able to focus and meditate

- Too much information (TMI) WARNING: if you haven't been touched by cancer and/or are squeamish, look away. Textbook poop every day, sometimes twice! If you have experience with cancer, you know this is a big deal. Let's be honest, textbook poop is a big deal for anyone over 50, really.

- Able to do ALL yoga poses, even headstand! Yay!

It's not all in my control. I know that. Still, I'm filled with hope and powerful empathy for my body. No matter what happens, I'm healing deeply. I understand what my friend Akua means in the quote at the beginning of this chapter. She's as wise as they come. She's equally as youthful as many decades of open-hearted curiosity and continuous learning make a person. She's also African-American, so she's endured a lot of challenges in her lifetime. Even in the midst of physical discomfort, she knows what it is to be well, to be surrounded, and to find joy in the midst.

I too am already well in all the ways that really matter.

I will keep fighting, living, and sharing. Perhaps some of this is helpful to you, someone you love, or the work you do.

Meanwhile, more and more, I will continue to empathize with my body, listen to my soul, and take good care of my whole self. I hope you can too. It feels good. ●

"I tell this cancer these things: thank you for teaching me to stop and listen; thank you for reminding me of what is truly important. You can go now."
— Belleruth Naparstek, Health Journeys Meditation

CHAPTER SIX • MAY 14, 2020

A Recovering Chemist Learns to Empathize With Chemotherapy

"I saw the angel in the marble and carved until I set him free."
— Michelangelo

As platinum drugs drip into my veins, one thing goes through my mind: It shouldn't be this way. Don't get me wrong, I'm grateful to have this option since I was diagnosed with ovarian cancer. Still, it shouldn't be this way. Why do I think that?

For starters, human bodies are not deficient in platinum. Platinum is a noble metal, but there is nothing about our divine design that requires platinum to live, heal, and thrive. So, I know an infusion of platinum into my body does not solve a natural nutritional deficiency. It's an unnatural thing to do.

Then, I think back to my time as a graduate student, earning a PhD in inorganic chemistry from MIT. My advisor made groundbreaking contributions to understanding the mechanism of cisplatin as an anti-cancer drug. The upside is that I remember the kind and smart people working in our lab who were good company for those four years. The downside is that I've been a "recovering chemist" ever since, and it's been hard work.

I wasn't one of the cavalier chemists who mixed things with ungloved hands while eating a muffin and teaching a class. (That guy lived until age 79!) Most of us were careful. We worked under hoods, in laboratory glove boxes, and with protective gear. We knew we were dealing with toxic heavy metals, dangerous acids, and solvents that you really shouldn't sniff. In 1997, a former student of my advisor—a Dartmouth College professor and mom, Karen Wetterhahn—died of mercury poisoning. It was incredibly tragic and inspired new safety procedures around working with mercury in labs.

Meanwhile, mercury-based Thimerosal continued to be used as a preservative in childhood vaccines until 2001. Monsanto's Roundup/glyphosate was ubiquitous in the grocery store produce of my childhood, altering our microbiomes like the potent killer it was designed to be. Convenient plastic was all the rage, imparting endocrine-disrupting chemicals into our food, water, the environment, and our bodies. The assault on our endocrine systems came from every angle, really—sunscreens, makeup, DDT, PCB. I could go on. Actually, I have before, many times.

As you'll read in the next chapter, I woke up from the myth of "Better Living Through Chemistry?" I swallowed the myth, hook, line, and sinker as a young professional—with some buyer's remorse and a passion for change. Why?

I left chemistry for the business world in 1994, in awe of the natural design, and grateful for how science helps us think. Still, I was happy to leave the lab bench behind for less lonely and more broadly-focused work. When I got pregnant and had kids, I started paying closer attention to the foods we consumed. Whole Foods moved in and upped the quality of organic produce widely available. The internet exploded with information about health, some of which was bogus and a lot that made sense...in a revelatory way. I appreciate having science as a background to absorb it all in with discernment. I came to see all the ways we've lived, especially in the United States in my lifetime, out of sync with how our bodies are meant to function and feel well. I made every adjustment I could, in real-time, as the information was available.

Our family struggled with some health issues along the way, but they were manageable and only served to enlighten us about how to live in harmony with the amazing design of our bodies and the natural world. We were doing a lot of the right work. It felt good. We felt better—together.

So, I always thought I would be one of those people who could avoid cancer or beat it holistically, even as I accompanied too many fit and fabulous family members and friends on this journey. Like many of them, I do not have the usual cancer-related genetic mutations. What I do have is a sensitive body that has to work hard to clear toxins. So, the idea of using chemical poison as a therapy to treat the results of our being poisoned environmentally sounded crazy. It still does! But believing I could avoid chemo was a luxurious dream in the absence of a serious cancer diagnosis in these modern times. It only took a few weeks, direct conversations with experts around the country, and a handful of pointed questions to my oncologist to understand that now, it's my turn.

Making peace with chemotherapy has been hard work, and it's ongoing.

Here's what I have come to understand:

- **In some cases, a body tips over an edge, and we can only regain safe ground with the most powerful ammunition available in the toolbox today.** Cancer can be like that. I guess that's why people use language like "war" and "fight" and "army." As one of our dearest physician friends says, there's a time for blending holistic and Western medicine. For me, this is one of those times. I hope that time never comes for you and respect whatever choice you might make. Here is what I know for sure: every diagnosis is different so generalizing isn't helpful, and empathic doctors are pure gold.

- **Our bodies are heroic, especially in the midst of an assault!** We are designed to heal, and heal we do, in ways deeper than I imagined. Our wholeness is not always dependent on our physical well-being. That's liberating.

- **Holistic care does not need to stop during the onslaught of necessary, but brutal, Western medical interventions like surgery and chemotherapy.** That's such good news for so many reasons, not in the least because it gives us agency. We are still here and able to fight, in the ways we were designed to do. I'm even more adamant and working as hard as ever, to support the natural healing pathways of my body. So far, so good. The cancer markers dramatically improved, yet I was feeling surprisingly well after two (out of six) rounds of chemo. I'm learning how to ride the cycle of assault/manage/recover without many of the worst side effects so far. I'm fortunate. In many ways, I actually felt better than I did BC (before cancer). The second round of chemo had been easier than the first. We have more figured out. None of this is linear or easy, and new hurdles can pop up. Dealing with chemotherapy is a lot of work for my 105-pound body. There have been hard moments, and being bald feels crummy (and cold). But if there were ever a time for a low-maintenance head, a pandemic is it!

So, riding the chemo cycle is what I've done. I have come to see these cycles as a chance to practice surveying the damage and recovering when the treatments are all done. Learning to recover from trauma can be transformative, especially when we are not alone. I am profoundly grateful to receive the boundless love and many gifts of this journey with a relatively clear head and open heart, as well as less pain and fear than I expected. Less fear means more empathy…even with chemo.

Artist friends have told me they "empathize" with their materials. It sounded strange at first, but they explained that the material is an active partner in their co-creative, artistic expression. Michelangelo put it in plain words when he said he carved away all the parts of the marble that were not his statue of David.

David was always in there.

So, rather than curse the platinum as it drip, drip, drips, I've made peace with accepting its help...for now. I can empathize with chemotherapy and its Western partners (e.g., IV antihistamines, growth factors, anti-nausea pills) and co-create my health and future. It's been a big leap for a woman who hasn't touched so much as Tylenol for a very long time!

Still, I hope and pray that in 10-20 years no one has to go through any of this experience. I dream that we learn, fast, how to clean up our act inside and out so everywhere is a Blue Zone of optimal health and well-being. The long hike from the top of the scientific mountain has taught me that ultimately, the answers to our health look and feel a lot more like swimming in a hot mineral spring, eating fresh whole food, and breathing uncontaminated air than anything cooking on my lab bench years ago. It's a lot easier to empathize with Pura Vida. Our bodies are designed for it! ●

CHAPTER SEVEN • JUNE 7, 2015

Better Living Through Chemistry?

If you consume allergy medicine, painkillers, or Doritos, please read this...

I love science. Specifically, I love how studying science helps us understand the world. I love it so much that I studied chemistry for a very long time. The world is beautifully designed. It's all far more clever than anything we humans can make. Therein lies the issue...

There is no question we live longer and mostly better lives due to incredible technological innovations. Penicillin. Effective chemotherapies. Diagnostics. But when you cross profit with science, bad things can happen—innovation without soul and marketing without a conscience.

Here are three cases in point:

1. **MSG (monosodium glutamate).** It is thought to be an innocuous flavor enhancer. It makes food dance on our tongue. It makes food addictive. If you consume anything processed from the grocery store and/or almost any affordable restaurant, you are taking MSG into your body. The federal government does not make food companies label MSG, so you'll find it under "natural flavor," "salt," and a variety of other euphemisms. So, it must be safe, right? No. First of all, in a society that struggles with obesity and the health costs—emotional and physical—of carrying extra weight around, we do not need food to be more addictive, do we? More importantly, for some people, including our daughter Sophie, MSG

causes migraines. "Hormonal migraines" have been a curse of women in our family for generations. Sophie had resigned herself to this fate, but then, she did the work. She did an elimination diet to understand the relationship between food and her body. The results were clear: eliminate all MSG, and migraines disappear. Forever. Over the course of her lifetime, she will not lie in a dark room, suffering from debilitating pain, unable to participate in the world. Frito Lay does not have the right to rob women and men of this time, just so they can grow revenues. No one said it better than an R&D chemist working in the food industry, speaking to The New York Times magazine a couple of years ago: "I feel so sorry for the American public." Indeed, but that's not all.

2. **Aleve (naproxen).** Many people take Aleve and its equivalents for a variety of aches and pains. It helps us get through the day, right? It helps us stay active as we age, doesn't it? Sure, for a while. But here is the deal. All of these NSAIDs (non steroidal anti-inflammatory drugs) are nephrotoxic, i.e., they poison your kidneys. How do I know this? My father, who was super-active and aging gracefully—picture gardening, cooking, playing with grandkids, yoga, Sudoko puzzles, healthy eating, lifting weights...used to take Aleve once a day for a month so his hip wouldn't bother him while playing golf. Now, in very small print, one can read warnings on the bottle that might have prevented what happened next. His lungs filled with water. His legs swelled to twice their size. He couldn't walk two steps without getting breathless. My mom was terrified. Long story short, perhaps the good news is that a brilliant team of doctors guided by my more brilliant mom found an underlying lymphoma which they then treated. My chemistry background has never been more useful than in helping my parents sort this out. Make no mistake about it, the kidney doctor confirmed that Aleve started the whole thing, compromising the filtration in my dad's kidneys to the point that he might have died then without my mom's intervention. The glass half-full view of these events is thank G-d they found the lymphoma while it was still early. We choose to look at it all this way. Still, Aleve certainly catalyzed a downward spiral in this case.

3. **Claritin (Loratadine).** Seasonal allergies seem to worsen at times. Our son Grant suffered from itchy eyes, a plugged nose, cough, sore throat...all of the usual symptoms. Tree pollen is the most likely culprit, and we'd given him over the counter medications, as advised by our pediatrician: Zyrtec, and then, Claritin. He was 11 at the time, and his body was changing. Eventually, Grant started suffering from extreme sadness and anxiety toward the end of allergy season. He's deeply sensitive,

so we listened and talked to him about the things that parents can reassure kids of...about growing up and the concerns that come with it. But none of that was reassuring to him. A lucky hunch led us to consider Claritin as the culprit, followed by research indicating this issue is all too common. The internet is littered with stories of depression and allergies. The more we discussed it with friends, the more we realized we were not alone. Some of the research focuses on the correlation between allergy symptoms and depression. Don't be fooled. It's most likely the meds, including Claritin. The good news was that after just a few days off Claritin, we had our boy back. When I told Grant that his eyes may itch, he said, "Oh, mom, that would be so much better than the terrible sad feeling!" Claritin messes with people's brain chemistry and emotions. It's scary to imagine what might have happened if we didn't sort this out. Talk therapy would have gone nowhere. Anti-anxiety or anti-depressant meds might have been suggested. What a pharmaceutical soup we'd be in! If you or your loved one is taking allergy medication, or oral contraceptives, or Accutane, or anything really, and suffering from moodiness (which affects a whole family), research your medication's side effects and don't stop until you have your answer.

There you have it. Chemistry is messing with our loved ones. Enough. I love chemistry, but I hate what we too often do with it for the sake of profit, unchecked. What does any of this have to do with empathy? Everything. Empathetic innovation would never allow MSG on the market, certainly not without a label. Empathetic innovation would take Aleve and Claritin off the market and/or put clear warnings on the bottles in big print—big enough to jump out at older folks and tired parents.

Do not assume you are protected. You are not. There is no scientist on the hill who knows what is best for your body and your loved ones. Her objective is usually profit. Even the best doctors don't have access to all of the side effects of common drugs, due to "scientific confidentiality" exemptions on disclosure. Thanks so much, FDA.

Your health is in your own hands. Wise consumerism is our best hope, and the transparency of the internet is of enormous benefit. Our family has learned to approach even these ubiquitous chemicals with extreme caution. I hope our suffering saves you some. ◉

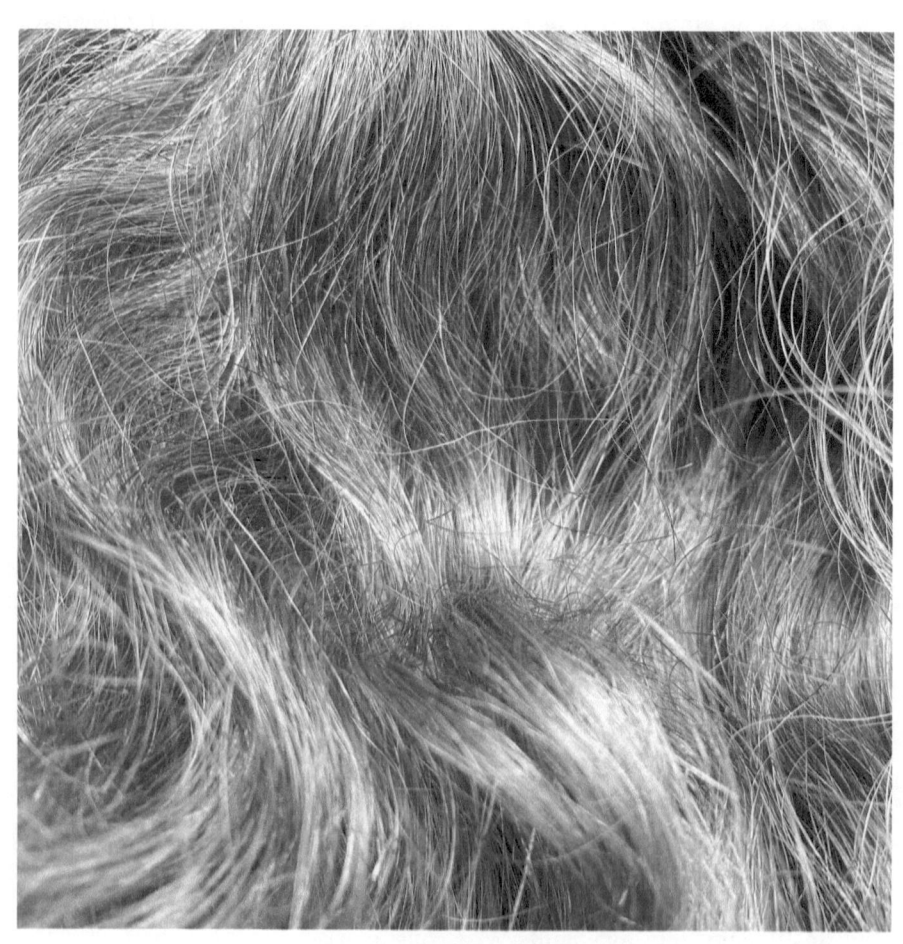

Jackie's hair prior to chemo

CHAPTER EIGHT • APRIL 23, 2020

Hair Today, Gone Tomorrow

"The root of suffering is attachment."
— Buddha

It's cold being bald. In summer, it could be fun to feel the cool breeze, dunk in the ocean whether it's hair washing day or not, or take a ride in a convertible without hair whipping my face. But when I lost my hair the first time, I was cold. I never knew. I'm amazed at my bald friends who never complain.

My friends and family have me covered, thankfully. Cute hats. Lovely scarves. A halo wig (with my old hair, pictured). I have options. Experienced friends explained gently but thoroughly what would happen. They kept me company, virtually, as the hair was going, going, gone. They sent me pictures of their beautiful bald heads and told me how to see the upside (the chemo is working, killing the fastest-growing cells...like cancer). That's good because it was also very, very sad to lose my hair. I was quite attached to it. Literally and emotionally.

Losing my hair has been a relatively fast but stepwise process.

Step 0. Long, wild, rebellious hair I planned to wear into old age. Thanks to Shelby Hersh for years of wonderful hair styling and indulging, yet moderating, my Chaldean desire for flashy blond highlights.

Step 1. "The pixie." Cutting enough hair to make the halo wig. Thanks again, dear Shelby, for making a hard thing easier and more stylish. (Halo wigs can be made by Chemo Diva via chemodiva.com)

Step 2. "The badass buzz cut." While sheltering in place, John "MacGyver" LeMay

37

consulted Shelby by phone, fired up the beard shaver (because that's how he rolls now), and took care of this business himself. Not bad.

Step 3. "The cue ball." If you've been through chemo, you know the hair comes out in bunches in the shower, even when it's short. It's crazy. I had a lot of hair. Then, even when it's short, it sheds onto your collar, making you itch as if you've just had a haircut without the cape...all day long. So, it becomes easier to proactively part ways with the hair that's left, even though it's difficult. I'll be honest. There were tears. I'm only human. I got halfway through shaving my head before I realized I couldn't do the back. Nothing about it was pretty. Enter MacGyver again, who helped clean up the mess, aesthetically and emotionally.

I've been lucky to feel surprisingly good in chemotherapy...so far. But being bald makes my status as a "cancer patient" unmistakable, to me. This adventure was not in my plan. I've adjusted to the person who stares at me from the mirror now, but it took a minute.

The hair is a metaphor for all of the losses somehow:

- How I thought I would look

- How I thought I would spend time

- How I thought I could manage health...and avoid hospitals, hopefully forever

As a yoga teacher, I know that attachment is the problem. The solution is not to lament the losses but to learn to live beyond them. The work is to lose the attachment, as I lose the hair. My Health Journeys app tells me about the gifts of cancer (and when Belleruth Naparstek says such wise things in that melodic and soothing voice, you believe her!). Cancer teaches you to slow down and realize what's important. In the big scheme of things, hair is not.

Humans get attached though, and I'm no different. I'm trying to lean into this opportunity to practice non-attachment, in a real, raw, and very personal way. It's a special kind of yogi boot camp. I repeatedly fail. In between seeking enlightenment, I rail against the physical and emotional toxicity making so many of us sick. I feel sad that the cold cap program was discontinued because of a pandemic. Cold caps and scalp cooling systems can help people keep some of their hair during chemo. Then, I realize losing my hair is just part of the deal. It's a chance to empathize with what too many people go through these days. The widespread fellowship I've received is both heartbreaking and beautiful.

And you know what? Practicing non-attachment is also freeing. Here are some things cancer is helping me shed that I won't miss: pleasing anyone else, focusing too much on the future versus the present, the illusion of control, and more. Letting go of all of these things opens the way for noticing more beauty, feeling more peace, and experiencing profound love and joy. Letting go makes room for presence and empathy.

As we say in yoga, it's a practice. So, I do.

I'll just keep my hat on for a while. It's warmer that way. ◉

CHAPTER NINE • APRIL 6, 2021

Cancer and the Fire-Breathing Dragon

It was terrifying to get an ovarian cancer diagnosis at the age of 51, in February 2020. I've been low and scared many times since. Not always, but many times. Before I was a cancer patient myself, I used to think of cancer as one of the biggest bullies of all. Rogue, mutant cells attacking unfortunate bodies from within. Cancer was the enemy to beat...to kill. A war with us on one side and cancer on the other, a fire-breathing dragon that required our biggest guns.

> "I imagine you sitting still in the face of a fire-breathing dragon. Hair rustled back with the force of all the air. Knowing you are perfect. You are safe. You have a deep knowing that is accurate. It is not a dragon."
> — Michelle Gerencser, MS, oncological nutritionist at Nutritional Solutions

- I was grateful that cancer didn't run in my family...until it did.

- I was relieved to have escaped the fight I saw too many people waging...until I didn't.

- I was glad I had so many tools for taking good care of a human body...until all that wasn't enough for mine.

I have more than two years of dealing with ovarian cancer under my belt now, and I see things differently.

Cancer is a Cry for Help
Our bodies are beautifully designed to live healthy, productive lives. It's incred-

ible really. When our daughter was born, my father-in-law marveled, "Built to last 100 years! Isn't that amazing?!" Yes, it is. None of us knows exactly how long we'll be here on earth, but we don't expect to be stopped short by disease at the scope and level we currently witness. Who out there doesn't have experience with cancer now—personally, in your family, or in your community? Our bodies are indeed assaulted by bullies, but I see them more clearly now.

- **Toxic chemicals are bullies.** Our bodies were never meant to process what we do now. Those of us who are more susceptible to toxins than others are not mutants. In fact, perhaps we are less epigenetically evolved/mutated than others whose bodies have adapted to safely process and remove pesticides, herbicides, industrial chemicals, endocrine disruptors, etc. Some of us get overwhelmed by these toxins and our immune system gets distracted, so we are unwittingly susceptible to more damage from what we take in (food, water, air, environment). "Cancer is a disease of genes mismatched with modern lifestyle," writes Nasha Winters, ND, and Jess Higgins Kelley, MNT, in the book, "The Metabolic Approach to Cancer." With chemical toxicity already challenging our bodies...

- Pathogens can be bullies. There are good and bad guys in the microbial world, as far as our body is concerned. Many of the parasitic actors (toxic molds, yeast, and pathogenic bacteria) are abundant in our food and homes because of unnatural practices that put expediency and profit ahead of health. Sustainability and green, clean buildings are not just good for the planet but crucial for our health and survival. Kids feel this truth in their bodies, so we see them getting active in this issue. Thank goodness, because being thrown into the disease management of Western medicine can be brutal.

- **Western medicine has many wonderful people, but many of the usual tools are bullies.** At the first cries for help, what we are offered too often shuts our body up and our intuition down. Creams. Pills. Procedures. They take away the pain or the itch, but the fundamental struggle remains—to not just eat well but to live by *actively detoxifying*. For those of us who grew up in the 20th century, this news has seeped into our consciousness in the background of going to school, working, and raising families. We did the best we could with what we knew, in our spare time. Our kids know better. They are also more in tune with emotional well-being and boundaries.

- **Bullies are bullies.** Whether they are triggering you in the media, your workplace/school, or even your family, toxic relationships have very real impacts on our immune system. What we take in is not just food, water, and air, but also emotional energy. Our kids know that trauma that is not transformed is transmitted. They might understand why people act with zero empathy, but they will hold boundaries. They won't put up with much of what we did. And that's great because their immune systems will not be on high alert with the potential to dysregulate and allow cancer cells to grow. And, yes, sometimes the bullies are even oncologists…like the renowned "expert" who offered her opinion without studying my case or bothering to listen to us. No collaboration? No thank you. Our bodies are the real experts and, therefore, must be included in the conversation. I'm lucky she was a bit player in my journey but shudder to think of her actual patients. It's hard to learn a better way when we are years into doing things a certain way, even if that way isn't working. Here is something I learned the hard way…

- **Chemo is a bully.** When our bodies cry for help in such a profound way as cancer forces us to, the predominant answer is still more toxic chemicals. Chemo is one of the biggest bullies of all, coming at us when we're at our most vulnerable. It literally kills. Yes, it kills fast-growing cells. There is utility in that to some extent. My former lab at MIT studied the mechanism of the chemo drug cisplatin 27 years ago, and I can't help but wonder why, after all those years, chemo is still the best answer for fast-growing cancers. Chemo is a big bully. Having been on a healing journey for some years, I have lots of standard and functional test results before and after chemo. It took courage to redo the tests and assess the damage, but I'm glad I did. Knowledge is power and key to preventing recurrence. Chemotherapy has serious systemic consequences that have to be more openly considered along with its impact on the cancer cells. Chemo harms our immune systems and gut microbiome, giving toxins and pathogens the upper hand for a period of time. Time heals, but proactive, strategic, bio-individualized healing interventions can heal our bodies and prevent a recurrence, faster and more completely. "Gold standard of care" does not reflect its name. Let's be honest; we all know it's cut, poison, and burn. Patients and innovative healers are pushing cancer care in more holistic directions. Someday, healing information *will be* standard, and care *will be* golden. For now, patients have to be resilient entrepreneurs, nonstop treasure hunters, and courageous scientists in the throes of Western medicine, not least because…

- **Cancer markers can be bullies.** Many of them are poorly understood and not well correlated with the state of cancer development. Not just ovarian cancer's CA125 which is notorious for false positives, but others too. Cancer patients are routinely terrorized by the numbers yet flummoxed by the fact that their markers do not relate to scans, how they feel, and progress on other dimensions. As one long-time ovarian cancer survivor put it, "That marker?! Oh, honey, I threw that out with the trash!" I'm not suggesting markers aren't useful, but that they aren't everything. Even more, I'm advocating that we need to do a much better job of understanding what they really mean...and so, how to truly heal.

- **Seeing the bullies.** Clearly gives us a chance to address them, personally and communally. Do I regret taking chemo? Sadly, no. With my type of cancer in 2020, I didn't have a choice at the beginning of treatment. Believe me, I tried mightily to get out of it! Am I sorry we don't have better choices after decades of a "war on cancer," billions of dollars, countless hours in labs, human and animal trials, and so many profitable drugs? Hell, yeah. Follow the money and you'll find the deliberate winners of this war on cancer; it's not the patients or their families. Our focus on genetics has been part of the problem. Proteomics—understanding how proteins are produced in the body—is part of the answer. But it's bigger than that.

Cancer is a Cry for Help, Not Just in my Body

Fifty years of creating the next patented chemo drug haven't gotten us very far. Real answers require listening to our bodies. Some people are doing just that. Curious, humble, and empathetic oncologists, tired of seeing patients suffer. Collaborative functional doctors who use meaningful tests to help us heal from the assaults of oncology and the upstream dynamics that led to cancer in the first place. All-in nutritionists who address body and soul, with tenderness, experience, and curiosity. Naturopaths and others who stop at nothing to heal themselves, developing and sharing new, effective solutions for previously intractable problems like mold toxicity and advanced cancers.

"A patient is unlikely to die from cancer, but from toxins accumulated in the body."
— *Dr. Max Gerson*

Most of the answers have been developed in a silo. The complexity of cancer really requires interdisciplinary answers. Adding up the pieces can be daunting. Then our bodies tell us when there are holes. We face down the fear, and more answers come. Through friends who channel, showing up at just the right time with what you need to know, even if it's just that you are not alone. Spouses who research, leaving no stone unturned...even when you don't always want to see what's underneath. Prayers answered with revealing dreams that leave you waking with a sense of knowing and peace. Our body and soul lead us in a healing direction if we can be quiet and plug into the divinity inside. That's how we're designed. That's what we can do. One of the biggest gifts of this year for me has been learning to listen deeply. There's a flow that's beautiful.

"Cancer has stripped me down and rebuilt me, better, stronger, more authentic."
—Carrie Kelley Kielty, Ovarian Cancer Warrior

Cancer is a Cry for Help, a Wake-Up Call

There is a blessing in not resting with *what is*, when *what is* isn't working. We all know too many sad stories; too many of us have lived them. We offer whatever support we can, with our hearts breaking as we watch friends and loved ones struggle with cancer diagnoses and treatments. Learning that yet another loved one/friend/colleague/child has cancer is devastating and exhausting. It's no longer my story that I was lucky enough to avoid cancer. But the truth is we are all unlucky to deal with the above bullies; they take their toll in a variety of ways. I'm taking aim there. That's a fair fight. One we can collectively win.

A cancer diagnosis is awful. The fight is intense and doesn't always end up the way we would like. But cancer itself does not seem like the biggest bully of all to me anymore. Cancer is not the fire-breathing dragon I thought it was. Cancer is a cry for help. If we remain still for a moment and shut out the noise, we can hear it. ●

CHAPTER TEN • JUNE 9, 2020

The Healing Power of Music Is Empathy

*"I will get well not out of fear of dying,
but out of the joy of living...and self-expression."*
— Belleruth Naparstek, Health Journeys Meditations, "Fight Cancer"

Has music ever made you feel less alone? I hear it. I see it. I feel it...differently now.

Music therapy is new to me. It's one of the perks of cancer for those of us treated at University Hospitals, which has one of the oldest medical music therapy programs in the United States—another Cleveland gem. Sure, I'd heard of it. I have even known music therapists and people who want to become music therapists. But I'd never been a recipient. Until now. I. Love. It.

Music therapist Tori came into my hospital room as I lay there post-surgery for ovarian cancer. I'd gained a whole new appreciation for the meaning of "gut-wrenching" while awaiting (ok, fearing) another five-six months of treatment with chemotherapy. She walked in, sensing how quiet my life force was at that moment. I'm not her first patient, and she knew what to do. I appreciated the gentle way she approached my so recently battered body and helped excavate my soul-in-hiding. She brought her guitar. She played. I think I wrote some of my feelings. It's hard to remember now exactly what we did that day. There was pain. There were drugs. I wasn't "home" in any sense of the word. What I remember clearly is that I felt a little better when she left. This was unexpected, as was the fact that I felt understood. Even in that moment. That's how the dance began.

So, when Tori called to ask if I wanted to continue music therapy with her

Music Therapist Tori

via Zoom (in the middle of a pandemic), I was more than game. I was curious and hopeful the work would continue to do something I couldn't do on my own, yet. I wasn't sure exactly what. Then, we continued. She asked me to reflect on my past, present, and future. It's always interesting and sometimes powerful to reflect on identity. Cancer brings a sharp point to that work, and lots of feelings emerge. Grief for what you have lost. Fear about the future. Uncertainty in the present. But alternately, it brings an appreciation for the foundation you have built, strength you didn't know you had, and hope for things you can still do now and envision in the future. She asked me to pick songs that represented my past, present, and future. Your current fight may not be cancer, but you probably have something challenging going on. Unfortunately, there is plenty of dis-ease and discomfort to go around these days.

What would be the songs that represent your selves—past, present, and future? It's a great question, I came to realize, because this kind of work helps you integrate them all which can be difficult. My answers? "I am Woman"

(Helen Reddy), "Bitch" (Meredith Brooks, and more recently, Ruby Amanfu), and "Freedom" (George Michael). Don't judge! It's the process that matters, not my taste. There is a disintegration of identity that can happen slowly over time and then acutely in life-altering moments. Re-integrating yourself and your feelings can be difficult, but it's vital to how we live. Music helps us move through that work, getting to places inside that words can't touch. Do you know what I mean? Doing this work, at a time like this, with a gentle therapist who deftly creates safe space for emotion and inspires creativity is a huge gift. It feeds my life force in ways that move beyond cognitive understanding.

Then, Tori and I took on the ultimate task. We (re)wrote a song together! How intimidating and how fun! I have always wanted to be a singer, thwarted only by a consistent inability to match pitch. Still, hope springs eternal. The song we used was one of my favorites, "She Used to Be Mine," by Sara Bareilles. The assignment: change the words enough so the song speaks to my story right now, out loud, with music. Yikes! It's a vulnerable thing to do, and there is also poetry and rhythm to consider. Incredibly, Tori made the work fun and easy (think MadLibs). It flowed mostly effortlessly and was finished in a couple of Zoom sessions. When she sang it, I cried. There it is. Emotion. It's an important part of the journey. But wait, there's more...

In debriefing the song, we discovered more. The whole process helped me describe, grant myself permission, and claim a word people often use in support of cancer patients and survivors: *badass*. I often hear it these days, and I can't say I mind.

What does "badass" mean to you? In which fight do you need to be a "badass" today? I'd like to think I could have imagined my way into this kind of learning, but the truth is, I couldn't. I am getting to places on this journey I haven't visited before. It helps that I like to travel, but the unknown is always scary, especially when physical suffering is part of the deal. But cancer brings the chance to realize and metabolize fear, over and over. To not let it be automatic. To not let it masquerade as anger. To not let it inhabit my body and rule my unconscious mind. I find it difficult work but liberating. Being human is inherently traumatic. Transforming rather than transmitting that trauma is tricky, difficult, and scary. When we can muster the transformation of trauma (rather than transmitting it to others), it's a badass thing to do.

It may sound ironic, but no one can be a badass without empathy. Empathy helps us move through and transform fear because we are not alone. We are held. We are loved, in the midst of it all. I am not alone. None of us is alone, but sometimes it's hard to see and feel that truth. One of the gifts of cancer is feeling that fellowship so fully and consistently. I have family, friends, angels, and healers of all sorts, including Tori. Being badass is really about being brave. There's Sara Bareilles' song again! I'm grateful to her and other singer-songwriters for being vulnerable and honest enough to share their feelings and stories in their art. It's such a brave thing to do. Music helps us not be alone. Music helps us change, in the ways we must in order to heal, individually and collectively. Music helps us be badasses, together.

So…If she can share hers, I can share mine. ●

"She Is Still Mine"

by Jackie Acho (*with help from Tori*) via Sara Bareilles

Verse 1
It's not simple to say
That some days I don't recognize me,
That these scars and this bare head,
Those drugs and these tears shed
Are taking more than I wanted.
It's not easy to know
I'm not everything that I used to be, although
It's true, I was never in cancer's dark center,
I still remember that girl.

Chorus 1
She's imperfect, but she tries.
She is strong, but she cries.
She's been hard on herself.
She's hard-working, too willing to help.
She is complex, but she's kind.
She is loved most of the time.
She is all of this mixed up and baked in a beautiful pie.
She is in there and used to be mine.

Verse 2
And it's not what I asked for.
Sometimes life just slips in through a back door
And carves out a person and makes you then wonder what's true,
And now I've got cancer,
And it's not what I asked for,
If I'm honest I know I would give it all back
For a chance to start over and rewrite an ending or two
For the girl that I knew,

Chorus 2
Who'll be badass just enough.
Who'll get tough when people get rough
So she'll see and believe that she just cannot help everyone
And then she'll be done,
And delight in the soul that's inside her,
Growing stronger each day,
'Til it finally reminds her
To fight more than a little
To light up the fire in her eyes.
It's still in there and used to be mine.

Outro
She is complex, but she's kind.
She is loved most of the time.
She is all of this mixed up and baked in a beautiful pie.
She is in there and she is still mine.

Heartfelt thanks to music therapist Tori of Eskenazi Health in Indiana, formerly with University Hospitals of Cleveland/Seidman Cancer Center. Tori left me in the caring hands of UH art therapist Barbara DiScenna, who encourages all the colors in the crayon box and notices "expressiveness" rather than the lack of training. What a gift!

Thanks also to Dr. Francoise Adan, Director of Connor Whole Health, UH, for these amazing programs that help so many patients, including me.

CHAPTER ELEVEN • APRIL 19, 2020

What Does Freedom Mean to You?
A Taste of Music Therapy

So many good conversations start with a great question. That's how it was in my final (boohoo!) discussion with music therapist Tori. Music therapy has meant a lot to me since first being diagnosed with ovarian cancer. The healing power of music is universal, whether you've had the blessing of music therapy or not. After our first conversation, the pandemic necessitated Tori and I continue to work via Zoom video. It didn't matter. Empathy transcends technology.

The Question, "What does freedom mean to you?" was poignant in many ways. First, it brought our work full circle. The song I'd originally chosen to represent my future self was George Michael's, "Freedom." Second, Tori asked this question after I had completed six rounds of chemotherapy, the first line of defense against ovarian cancer. Visualizing freedom also felt like a good thing to do, because it turns out that I needed more infusions. Some cancers are wily. Although I've made peace with chemo, it's not fun. Sustained remission requires a full court press, including discovering new ways to cure cancer from the inside-out by empathizing with our bodies. Don't worry. We're on it.

But...**freedom**. I yearn for it in many ways.

Freedom from:
- Tests and scans and contrast dies.
- Chemotherapy and all pharmaceutical interventions.

- All the side effects and awful trade-offs associated with all of that s**t.

- Disease intervention vs. prevention. No offense to all the caring doctors out there, but we've been seeing way too much of each other lately.

- All food sensitivities. On this front, thanks to extraordinary integrative nutritional advice, I've made surprising progress *while in chemotherapy*(!)

- Running with a mask while in chemo during a pandemic and managing my cortisol because many people chose not to wear masks. For me, Covid was a major risk factor as I was immunocompromised.

- The vast array of supplements and herculean effort it takes to feel ok during the assault of chemotherapy and Western interventions for cancer.

> "In our response lies our growth and our **freedom**.
> Everything can be taken from a man but one thing:
> the last of human **freedoms**—to choose one's attitude in
> any given set of circumstances, to choose one's own way."
>
> — Victor Frankl, Austrian Neurologist/Psychiatrist,
> Holocaust Survivor, and Author of "Man's Search for Meaning"

Freedom to:

- Enjoy as many healthy foods as a healthy body can and should. I'm a cook and a foodie. This is not just a small part of who I am. It's not just nice. It's essential to my joie de vivre. If you've ever eaten my cooking, you know. Also, please bring on the occasional mold-free, organic wine! Has anyone else gone through the pandemic stone-cold sober? I didn't think so.

- Do all the healing things that feel good and right and productive for a human body. I've leaned into all of this already, and it feels so good. It's also working to heal my body and keep me feeling like myself throughout chemo.

- Travel! We love exploring new places, culture, and food. More of that in the future please. Travel is nourishing in so many ways to the human spirit.

- Use the "ovarian cancer card" to say no, avoid emotional toxicity, take care of myself and my family. Hey, I've earned it.

- Dance!!! Alone, with John (and Grant and Sophie), at weddings, and in competitions even. That may sound like a joke, but I'm serious! The last thing I had to quit before we took on this cancer project was dancing in GroundWorks Dance Theater's annual dance fundraiser competition, "It Takes Two." I was slated to dance with Executive Artistic Director David Shimotakahara, who makes clear that dancing is empathy in motion.

What's not to love? I may have been otherwise occupied this year, but I plan to dance triumphantly in the future and bring as much attention to this wonderful organization as I can.

Those are the things on my freedom shortlist. What would be on yours?

Here comes the audience participation part and your chance to taste music therapy!
Your constraints may not be cancer-related, but you are human. So, you probably have things that keep you from feeling "free." It may be individual, e.g., a job you don't love, an emotionally toxic relationship, or an addiction you have to keep at bay (all those pandemic baking posts sure do look yummy). It may be societal or situational. Systems of oppression are everywhere, even in a "free" country. Get some paper and a pen. Really. Do it. This won't take long

Ready? Here we go:
Step 1. Write down your answer to the question, "What does freedom mean to you?" Don't overthink it. Just put what comes to mind in 5–10 minutes.

Step 2. Pick a favorite song that helps you feel free. Maybe it's "Me and Bobby McGee," or "Freedom Highway," or maybe "Roll Me Away"...whether you're a biker or not...or, how about this memory?! "Free to Be You and Me." What other songs make you feel free? I'd love to know and add them to my Freedom playlist. Now, close the door, and dance like nobody's watching because it's true! Nobody is watching. If dancing is not your thing, just close your eyes and listen. Sway or sit still. Absorb your freedom music however you wish. You are free to make that choice and so many others. Take your time. Listen to the whole song. We'll wait.

Well, how did that feel? Can you imagine a future that is more free? I did. It helped me empathize with my future self, toggling toward the hopeful side of grief and loss that's inevitable at times with cancer. It helped me visualize and choose life over fear again, even when so much is out of our control. It also helped me realize the freedoms I have now. The irrepressibility of the human spirit is alive in every circumstance. It's stunning, really. As Victor Frankl and others have said, we are free to choose how we respond. No one can take that away from us. Ever.

The truth is, I have so many unexpected freedoms even now, fighting ovarian cancer, in the midst of chemotherapy, during a pandemic.

I am free to:
- Vote

- Choose love over fear

- Think! #NoChemoBrain
- Type, without neuropathy
- Run, practice yoga, lift weights
- Help move our daughter and son into college
- Cook, taste, and digest healthy, delicious food
- Create...a meal, a post, an imperfectly perfect piece of expressive art
- Do inside-out cancer research and make choices that help me survive and thrive
- Even...dance. Even now. It may be a while before I get to dance at a wedding, compete, and do the lift again, but I will.
- Evolve my soul, especially as my body ages and earthly attachments fade away. The grace of such vulnerability is the clarity it brings.

I hope you enjoyed this little taste of music therapy and will find ways to let music heal you...helping you find your own freedom, over and over again. I know I will. ⚬

"Freedom's just another word for nothin' left to lose."
— Janis Joplin, "Me and Bobby McGee"

As a parting gift, Tori wrote a song about our time together, my cancer journey so far, and kicking up to the surface. Yes, I cried. That's the therapy part.

"Waves, for Jackie"
by Tori

It's not simple to say and it's not what I asked for

These waves so strong, whipping me to the shore

The drugs and the tears and the scars and this bare head

Choosing not to transmit but transform instead

So I'll kick up to the surface, get back up on that surfboard

Ride those waves again and again and again

Surf's Up! LeMay Family, 2017

There's so much out there for me, and this world can be scary, but I choose life over fear again and again and again

In this life there are waves that will knock you down without ever knowing why

I've learned to sit comfortably in the mystery of this life

So when they ask how I am, I'll say, I am well in all the ways that really matter, hey

And I'll kick up to the surface, get back up on that surfboard

Ride those waves again and again and again

There's so much out there for me, and this world can be scary, but I choose life over fear again and again and again

Thank you for helping me to stop and listen;
Thank you for teaching me how to let go;
Thank you for reminding me of what's important;
Thank you...And now you can go

Watch me kick up to the surface, get back up on that surfboard

Ride those waves again and again and again

There's so much out there for me, and this world can be scary, but I choose life over fear again and again and again

CHAPTER TWELVE • JULY 21, 2021

 Nontoxic Cancer Therapies That Work

My inside-out healing experiment continues. Of course, I wish I were just...done. But the reality of some cancers, including ovarian, is that traditional oncology doesn't have good answers. Yes, I accepted surgery, even though it was brutal. Yes, I accepted chemo, even though it empowers cancer stem cells and pollutes already challenged bodies. No, traditional oncology does not understand the cancer markers or how to heal most patients like me. So, ringing the bell and taking a rest was never an option for me and most people with ovarian (or pancreatic, appendiceal, etc) cancer. That's the bad news. The good news is that the alternative/naturopathic/functional community is working hard on truly healing alternatives. Could I have done these things from the beginning? I wonder...

Are they working now? In many ways, yes.

How do I know? Some cancer markers moved in the right direction, as have many pre-cancer terrain blood markers. Do these therapies in aggregate cost less than traditional treatments? Yes, some are even *free* lifestyle choices. Should insurance pay for these things instead of/in addition to traditional therapies when they don't work? Yes. Should they *at the very least* educate doctors so they might help patients more? Hell yes. Why don't they? Well, we've talked about that before. The short answer is lack of empathy in research and medicine—lack of empathy for people suffering and dying. In any case, we can educate ourselves.

Let's get back to the good news.

Here are the nontoxic therapies that work in my experience and data:

1. Terrain assessment/supportive supplements and diet. Your body terrain is the state of your inner environment. It includes your nutritional status, metabolism, immune function, microbiome, environmental exposures, and other factors. Your terrain can affect how a tumor grows and spreads. This is assessed through a much broader blood panel that looks to determine some of the conditions in your body that might be supporting cancer growth and then recommend interventions through diet and supplements.

2. Off Label Pharma – there are a variety of off-label (used for something other than originally approved/intended use) pharmaceuticals that have been shown to have beneficial effects in the treatment of cancer, often in concert with chemotherapy. Examples include low-dose naltrexone, doxycycline, metformin, statins, bisphosphonates, ivermectin, itraconazole and ritonavir.

3. Toxin Cleanup – mold, heavy metals and other toxins can distract the immune system, reducing its focus on fighting cancer. There are a variety of tests to determine if you have toxin overload and binders that can help remove the toxins from your system.

4. IV treatments – e.g. Vitamin C, resveratrol, quercetin, phosphatidylcholine, and many others.

5. Modified Ketogenic type diet – There is significant research that suggests glucose is the most efficient fuel for cancer growth and should be limited. A ketogenic diet primarily consists of high fats, moderate proteins, and very low carbohydrates.

6. Hyperthermia
    - Full body only available outside the US
    - Local available at some integrative clinics in US

7. Oxygenation
    - Hyperbaric oxygen
    - EWOT (Exercise With Oxygen Therapy) exercise while breathing oxygen through a mask.

8. Ferroptosis – An intracellular iron-dependent form of cell death that is distinct from apoptosis, necrosis, and autophagy. Studies suggest that ferroptosis can play a pivotal role in tumor suppression, thus providing new opportunities for cancer therapy.

9. Plant based – Helleborus, Mistletoe, Oleander

10. Low voltage electric field therapy—emerging treatment that is thought to selectively disrupt multiple cancer cell processes while sparing healthy cells.

I'm not saying that chemo didn't work for you if it did. Nor am I recommending you skip traditional oncology if you get a difficult cancer diagnosis. Doing what is right for your body is all that matters, and **you are the only one who gets to decide.** Lots of people have opinions, but the truth is no one can take this journey for you and you get to decide how, when, where, what, and whom. If you do accept traditional therapies, my experience suggests an integrative approach with nutritional advice can make a huge difference in tolerating and optimizing the outcomes of such imperfect traditional treatments. Integrative support gave me a surprisingly high quality of life, even in the midst of the onslaught.

What I am offering here are proven healing modalities you can choose to add, especially if traditional chemo fails you...and please, don't accept any narrative that says you or your body "failed chemo." How obscene to say a human body didn't heal while absorbing some of the worst poisons known to man, manufactured in a lab with profit as the primary goal. What does it even mean to fail? Markers that don't come into range...but no one understands them. Maintenance drugs that can kill you in other ways (e.g., a heart attack, Parkinson's, Alzheimer's). Sitting on pins and needles because recurrence rates are so damn high, while trying to "stay positive," "have faith," "keep calm and carry on." Yeah, I meditate and pray, but to deal with that kind of uncertainty, this scientist needs more solid, scientific, and non-toxic therapeutic ground. It's out there, just nowhere in the halls of our most storied medical institutions.

I've also tried many other healing modalities recently and through the years, many of which I continue to use therapeutically. Here's a partial list: acupuncture, healing prayer, walking in nature, grounding (also known as earthing), castor oil packs, getting plenty of sleep, saunas, coffee enemas, cranial-sacral therapy, cranial osteopathic manipulation (helpful for putting abdominal organs back in place after major surgery), laughter, meditation, Eye Movement Desensitization and Reprocessing (EMDR), Emotional Freedom Techniques (EFT) such as tapping, and rebounding. And yes, I do enjoy a warm bath!

All of those means of self-care have a place but did not move the needle on my cancer markers as much as the eight targeted therapies listed above. Part of the challenge in this work is to prioritize because there's only so much we can do. I've also tried juice fasts, eating vegan, and eating paleo over the years...I wish those worked for my body, but they didn't. In hindsight, mold toxicity and detoxification gene variants made those options more challenging than healing for me when I practiced them. You have to find what fits your body now. The right partners will work collaboratively to bio-individualize your healing rather than promoting dogma.

Now that some cancer markers are moving in the right direction, we are encouraged. The evidence is, I have some of what we need with these therapies. Some of them we figured out on our own. Now, we're relieved to be in the care of a naturopathic network that has been practicing non-toxic cancer treatment and prevention, thanks to Dr. Nasha Winters. Her book, "The Metabolic Approach to Cancer," was one of our bibles from the beginning. If you want to prevent cancer or support your current treatments, you might find it an invaluable resource. If you want a capable and empathetic partner in this work, her network of practitioners might be able to help.

I'm not going to pretend any of this is simple or easy. It's not, yet. It's experimental. It takes time, discipline, and emotional fortitude. Sometimes aggressive cancers need more, like chemo. The traditional cancer researchers are not saving us, but that's ok. At some point, enough courageous and entrepreneurial researchers, doctors...and even patients willing to experiment and share...will be out there, connecting with each other and communicating about what really works, in line with the divine design of our bodies and the planet.

Then and only then, we will finally win the war on cancer.

We'll stop cancer before it starts, through individual education and choices as well as collective action (e.g., cleaning up our air, water, and food system). We'll support our bodies' natural ability to get ahead of the cancering process if and when it starts, rather than destroying patients' immune systems. We'll do all of these things rather than continue to bear witness to the suffering of our loved ones (and sometimes ourselves). We all have more power than we think in this fight.

The next time you have a good, long, comforting soak in a warm bath, you can dream about all that.

I know I will. ⬤

Turkish market spices

CHAPTER THIRTEEN • NOVEMBER 15, 2021

The Adventure of a Lifetime

"Oh, wow, oh wow, oh wow."
— Steve Jobs last words

Istanbul is a special place. The spices and flavorful food. The colors and architecture. The markets and history. Also, it's personal. Our daughter is named after the Hagia Sophia. My college thesis advisor, Seyhan Ege, was Turkish. Now, our best hope for finally achieving remission from ovarian cancer is in Istanbul. The American "gold standard of care" failed me, as it does the vast majority of ovarian cancer patients. The truth is that I was told to go into palliative care/hospice in August 2020 by an "expert" with a typical lack of curiosity and imagination. Nontoxic therapies got me through many healthy months since then. I kept running, doing yoga, working, cooking, eating, hiking, enjoying my family...but those naturopathic interventions were still not enough to achieve remission, unfortunately. My ovarian cancer is aggressive.

Chemothermia is an integrative oncological clinic started by doctors who were tired of watching patients with difficult cancers die too early and painfully from the same treatments we've given them for decades. How refreshing. What do they do there? The short answer is they combine traditional treatments like chemotherapy (low-dose, bio-individualized) with nontoxic therapies that stress cancer cells (e.g., local and whole-body hyperthermia, hyperbaric oxygen, ketogenic diet) and protect healthy cells (e,g., IV nutritional infusions). In many ways, they do all-at-once the multiple therapies I've employed over the last two years. They've published remarkable results, including a Cleveland-area patient who shared her incredible story with us, from near-death to remission in six months. Traveling internationally when you don't feel well is daunting, but we've remained hopeful.

I'm also at peace.

I did everything humanly possible to heal. What I learned about cancer, life, and love is in this book. It's also in the hearts of John and our kids. I've enjoyed my work, a luxury I never took for granted. I've lived a full life. Our home has been full of peace and love. I've traveled around the world for pleasure and work. I'm so grateful I could work around raising our kids. Memories of doing simple things with them and as a family…picnics, reading books, creek walking, cooking, swimming in the ocean…fill my head and my heart. I was fortunate to meet and marry the best partner I can imagine in this adventure of life. I regret nothing about our choices and how we spent our time.

Still, cancer should not be this common. It should not force lousy choice after lousy choice on a relatively young woman and her family. I will stay in Istanbul for six months, missing a big chunk of our son's senior year of high school ("the boring part" he sweetly reassured me, now that soccer season is over). Still, it's not right. I'm certain this epidemic of cancer is not part of the cosmic design but rather a problem of toxicity we humans have created. I'll continue raising that flag for as long as I'm able. At least I grew up, had kids, raised them, and enjoyed several decades. Many are not so lucky.

No matter what happens now, I have faith…

- That love lives on, and I can (not in a creepy way) still be part of the lives of my loved ones even if I'm not here physically.

- That at some point in the next year, my body won't hurt so much anymore.

- That our kids have what they need. I couldn't be more in awe of who they are or excited about the good they will do in the world and the amazing lives ahead for them.

- That our friends and family will embrace John, Sophie, and Grant, with empathy as they have always done.

- That the transition from this life holds a kind of magic we only glimpse until it's our turn to go. If I can't say, "Oh, wow" out loud when it's my time, I trust I will feel it. That transition is the greatest adventure of all, really, and we will all take it. I'm still hoping for some pizza and wine on the other side (and many other yummy foods my human body can't process anymore)!

Still, I pray...

- I can be at all the graduations, dance at weddings, rock grandbabies, and continue to make holiday meals.

- I can be a sounding board for all the decisions to come, including the most important of all...life partners/co-parents.

- I can stick around for the fun part with John...and put my arms around him for the rest of my life. Oh, how we loved to travel and looked forward to more in retirement.

So, we went off to Istanbul together for one more adventure. It's not what we had in mind when we imagined "retirement" travel, but hopefully, this trip enables more in the future. I've downloaded Turkish lessons on my phone and look forward to breakfasts with olives, baba ganoush, and spicy baked tomatoes. As I feel stronger, I will enjoy strolling through the markets and the warmth of the culture. Mostly, I look forward to finally getting the help I need, the possibility of a real remission, and maybe some rest. ●

CHAPTER FOURTEEN • DECEMBER 6, 2021

Learning From Other Cultures
What I Could Get in Istanbul That I Could Not Get at "World-Class" US Healthcare Institutions

The answer is simple: a chance to live.

In the fall of 2021, I could not eat. I had the equivalent of labor pains all day long. Our oncologist gave us the devastating news that I had two to three months to live, and it was time for hospice. Then tussled my hair and left John and me sobbing and holding each other in the room. I guess these moments are awkward for the doctor too, even after 40 years, telling 80% of his patients similar news. He tussled my hard-won, newly-grown, post-first-line chemo hair. In many ways, it was the most useful news we received in two years. We knew we had to move on.

I evaluated treatment protocols at numerous top medical institutions in the US and can testify the treatment recommendations are very similar. I endured "gold standard of care" surgery and chemo in the US, April through September 2020. Adjuvant/integrative advice made chemo as tolerable as possible. We found all of this advice on our own, consulting countless experts. We had to separately check blood markers, find supplements, understand deep nutrition, detox the chemo, detox from mold, settle MCAS, etc. None of this is part of the gold standard. I finished with markers out of range so worked a wide range of nontoxic, anticancer therapies diligently for months afterward, likely buying healthy-feeling time.

But we always knew I was in danger. It was also exhausting, physically, mentally, emotionally, and even spiritually. Then, I started feeling unwell. Fluid accumulated in places it shouldn't. My energy plummeted. My appetite disappeared; it became painful to eat. Running three times a week, rock climbing, weights, yoga...became walking around the block. Eventually, I wasn't even able to do that. Poor Rocky languished at my feet. Treatments can be brutal, but so can aggressive cancers.

So, we went to work again, because acceptance of a dire fate didn't feel right, yet. Our daughter has always had faith we'd figure things out because we healed health issues for her. (At the end of this chapter, read my article, "Empathy is Powerful Healing Energy," published in The Energy Healing Magazine, May 2019, about Sophie's path to better health.) Our son explained that his mom dying too young just doesn't feel like part of his story. John did what he always does. He dug in. My family literally kept me from giving up. I'm a fighter, but severe pain has its way with a person.

After two years into this battle, I started treatment again weaker than I did in the beginning. Still, there was hope in Turkey. There are many reasons to be positive in Istanbul. After three weeks there, I had completed one full cycle of treatment, out of several. I can now tell you exactly what's different. It's truly empathetic care.

> "By the time you think of what you need, we've already given it to you."
> — Dr. Abdul Kadir Slocum, Chemothermia, Istanbul, Turkey

Can you imagine how restful that is for John and me, finally? So far, everything he's said has been true and every problem has a solution. The treatment cycle is very different and all-inclusive of the many proven therapies for my cancer. Chemothermia's published case studies speak for themselves, as do former patients enjoying remission. What I experienced is not experimental; it's just not available in the US, for many reasons. None of those reasons are patient-centric or reasonable. That is, if our goal is to cure people and give them more years of quality life. Shouldn't that be our goal?

As a published scientist with too much experience on this end of cancer treatment, I've been both fascinated and encouraged by how the 10-day cycle goes:

Days 1 and 8: Start with an 18-hour fast to lower blood sugar and hyperbaric oxygen therapy (HBOT) to stress cancer cells and protect normal cells, insulin injection known as insulin potentiation therapy (IPT) to lower blood sugar further, low dose chemotherapies (a cocktail proven in vitro to attack my personal cancer. John verified that fact through testing done at the Nagourney Cancer Institute. I received a high-dose vitamin C infusion, lunch with carbs — whatever I wanted! With yummy pomegranate juice, vitamin B infusion (to prevent neuropathy and more), more chemo, iron infusion (to cause ferroptosis and based on my blood work), more chemo, antioxidants, more chemo, local hyperthermia (one hour), more chemo, then whole-body hyperthermia with chemo on board (2.5 hours). That's the hardest part. Imagine being in a 112 F sauna while taking chemotherapy. At least I'm used to saunas. I hope John's memory of the raging bitch I become toward the end will be as short as mine of the suffering.

Thanks to friends for the audiobook and funny movie recommendations that provide some distraction. Then, a saline drip to re-mineralize and rehydrate, and the chance to go home. 8:30 a.m.–5 p.m. A good day's work. All in one place and the managed transitions right on time. The staff is very nice and attentive. The nurses place IVs in one, relatively painless stick. It's all just very thoughtful.

Days 2-7 and 9-10: More HBOT and local hyperthermia, nutritional infusions/shots/tinctures titrated to my blood work, usually including vitamins (e.g., B's, high-dose C, D+K), high potency antioxidants (e.g., dimethyl sulfoxide or DMSO), and immune support.

After the 10-day treatment cycle, I had 10 days to recover. During the recovery period, I would take a small handful of supplements and pharmaceuticals, proven to fight cancer and treatment side-effects...which their pharmacy dispenses before we leave the clinic. No guessing. No chasing. No hassle.

Repeat four times. Check scans and markers. Repeat five more times, if needed.

Stability, and if I'm lucky, finally remission.

My symptoms aren't gone yet. I'm frequently exhausted. The treatment days are brutal...but I'm more alive than dead now, and that's saying a lot.

When we went out to dinner the first time in Turkey, it was the most normal thing we've done in two years. Date night with my honey. Most importantly, I could eat without much pain anymore. I hadn't left the apartment other than to go to the clinic or downstairs for breakfast since we arrived. So it was a bit of an effort to get out, but totally worth it.

Where did we go and what did we eat, foodies among you want to know?

Vogue Restaurant and Bar, Istanbul. Let's start with the view! We were surrounded by the Bosporus and Sea of Marmara. We could glimpse the Hagia Sophia (our daughter's namesake).

The food was outstanding: tender and delicious tuna sashimi (keeping low carb and gluten-free to fight cancer, otherwise I would've gone crazy with the sushi); Vogue salad which was very fresh, beautifully composed, and quite large. I've taken enough food home for lunch. I had black cod, one of the best pieces of fish I've ever eaten—buttery and sweet. The preparation was very subtle which was appropriate because the fish was so flavorful, substituting sautéed spinach (low-carb), but the pickled vegetables were a highlight for me. There is a Chaldean dish we make called Turshi which my dad and I love, and these were similar. We may have split a glass of dry red wine, again something we have not done in two years, and it was so delicious to both of us in every way. John had grilled Seabass over fennel confit. Then we ordered two desserts. One a San Sebastian cheesecake. I just tasted it but that was very satisfying. Best. Raspberry. Sauce. Ever. We also had decaf lattes, and John had the bread pudding. We took a taxi there and back. It's only about a 10-minute ride. The neighborhood was happening! We couldn't wait to try the other two restaurants recommended by a new Turkish friend. I'm not in the habit of taking pictures of food, but next time I'll try to remember!

My job there was relatively simple: eat, rest, and heal. Throughout the journey, I rested in the arms of the Chemothermia team, and of course, John. I'm grateful that he, too, could finally get some rest. ◉

Empathy is Powerful Healing Energy
(Originally published in The Energy Healing Magazine, May 2019)

Healing is hard work. I know from experience. My daughter started getting hemiplegic migraines at age 11. Besides the aura and horrible pain, she would be paralyzed in half of her body for hours. Western doctors assured us that the migraines "weren't harming her." I, who never took my eyes off my daughter, can assure you, they were. Traditional medicine offered preventive pharmaceuticals with horrible side effects. I shudder to think of how she'd be today if she started those drugs at 11. We said, "No thank you" to all of that and began a holistic healing journey. Around that time, perimenopause hit me like a ton of bricks. I needed healing too. So, we were in it together. Fully. With empathy.

Empathy is Human
What is empathy? Empathy is the ability to feel and understand the inner emotional experience of another, and have an appropriate emotional response. Empathy was translated from the German word *Einfühlung*, meaning "infeeling" or "feeling into," coined in philosopher Robert Vischer's PhD thesis in 1873. Empathy represents a complex soup of cognitive, emotional, and physical responses that are a unique part of the human experience.

Empathy is generally differentiated into two major components. Cognitive Empathy is a thinking activity. Some people call it imaginative empathy. Affective empathy is a feeling activity. When your child is hurting and you hurt too, that's your affective empathy talking.

Empathy is Healing
Empathy heals. How? Have you ever been so sick, you could barely get out of bed, but then somebody understood? Somebody helped. Your friend brought soup. Your husband made tea. Your mom called. They didn't give you pills. They didn't even physically touch you, but their kindness and understanding helped you remember you're not alone.

When you're healing from something more than a cold, it can be a long and hard road. Detoxifying is not for the fainthearted. Mini victories (a migraine-free month!) can be interspersed with healing crises (the worst earache ever). Moving through fear and uncertainty is difficult. You can't eat what you used to like or perhaps even do some things you used to enjoy. Sitting alone with those losses feels more like deprivation than progress. With a companion on the journey, it's easier to keep your eyes on the road ahead. It's easier to have faith and hope. Friends don't let friends detox alone. Neither do parents and children.

Empathy is Power

My daughter and I have been side-by-side healing for some years now. Migraines are in the rearview mirror, thank goodness. Hot flashes and many of the other issues of menopause are not my constant companions anymore either. We're not done. Our toxic world ensures plenty of work to do.

Professional healers come and go. They bring intuition, ideas, and knowledge. They read our tests. They answer our questions. They sometimes understand how we feel because they've been down a similar road before. But they do not have eyes and ears on us. We do. Empathy is a contact sport.

We help each other walk the line of detoxing and living life. We commiserate and problem solve when we don't feel well. We celebrate milestones and little victories. We help each other stay strong while others devour hors d'oeuvres and pastries we don't eat. We create and share delicious food and drinks that heal our bodies. We look to the future, with some sense of control over health issues that used to plague us. Most of all, we are not alone. Empathy is powerful healing.

What could the healing power of empathy do for you?

CHAPTER FIFTEEN • NOVEMBER 21, 2021

 Reasons To Be Positive in Istanbul

It's hard to stay positive when chemo fails, whether you're the patient, a caregiver, or someone rooting for us. The cancer fight is so brutal. The effort—*intellectual, physical, mental, emotional, spiritual*—is so daunting. It's exhausting and tempting to call it a day. To say, I'm done. Time to rest. I've gone that low. Severe pain is a game-changer. So is your oncologist recommending hospice. But then, the embers of the human spirit can ignite again with even the slightest hopeful breeze.

The news of our trip to Istanbul and the direness of my situation may have seemed sudden. The truth is John and I have been clear since early July of 2020, that I wouldn't be one of the lucky ones finishing "gold standard" American treatment in remission from ovarian cancer. We watched as the cancer markers declined at a slower rate, realizing the limitations of the care I was receiving. Really, any statistician would say the same as 80% of women with my diagnosis don't make it. Still, in many things, effort-in can translate to hoped-for results. We did everything we could around the standard treatment. In many ways I was able to live with great quality of life, and even hope, for months.

Ultimately, cancer is not an effort-in equals outcomes game for too many of us. It could be. I hope it will be someday. That would require a radically different approach to research, medicine, healthcare overall, and the way we care for the planet and our environment. Not all of it is in our personal control. Yes, of course, we pray, but there are also physical realities because we are the hands and feet of whatever universal force designed this beautiful world. We are prayer in motion.

And now, we have good reasons to be positive in Istanbul.

There are people who continue to push the boundaries, invested in helping truly prevent and heal from cancer (versus publishing the next paper, looking smart at a conference, curiously willing to let the vast majority of patients die over decades-long careers, profiting off the next "blockbuster" drug that gives us an extra month of low-quality life, etc.) I wish we didn't have to learn all of this the hard—**no, brutal**—way, but here we are after more than two years of fighting Stage IIIC high-grade serous carcinoma in an ongoing pandemic.

We've learned some important news in the first two weeks of treatment in Istanbul:

- The worst of the frontline poisons (Taxol/paclitaxel) given to me in chemotherapy in 2020 **was one of the least impactful chemo drugs** *in vitro* on my cancer cells. Oh, we know from *in vivo* experience in my body that it did plenty of damage to my hair, gut lining, and other healthy tissues, but not my cancer. Yet, paclitaxel is still part of the "gold standard" of care for all ovarian cancer patients. Sure, results in a test tube are not identical to results in a body, but it's safe to say the experiment in my body confirmed the findings that Taxol was not effective against my cancer. Wouldn't it be smart to do this kind of testing of chemo versus the cancer cells ahead of time?! Like much of the science John and I ended up learning and employing, chemo versus cancer cell testing is available in the US, but it's a needle in a haystack we had to find ourselves. John found this gem talking with Dr. Robert Moss (of the *Moss Reports*, a great resource on cancer and integrative and alternative therapies). The Nagourney Cancer Institute does the testing. Thank goodness John found them.

- The PARP inhibitor (niraparib/zejula) drug I was given after chemo, was similarly **one of the least impactful drugs** against my cancer cells. It ruined my digestion, spiked my blood pressure to the point of concern about a stroke, and made me feel slightly crazy (in no small part because of the carcinogenic and toxic artificial colors in the capsule shell). Really, GlaxoSmithKline? Is your branding (GSK) worth our suffering? I was a candidate for this astronomically expensive and profitable drug because I tested positive *not* for a cancer gene like BRCA (for which the drug was designed—part of the genomic bias of cancer drug design, helpful for the 5% of patients with cancer genes) but a so-called "human repair deficiency gene," more likely a function of methylation issues which should be resolved in my body with vitamin B supplementation instead.

- So, I finished "gold standard" chemo with cancer cells not only alive and kicking but most likely empowered, smarter from the fight against crude and ineffective tools, thriving against an immune system depleted from the treatments. No amount of discipline, prayer, meditation, or volume/variety of nontoxic therapies could get ahead of cancer at that point. We didn't know all of this information at the time, but I'm grateful to realize it now. In hindsight, it's good news because it explains a lot. I still believe wholeheartedly in a non-toxic approach to cancer treatment in most cases, including people who finish chemo with cancer markers in range and those with slower-growing, earlier-stage cancers. Chemo is still obscene and crude. Nontoxic approaches absolutely work. I'm watching others have great success. For some reason, my assignment has included a more aggressive cancer, a full tour of symptoms, and a widespread search for therapies.

- **So the best news of all** is that the drugs the doctors here at Chemothermia in Istanbul used in my treatment were shown to be *effective* against my cancer cells *in vitro*. These drugs, given at lower doses and metabolically delivered, combined with many of the nontoxic therapies I've already been using, have a fighting chance of killing the cancer cells—rather than me. As Drs. Slocum and Iyikesici told us, "You simply need effective cancer treatment." It sounds so easy when they put it like that. Effective treatment and some discipline on my part (e.g., healthy ketogenic diet, continuing nontoxic therapies here and then at home) have a chance of healing my body. **Then the doctors emphasized that 51% of the outcome depends on staying positive. Since I'm a scientist at heart, it really helps that we have some good, logical reasons to be positive about this round of treatment.**

There are other reasons to be positive in Istanbul...

I'm an exchange student at heart. I went to Spain for the summer when I was 16 and never stopped loving being immersed in other cultures. Istanbul does not disappoint. I've started reading Turkish history (fascinating), studying the language (not easy, but Pimsleur is a great way), and learning about the food and cooking (which became more fun as I was able to eat...and yes, a variety of wonderful olives are at the breakfast buffet, just as I remembered).

John shares this love of cultural immersion. The uncertainty is more exciting than burdensome to us, which makes the adventure together fun. Did you know that Istanbul has 15 million people? That makes it the biggest city in Europe. Double the size of New York City! It's at the crossroads between Europe and Asia; you can literally walk across a bridge between continents. Istanbul is also close to so many wonderful places in the world. I'm dreaming of better times as a family exploring historic sites, relaxing on beaches, and frolicking in the seas.

The adventurous part of this trip is a good distraction from the pain and seriousness of our situation. Pain gets in my way too often still. Walking this hilly city (reminiscent of San Francisco) is out of the question. Effective treatment should change that. Turkish people have been warm and kind. The people at Chemothermia are making everything as easy as possible in difficult circumstances. They've done this work for more than a decade and know what they're doing.

We are wasting no time. We decided to come on November 10th, left on the 16th, arrived on the 17th, had testing on the 18th, discussed results and a treatment plan on the 19th, and began treatment on the 22nd. Not a moment too soon. Here, I have the chance to live. At home, the conversations with hospice were all too real and painted a clear picture. I asked, "What makes for a peaceful passing?" "Acceptance," was the answer. I accept that none of us gets out of this life unscathed. I don't accept that cancer is taking so many of us, brutally and unnecessarily, too young.

"Knowledge is your problem," the hospice social worker told me. Yes, it is. Even as I continue to muster the *personal peace* to walk through whatever is required of my body and soul, I cannot shake the knowledge that the systems are so broken and so many people are suffering. In many ways, we treat our dogs more humanely than cancer patients in the end. Knowledge wakes us up and shakes us out of accepting current realities that aren't serving humanity. The truth really will set us free when we collectively understand it.

The Turkish doctors told me to surround myself with people who could help me be positive; they were glad to see John sitting by my side. He's the best. Many other friends and family also came to mind. Their words throughout these two years have been amazing, empathetic, and uplifting. It's kind of bizarre...as if I get to attend my own funeral while I'm still here. It's heart-breaking and touching. Let's remember to tell each other all the wonderful stuff anyway, even when life isn't so dramatic.

For me, of course, our kids have been front and center. They've had to grow up too fast in these last two years. They're up for it, but it's still not right. It's hard to describe the depth of their caring, empathy, and maturity as we've shared the news of this cancer journey all along the way, good and bad.

> So, when the doctors said, "Surround yourself with people who help you feel positive," my subconscious did an interesting thing ...

Still jet-lagged and struggling physically, I came back to our Turkish apartment and fell asleep. I dreamt we were all together as a family. The kids were little, and we were having the simple kind of fun we did in those days. They gave me hugs. Preschooler/toddler hugs. The spontaneous, passionate, full-body kind. It filled me with warmth. I'll call on that feeling when treatment side-effects set in again, hopefully not as bad as before.

Teenager hugs are great too, and I got some good ones before we left Cleveland. Many friends wrapped their arms around our kids metaphorically and physically while we were away. It's astonishingly beautiful. There will never be enough words to express the deep gratitude and peace we receive because of that gift.

With the first treatment in Istanbul, we sought early signs of progress. It's very basic at the beginning, such as can I eat without pain? I was followed carefully with blood tests and scans. I shared fun pictures and adventures with health updates. In future chapters, I hope you'll enjoy virtually drinking delicious coffee and taking in the beautiful architecture and sea views.

Meanwhile, I'm thankful for long-distance company and empathy. It adds up. I couldn't get to 51% without it. ●

Part 3

Harvesting the Profound Emotional and Spiritual Lessons of Cancer To Grow Your Soul

CHAPTERS

16. Resilience	83
17. Keeping Company With Cancer– aka Entering Sacred Spaces	89
18. Eat Food Is Medicine	97
19. Pray Faith, Science, and Healing	101
20. Love The Best Medicine	105
21. Lost and Found Reflections on Two Years of a Cancer Journey	111
22. Appreciating the Simple Things	115
23. Divine Inspiration	121
24. Keeping the Faith…In Science	127
25. Dreams Instead of Resolutions	131
26. Treat Yourself Well	135
27. Chronic Illness A Master Class in Appreciating the Gift of the Present	141
28. I Am Still That Girl…Integrating Our Lives	145
29. The Healing Power of Good Friends Is Empathy– Getting Your Own Triggers Out of the Way	151
30. Home With a Capital H	155

CHAPTER SIXTEEN • OCTOBER 15, 2020

 Resilience

If you told me a year ago that I'd be thrilled to watch my eyelashes grow back after my first bout with chemotherapy, I would have been horrified. But it's true. Such is the resilience of the human spirit, to celebrate this little victory rising from the ashes of chemotherapy to treat ovarian cancer. Signs of growth propel us forward, and I'm not particularly unusual. I've watched others navigate the cancer journey with a combination of strength and grace that feels beyond human, looking from the outside. This is happening for too many people and way too many kids, many with stories that are tougher than mine.

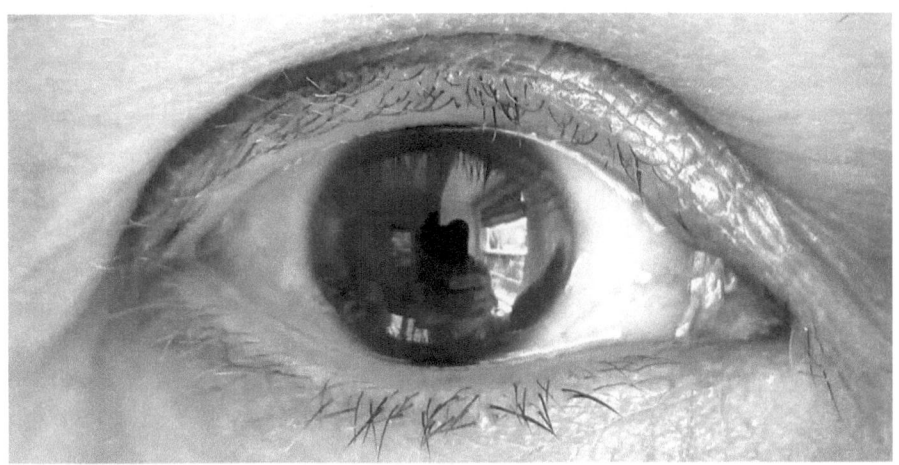

My eyelashes growing back

I've come to understand that resilience is really a sign of humanity in action, whether we are struggling with a difficult health issue or a global pandemic that just won't go away. We carry the seeds of resilience inside. In parched earth, they are watered by good company. Empathy helps our resilience grow. Think of the phrase, "What doesn't kill you makes you stronger." ok. So long as you are not alone. Even as he inspired that quote, Nietzsche showed how miserable it was for humans to live isolated.

Not everyone can sit with others in painful places. It hurts. That's what drives the desire to fix, deny, or put a positive spin on things. "You've always been so healthy! You'll be fine! I just know it." Others' pain triggers our own which is too often unresolved. Parents get a sharp lesson in this truth, over and over. It's a lifetime sentence. When our kids are hurt, we hurt too. Sometimes we feel it's most helpful to deny or try to metabolize difficult feelings for them. That's not empathy, and it doesn't build resilience. But when someone can lovingly hold space for difficult feelings to pass, remarkably, little by little they do. Empathy helps us move through fear, even when we can't fix everything. What's most memorable afterward is that we were not alone.

I'm not saying that challenges aren't sometimes downright awful. The treatments for cancer are brutal. Cut. Poison. Burn. Surgery is an assault on the body, and it takes time for our subconscious to let that go. I hope chemotherapy becomes obsolete in my lifetime; it took every tool in the box to walk my body into the infusion center seven times, then more. From what I've seen, radiation doesn't belong in the human repertoire either. What I am saying is that when I reflect on that time now, what shows up in my body is the love and support (warmth and tingling around my heart) more than the physical pain and emotional fear (heaviness in my gut). I am not resilient alone. I am resilient because I am *not* alone. Empathy helps us move through pain, suffering, and fear and not be overwhelmed by it.

What made the Covid pandemic difficult for many of us (who are lucky enough to have shelter, food, and emotionally peaceful homes) is that it separated us from humanity in so many ways. It was hard to connect with our people in the old ways for a long time. We Zoomed. We met outside. We watched sports wearing masks. We didn't often get to hug, shake hands, or read facial cues. The kids were especially creative. They dragged TVs outside and bundled-up to watch movies together. They built forts, creek-walked, had picnics and hosted socially-distanced outdoor sleepovers in tents, and went on hikes (stuff they might have scoffed at otherwise as teenagers). Even though we love to celebrate individual resilience in kids especially, they got through this pandemic *together.*

All this celebration of resilience belies a problem though, especially vis a vis the kids.

Resilience is all the rage. We love to talk about how well today's kids are weathering the pandemic...the toxic national dialogue, lock-down drills, increasing food sensitivities/allergies/health issues, bullying, intense competition getting into college followed by the disappointment of online school, the challenge of finding a job in these very strange days, the impact of racism or [*insert your challenge here.*] "The kids will build a better future!" we say, but aren't we responsible for building the future they face now?! We can't abdicate that responsibility now.

Cancer is similar. We love to root for people to, "Beat the s**t out of this horrid disease!" Not everyone does though, and it's not their fault or their bodies' fault. The rise in cancer isn't an opportunity for more people to practice resilience so much as a flashing red danger sign about the toxic soup we've created around ourselves. So many of our challenges are human-made problems. Rather than constantly celebrating the various gymnastics more and more of us do to overcome these challenges—*to be resilient in the face of trauma*—how about we focus even more on getting rid of the upstream causes?

When it comes to resilience, few people can encourage my personal healing more authentically than our daughter. Sophie started getting hemiplegic migraines at age 11. **She healed herself naturally without pharmaceuticals over the course of the next several years.** I helped. (See end of Chapter 14.) It wasn't easy. So, from that deep place of experiencing the power of natural healing, persevering in the midst of the fear and pain, and knowing me/her mom, she is one of the only people who could get away with saying, "I expect nothing less" about my progress in the cancer journey. She's earned it. I relish it. I actually laughed!

We can never escape pain and suffering completely. Human beings don't live forever, so there is no life without loss or love without grief. Still, how much pain and suffering are we not just abiding but **manufacturing**, directly or indirectly, at close range and from a distance?

- How do our words and actions contribute to or minimize emotional and physical toxicity and trauma in our families, with our colleagues, and out into the world? Including social media. Including using your voice to vote.

- How does our economic system incentivize mental and physical well-being versus disease? We can't change everything, but we all have some power to choose how we take care of our bodies and our families...what we take in, how we spend time, whether we empathize with the natural design or not.

- What else do you see upstream of the traumas you have endured? Start there.

Let's continue to celebrate resilience.

We will always need it. And the emotional wherewithal to move through pain without folding will always be a function of empathy—tapping into the stores we built as children, then replenished as adults in loving company. but, let's take some of our energy and ask, "What should we change so no one ever has to go through this s**t again?!" Then, change it. Too much suffering is human-made and entirely unnecessary.

Every generation wants the next to have a better life. Continuing to beat the drum of resilience makes a hollow sound, if we don't combine it with work aimed at smashing sources of human-made suffering we can see and could change. I wonder what that could be for you? Not everything at once. Just. One. Thing.

I find meaning in this surprise cancer journey by reflecting on this often dark space, bearing witness, and doing inside-out research on alternative forms of healing that are scientifically sound. From the inside, there is more clarity about what has to change. Right? We don't have to fix everything, but we can choose something we know intimately and do something no matter how small. Change is hard, but we can be resilient together. We can heal.

We should expect nothing less. ●

Sharon and Jackie at South Chagrin Reservation, Cleveland Metroparks

CHAPTER SEVENTEEN • OCTOBER 9, 2021

 Keeping Company With Cancer–aka Entering Sacred Spaces

Co-written with Sharon Sobol Jordan

Sharon and I have worked together and enjoyed friendship for close to two decades. We knew the outlines of our personal stories but didn't frequent the deep end until March 2020. That's when we started walking and talking in the woods, every Sunday. That's when I entered the sacred space Sharon knew all too well, and the beautiful Cleveland Metroparks were just the right backdrop. Sacred space. Sacred conversations. Dealing with a difficult cancer diagnosis for yourself or a loved one thrusts us into an in-between space that's hard to comprehend intellectually until it happens to you. Then there is no choice but to feel it in your own body and soul. You care about this world, but you think a lot about what's beyond. Sharon and I are not experts in these difficult conversations, but we have had lots of practice. In case it helps in your own sacred conversations, here is that story.

> "I'm glad to bump into you now; I just haven't
> known what to say since your diagnosis."
> — A Friend

> "Well, that's a wonderful thing to say actually. It's simply the truth."
> — Jackie

Jackie: When our family shared my ovarian cancer diagnosis in February 2020, we felt an outpouring of love and support despite the start of the pandemic. I'd known Sharon for years, including the story of how she had lost her first husband Pat Jordan to metastatic melanoma 26 years ago when their daughter Anne was just 13 months old. As a leader who was a hands-on parent, devoted to Anne, I admired her very much. My own kids were very young when we first started working together. I was relieved, inspired, and overjoyed to find an accomplished CEO who had a wonderful relationship with her then pre-teen daughter. The boundaries she pushed to be present for Anne were unusual for the time—working from home when needed, being truly present with Anne when she was with her, and surrounding herself with a supportive network of family and friends but staying front and center in her daughter's life.

None of this was easy. That much I knew. What I didn't realize...what we never discussed...was what it truly felt like to lose a beloved spouse and co-parent of your child so young. Sharon was only 35. We had never discussed what it meant to live in the aftermath of such a profound loss. It had been decades, and I'd never met Pat. Delving into that time too much felt intrusive, and I really didn't know how to manage my own feelings imagining such a loss. Who does? Sharon had also lost her mom two years prior after a very unexpected and difficult battle with lung cancer. I had met her incredibly talented mom and offered what support I could. It was a privilege to hear more of her amazing story at the funeral.

Little did I know that a short time later, my husband John and I would be entering this space of fear and trauma, but also having profound conversations about life, death, and love.

The first thing Sharon did was offer support to John. She knew firsthand what it was to walk a cancer journey with a beloved spouse. As I recovered from surgery, she reached out to me. Would I like to walk? Yes, yes I would.

Moving was good for my body. It was also healing to be with a longtime, empathetic friend. Rain or shine, hot or cold, I walked with her sporting pandemic masks, snow pants, brand new pixie-cut hair, scarves over a bald head, and the pixie redux later on. We walked as my surgical scars healed. We walked through the assault of chemo. At first, I thought it was incredibly generous of her to enter this space with me after all she'd been through. That's when she explained, it was comfortable. It was a two-way street. It's hard to express what a gift that was and is. She was not pitying me. She was not trying to solve my problems. She was listening. She was being with me. That's...well, pure empathy.

Sharon: Jackie and I were not very engaged in each other's lives when I learned of her diagnosis. The circles of our personal and professional passions had overlapped less than usual for the few years prior. But that didn't concern me. My instinct was to move towards her.

I think we both knew we had something special from the start. When I became CEO of The Centers for Families and Children, our board made it clear that the first order of business was to update our strategic plan in line with my vision for our organization. I had big ideas and plans, and was determined to find a consultant to co-design and facilitate a new and different kind of process with me. I talked to many wonderful, well-qualified professionals but no one seemed quite right. A trusted friend and colleague urged me to meet Jackie. After a successful run at McKinsey, she had recently left to start The Acho Group to do work her way and create better work/life integration. I met her, hired her, and we got to work. To get started, she proposed to me an exciting framework for the work ahead. I interrupted her as the two of us sat together at the conference table in my office and exclaimed, "I'm so glad that I picked you!" Without missing a beat, Jackie turned to me and calmly replied, "What makes you think *you* picked *me*?" We laughed and got back to work. The perfect partnership. The beginning of a life-long friendship.

Cancer and the various losses it brings are familiar territory for me. I have traveled this journey alongside too many people I love. Too often, I have been left to continue on without them. They have shaped who I am, somehow making me different in ways I don't fully understand and rarely allowing me the space and time to explore.

When Jackie and I first met, my husband Pat had died about 11 years earlier. I had a busy life, doing what was expected of me and doing it very well. In addition to serving as the CEO of one of the oldest and largest nonprofit human services organizations in the state, I was an active, engaged parent to my then 12-year-old daughter, connected and involved in the community, and managing a blended family having married again a few years earlier. I was doing this so well in fact that people rarely if ever mentioned Pat to me at all. Why dwell on the painful past? We are beyond all of that, right? All better now.

According to the TV-character *Ted Lasso*, the happiest animal in the world is a goldfish. "It's got a 10-second memory," he tells us. Unfortunately, I am not a goldfish. I have enjoyed a full and active life over the past 26 years and through it all, I thought about Pat every day and still do. I missed Pat every day and still do. I loved Pat every day and still do. I haven't moved on. I move forward and carry him with me—forever changed by the life we lived together and the future we will never have.

So when I learned of Jackie's diagnosis, I moved towards her. I didn't want her to feel alone. Even more so, I wanted to be with her. I wanted to keep her company with cancer.

Jackie: Week to week, we shared our news. Personal. Professional. Health, in every sense, physical, emotional, spiritual. Sometimes I was grappling with a bad result or test. Sometimes I was rejoicing in a new idea or connection (e.g., mold, MCAS, and cancer) or progress in healing (clearing mold, yay!). Sometimes I was railing about why so many of us are suffering with cancer in our own bodies or our loved ones. The content of Chapter 4, "Worn-Out Genes," began as conversations with loved-ones long before they were public. I'm lucky to have Sharon and a handful of other understanding, empathetic people walking beside me. Although no one is in my body—no one who can take this walk for me—having company is healing.

Sometimes it's hard for people to keep company with cancer [or insert other life-threatening traumas] though. I get it. So many things get in the way. First, there is an American cultural norm of rooting for the underdogs, so *long as they win.* Staying positive! Extolling people to be strong, pull ourselves up by the bootstraps. The truth is that attitude matters, but it's not nearly everything. Overcoming cancer requires a multifactorial and bio-individualized approach. Even then, sometimes bodies are too sensitive to this toxic world and the primitive treatments offered (cut/burn/poison). It's not the fault of patients or their families. I guarantee they did their best and are heroes, no matter what the outcome. Because of everything that gets in the way of keeping company with cancer, what I've seen with friends is that the journey can be very lonely even when surrounded by people.

Keeping company with cancer, in my experience, is simple but not easy. Simple, because it's about being with. Not easy, because to sit with someone else in painful places is very often triggering. Maybe you have horrible memories of your own health traumas. Maybe you lost someone you loved, even though you all fought ferociously. Maybe you are too scared to lose the person who is suffering for any number of reasons, so that you can't really look at or hear the truth of what they face. Maybe you are simply scared of your own mortality...that you could be me. All of that is reasonable. All of that stands in the way of us entering sacred spaces together.

Sharon: People like to focus on silver linings. Pat's death destroyed our young family and ended our dreams. It left me grief stricken, traumatized, and broken. That doesn't change or fade or get better with time. His death will always be tragic, heartbreaking, and devastating to me.

And yet they told me that I was stronger, more resilient, even heroic for surviving his death. They told me that I had an enviable relationship with my daughter—such a strong bond, incredibly close—that never would have been possible if I hadn't raised her on my own.

In my pain, I wanted to believe something good could come from something so terrible. But here's the truth: My strength, my resilience, my bond with my daughter did not come from surviving his death. It came from being a part of his life. I was the family he chose, and he was mine.

Within hours of his death, I found out how lonely this loss would be for me. Not only was I living my worst nightmare, but I was living everyone else's as well. No one wants to talk about it—it hits too close to home for just about everyone—we all just want it to be over and done. As one person said to me at my husband's wake, "Don't be sad. You will be married again before you know it."

So I carry him with me, but I carry him with me alone. Before cancer, Pat and I were on course for an amazing life together. Without him, I was a young widow and single mom that once had it all and lost it. And that triggers most people's greatest fears—ranging from "I don't want to say the wrong thing" to "I don't want to be you." Also, people need to move on. Other things come up in their own lives and the lives of the people they love. We only have so much bandwidth to deal with it all.

Whatever the cause, the effect is distance, isolation, and loneliness for those of us on the other end. Every now and then, I meet someone new who realizes that I am Pat's widow. They say some version of, "I have a great story about Pat, but I probably shouldn't tell you. I don't want to make you sad by reminding you of all of that." I insist they tell their story and truly love these moments. They are the moments when I am allowed to be *all* of me—everything I am today *including* Pat's chosen family and the life partner that lost him.

In these moments, I always wish I could find a way to explain that losing Pat is always with me. To ignore it is to deny an indelible part of me. It is the lens through which I see and experience the world. To act as if it is over and done, like an unfortunate chapter in a now happy life, is not authentic. It is not true. It is not how the story goes. Maya Angelou said it so well in her poem, "When Great Trees Fall."

> *...And when great souls die, after a period peace blooms, slowly and always irregularly. Spaces fill with a kind of soothing electric vibration.*
> *Our senses, restored, never to be the same, whisper to us. They existed.*
> *They existed. We can be. Be and be better. For they existed.*

Throughout the years, I have been embraced by an incredible community of family and friends who loved Pat and me. I have never been good at asking for help but certainly am grateful for all they have done to make life without Pat somehow work. And yet when conversation went there, it tended to be and still is understandably uncomfortable, emotional, and infrequent. I need, I want these conversations. We all have struggled with what to say or do, *including me*. The people who love me genuinely want to make this better for me, but how? I truly want the people I love to see who I am now, but how?

Walking with Jackie has created that space. We each bring our "list" of the thoughts, ideas, and questions that don't seem to fit anyplace else during our week. We don't expect answers. We are spending time together in it, comfortable figuring it out as we go.

Jackie and Sharon: So, what does it feel like to empathize in a mutual way? How does it work? What do you say? Here's how it works for us...

When there is good news, we celebrate together. We acknowledge that the journey's not done, the game's not won, but there is a chance to catch our breath. When there is bad news, the answer isn't "You're strong! Stay positive and you'll get through this!!" or "maybe it's a fluke?" or "I can't bear to think about that." The answer sounds more like, "I'm with you. Your people are right here. You're not alone."

Jackie asked and heard the story about before and after Sharon's husband Pat died. It was one of the most profound conversations of her life. You know those moments that feel outside of time and space? Pat's courage and devotion to his family right up to the end sounded so right...like something we'd like to have faith we could do when necessary, hopefully later rather than sooner. None of us is getting out of this alive, and staying present in loving relationships is one of the best things we do in the end. In many ways, that requires more courage than surviving. Understanding Sharon's love for Pat also helped Jackie understand what John carries, and how that love lives on with every memory, story, and feeling. Years don't diminish any of it. Despite what might sound sad or depressing or scary about delving into Sharon losing Pat, Jackie felt none of that. The story was sacred and universal. Big loss is the price of big love.

The more we ride the rollercoaster of ups and downs (in Western medicine especially), the more we realize some of that ride is mythical. Sometimes, we can choose not to buy the ticket. Cancer is not the fire-breathing dragon, in many ways. Such a perspective would be hard to achieve without some company. At least, it would have been difficult for us. The conversation is also not just about cancer because we are still here, living.

"Get busy living or get busy dying."
— Andy Dufresne, played by Tim Robbins in the movie,
"The Shawshank Redemption"

We talk about politics. Who doesn't in these crazy days?! We talk about strategies for work. We talk about hairstyles. Healing modalities. We talk about childhood experiences, transforming trauma, and emotional growth. We laugh about ironic and simply funny situations. We talk about books, music, spirituality...you name it. Mostly, we don't spend much time on small talk. We go straight to the deep end of the pool and start synchronized swimming. We're ready for anything. Good news. Bad news. All of the messiness of life. We know we don't have to fix it all or make it better. We know how healing it is to just be, together, with what is.

That realization is one of the biggest gifts of entering this club of cancer survivors. Life truly is mysterious in so many ways. Entering sacred spaces together is a wonderful way to be together...to make time to stand still...to be present to the majesty and awe of it all. No matter how much we intellectually understood that "life is short," we can't think of a better lesson to internalize or another way we could've done it. Not so we get comfortable with dying...but so that we live and love with abandon while we are here. ●

CHAPTER EIGHTEEN • DECEMBER 11, 2021

Eat
Food Is Medicine

Too many cancer patients die of malnutrition. I understand now how it happens, between the pain and the havoc cancer and its treatments wreak on the digestive system. Cachexia keeps our bodies from using the nutrition we work hard to intake. In many ways, that's what was going to get me. Not now. I'm eating, digesting, and enjoying food again!

Food has always been an expression of love for me. Cooking. Sharing. Creating. Cooking with my children and husband. Reading food science for fun. What chemist doesn't? It's fair to say I have a cookbook addiction, which food blogs now satisfy as well. My taste memory is one of my superpowers. If you've made me a good meal, you can be sure I remember it clearly and fondly. Thank you!

From grandmothers who cooked whole food (one Southern, one Middle Eastern), to travel experiences (e.g., taking notes in the kitchen as an exchange student in Spain; cooking classes in Tuscany, Vietnam, the Netherlands), to giving and receiving healing foods during times of trouble or illness. Food can transport us and bring people together. I've considered careers in food but always came back to food as life, rather than a livelihood. Food is a tangible way to nourish and empathize.

Love of food contributes not just to health, but to my will to live. So it was devastating to have mounting food sensitivities, then not be able to eat at all without pain. Thankfully, I'm in a good place now. I have always tried to walk the line between taste and health, which is not always easy given the changing landscape of nutrition science. For people with advanced cancers, there is mounting evidence that low-carbohydrate, veggie strong ketogenic eating heals. That may sound constraining. It's not really. I've healed issues for myself and my family in different ways at different times, but clean eating is always the foundation. Testing shows gluten-free makes sense for me, but that's not so difficult anymore. So it's wonderful to see our food system cleaning up its act. Healthy food is a human right, not to mention an economic issue, and should be easy and available. Junk food makers should have to pay the downstream costs of their devastating impact on our healthcare system and lives.

When we decided to come to Turkey, one of the draws I mentioned was breakfast. You foodies understand. They put out an enormous spread every morning in the restaurant downstairs at our apartment. Cheeses, meats, eggs, fruit, cucumbers, tomatoes, arugula, yogurt, olives, breads, etc. I wonder how you'd build your plate?

Turkish breakfast, including menemen

Family dinners are sacred, and going out to dinner with my husband is one of my purest pleasures in life. How lucky we are to linger over a good meal and great conversation, sharing our lives, hopes, and dreams. Solving problems. Finding solace in company in times of trouble. Dinner with friends too. It's all good.

Istanbul is twice the size of New York City. Not only is there beautiful Middle Eastern food that feels like home to me, but you can find pretty much anything you desire. John and I are "Door Dashing" like teenagers here. As I get more stamina, we have a kitchen and will cook more. Since we've been out and about in Istanbul, more recommendations have poured in. This time, we tried Sunset Grill & Bar. Here go you, foodies...

We both started with the garden salad: a fresh, crunchy composition that engaged all the taste buds with beetroot, avocado, pine nuts, coriander, cherry tomatoes, cucumber, and pomegranate syrup sauce. We shared a beautiful bowl of umami in the form of tuna sashimi (maguro and toro).

Then, I had baked black cod marinated in miso sauce. A pretty perfect rendition of this classic, with fresh, buttery fish. John had mixed seafood sautéed with lemon peels and basil with baked red pepper, shallot, and kalamata olives. Super fresh and tangy.

We shared a side of Asian spinach, and I tasted John's wild mushroom risotto, rich with truffle oil, thyme, and parmesan.

I enjoyed a beautiful decaf cappuccino and some fresh pomegranate seeds.* (Look Dad! I'm getting pomegranates here!!), along with a little taste of John's pumpkin cheesecake with raspberry and mango sauce. #chaldeanfoodies

> *My dad once mailed pomegranate seeds to me in Boston because he wasn't sure I could buy them there. It took two tries, but I enjoyed them. As my Southern grandma, Minna, said at the time, "That's good, hard lovin'!"

Following 10 days off, I started another 10-day treatment cycle. The upside? The powerful insulin potentiated therapy (IPT) benefits from high carb meals on chemo days. It really helps to dream about and plan what I'll have. Pomegranate juice. Homemade rosehip tea.Gluten-free granola. Fruit. Potstickers. Lentil soup. Anything with rice, especially dolma and maki. Gluten-free pizza and pasta and gnocchi! French fries with mayo!!! Gluten-free tarts and German chocolate cake. Yes! All of this is available here. And don't worry, I've learned how to hack a keto version of everything now, so I won't be deprived later either. But, it's still nice to have an upside to chemo days...in addition to knowing cancer cells are dying.

One last encouraging story. I walked to the nearby organic grocery store with John the other day and shopped. Getting around is still such an effort, but my body is stronger now that I can eat and move. I love going to grocery stores in other countries, finding local treasures like fresh pistachios, rich yogurt, and pomegranate juice. ●

> "You never know how strong you are until being strong is your only choice."
> —Bob Marley

Galata Tower at dusk

CHAPTER NINETEEN • DECEMBER 18, 2021

Pray
Faith, Science, and Healing

Why do bad things happen to good people? Forget about *my* cancer. What about kids? Babies? What did *they* do to deserve suffering? Innocent people die from cancer, war, neglect, violence, and more. If we believe in a good G-d*/Spirit/Yahweh/Adonai/Universal Presence (whatever name you prefer), should we be angry that she/he/they allow bad things to happen? These are the kinds of questions that go through our minds when we suffer. Certainly, they have gone through mine.

Being in Istanbul, we hear Salat, the Muslim call to prayer, from nearby mosques five times a day, starting before sunrise. It's a beautiful sound and reminds me to stop. To reflect. To pray. Just listen.

For what do I pray? That our kids are safe and healthy. That my husband is safe and healthy. That I heal from this cancer and have a chance to keep working, loving, and enjoying life in this world. It's a comforting habit. Curtis Jackson, better known as 50 Cent, said, "You either worry or pray. Don't do both." Worry is an illusion of control, but a difficult habit to break. It helps that praying feels better.

I also pray for others who suffer, that they find peace and comfort. But I do not blame G-d for human suffering. I blame us. I am not angry at G-d. I'm not even angry with us anymore. I am frustrated. Why? We keep failing to see

G-d is written this way out of respect for religions that hold this practice sacred.

that the root of human suffering comes back time and again to our lack of empathy and love for each other and our planet. Yes, empathy—deep understanding and resonance—with the original, wonderful, beautiful, glorious design of this planet and universe.

So many of us have cancer now because our human bodies were not designed to process the crap we have put into the environment, our food, and our bodies for far too long. Our genes are worn-out. Cancer and so many other diseases are epidemic, but profitable for some, from start to finish. I say this as a recovering chemist. I was so fascinated by the way the world is designed. I loved teaching, but was lonely at the lab bench and decided I didn't want to make chemicals after I finished my PhD at MIT. I shifted gears and went into business. Along the way, I got an inside-out view of how and why we choose to do the research we do ($), make the products we do ($), and fail to clean up after ourselves ($).

One other thing was clear back then. Faith and science are not incompatible. The more I learned about the way the universe is designed, the more mystical and magical it all seemed. A common problem with science—and the reason people are distrustful nowadays—is arrogance. We *didn't make any of this world. We're just scratching the surface of understanding it.* We don't control it either, but we pretend we do at our peril. We interfere, design, patent, isolate, synthesize, too often only with profit, power, and promotion in mind. Not the future. Not our health. Not our children. Therein lies the problem.

Jackie and her family in the Hagia Sophia

I don't believe in a vengeful or uncaring G-d/Designer of the universe. How could she be? Look at the beautiful gifts all around us! Take a walk in the woods. Dip your feet in the ocean. Watch the sunrise and sunset, right where you are. I take inspiration from science here. There is no such thing as dark, just the absence of light (photons). There is no such thing as cold, only the absence of heat (energy). I believe there is no such thing as evil, but there is the absence of empathy and love which leads to evil human behaviors and outcomes, usually things we do to each other directly or indirectly. It's up to us to fix this.

So, then, what's the role of G-d and prayer in healing? Will faith help reverse my cancer? Do your prayers help me? Definitely. Every note of encouragement, care, and prayer lifts my spirits. Incredibly, I've been the lucky recipient of virtual healing prayer with a small but dedicated team of earth angels every single week since I was diagnosed. I grew up Catholic, spent many happy years at St. Paul's Episcopal Church, am a certified yoga teacher, and have enjoyed studying and practicing other religions with friends, especially Judaism. But these healing prayer nights have been some of the best, most profound spiritual experiences of my life.

I don't expect an instantaneous miracle. I know my body is physically challenged, here in this earthly plane. I know it's up to me to intervene. What I seek—what this group gives me—is the time, space, and connection to a higher reality to discern what to do. What not to do. Who can help? Who cannot? They give me peace in the midst of confusion. They give me comfort in the wilderness of physical suffering. I feel the presence of human empathy and the company of something more divine. Sometimes, I have even felt joy, which is important momentum through the highs and lows of the bumpy and unknown road ahead.

When I am healed, I know this spiritual practice will have played an important part. I also know that every kindness, every word of encouragement, every angel-inspired action our family has received (putting lights up at our house for the holidays!) is inspired by something bigger than ourselves. One of the few good things about experiencing cancer as a family is seeing G-d in so many people around us, over and over. It lifts us emotionally, physically, and spiritually. It's powerful.

So, when people do heal from cancer, is it a miracle? Please don't say that to the woman or man suffering through hours, sometimes years, of chemo, hyperthermia, special nutritional programs, etc. It's hard work. We'd love to skip the suffering and go right to the miracle, but we are the physical embodiment of the divine on earth. We have to do our part. We have to do the right work. For me now, this means making good decisions about how to heal my body and having the discipline, endurance, and resilience to see them all through, renewed by some of the biggest, broadest experiences of love in my life.

But I'm just one person with one issue. Our human-made problems are so much bigger. Cancer should not be part of the human experience, yet it's all too common. We need to wake up, be much better to each other, act today with the future in mind, be much more responsible stewards of our environment and planet (no, we can't just colonize Mars), and leave this world a better place for our kids. Together, we can do this. It's not too late. ●

CHAPTER TWENTY • JANUARY 1, 2022

Love
The Best Medicine

I am alive today because of love. That's true for all of us. At least one person loved us into being, growing, and sticking around for the fun. Parents. Spouses. Children. Friends. They give us empathy which is how we internalize the practice for ourselves before we have words...and also when words fail us. Empathy starts at home and is a gateway to love. But it's especially true for me now. Since my ovarian cancer diagnosis, the epicenter of my healing and living has been our family: Grant, Sophie, and John LeMay. Being together in Istanbul for a week was the best medicine I could have had there.

Our son Grant loves life. His enthusiasm is reminiscent of the character Dani Rojas in the TV-show *Ted Lasso*, and not just because he loves futbol/soccer too. While we have enjoyed watching him play all these years, Grant does everything with a *joie de vivre* that makes you not want to miss out. He loves his family, friends, good food, sports, music...life. And he's a realistic optimist. It's a great way to be. When things got as low as we can imagine for me healthwise, we were all crying. It was Grant who suddenly got very calm and said, "No, this is not part of my story. My mom does not die while I'm in high school. I know it." And I believed him and...so far, he has been right. But part of his being right was convincing me from the inside out. It's the ultimate form of what we like to think of as leadership really, to be able to inspire someone to do the impossible. Out of love. What a gift.

Our daughter Sophie is brave and powerful. Everything important I've learned about the natural healing and adjuvant care that's kept me feeling unusually well during brutal cancer treatments, and alive longer than I should be, I learned in partnership with Sophie. When she got hemiplegic migraines at age 11, we realized Western medicine had nothing good for her. We embarked on a natural healing journey that would take us through many philosophies, practitioners, and healing modalities. We adjusted. We shifted. We learned how to discern dogma from what worked in our own bodies. We worked hard to continue to make eating healthy food and taking good care of ourselves fun, rather than deprivation and a burden, even as she watched friends eat school lunch while bringing her own for years. We did it. She lives migraine-free, healthy, and happy.

She's studying biology, narrative journalism, anthropology, sociology and is interested in Blue Zones and healthy living. One of the dreams sustaining me through treatment is getting to go to Ikaria, Greece with her and our family. The power of learning and practicing all of that good living as a teenager is astonishing to me, both in that she managed to go against the grain yet maintain great friends during a difficult time, and that she now has it inside of her. Her unwavering faith in our ability to figure out this challenging cancer situation makes me a believer too.

My husband John never ever gives up, even when I kind of do. He researches options and thinks ahead. Discerning the good from the bad. Protecting me from the latter. Gently nudging me toward treatments that have a chance of working. Oh, he was right there with me when hospice came to call, ready to "walk me home" if that's what I was ready to do. If that's where I was. He was also right there when I knew it was time to travel to Istanbul. We were on a plane within two weeks. Kids. Jobs. A house. A dog. A world away. It seemed crazy, but also, it was my best shot at living, and we both realized it. John LeMay is like the TV character McGuyver. He makes s**t happen like no one I've ever known. It's such a comfort to be in a partnership with someone you can trust completely, who figures everything out somehow, grows along with you, and holds you up when you can't do that for yourself.

We had a peaceful and loving marriage before all of this went down, but going through this fire has left us both with a sense of the depth of our love and commitment that we hope to enjoy for a long time to come. We've worked really hard. Sometimes, I felt guilty about that…like, maybe it would be easier for him and our kids if I weren't here anymore. I've even said that out loud. The look on his face shows me how out of the realm of possibility that is for him. Incredibly, somehow I still feel beautiful in his eyes…bald, wasting away, swollen with fluid in places it shouldn't be. I don't understand it, but I'll take it. All. Day. Long. Oh, we have our moments, like any two people together 24/7, through thick, thin, and a pandemic! Through it all though, I really want to stick around for the fun part with John.

Outside of this epicenter, we are surrounded by family. Longtime friends. Colleagues. New friends in Istanbul. Showering us all with love and affection from near and far. Physically helping us with our kids, our dog, our home. Feeding us literally, emotionally, and spiritually. So much encouragement. So many prayers. There simply aren't enough words to express how deeply we appreciate it all. It sustains us. The words and care breathe life into us.

Does all of this love guarantee that I will live? Not necessarily. Does it mean that I will feel exquisitely beloved until the end, hopefully, many years from now? Yes. Does it make me well and whole in all the ways that really matter, no matter what happens in my physical body? Yes. Even after people pass from this earth, they live on in our loving memories and stories. I find comfort and inspiration in that. For all we know, life beyond this physical plane is pure love. There sure would be less to fight about without any bodily needs, hurts, or pains. It helped a lot. Sometimes, when I realized what a long-haul I was in for, I got depressed. It can be difficult to take the long-view when the finish line is uncertain. There's so much to appreciate here, but there is no place like home...where our family is.

Our family enjoyed being in Istanbul altogether. It felt magical to me. Our teenagers flew across the world to bring home to us!! We enjoyed great meals together, and a cruise on the Bosporus, offering the best perspective on this amazing and beautiful city.

It was a spiritual experience to be with our grown children in the Hagia Sophia where we were inspired to name our daughter more than 20 years ago. We drank in sights full of wonder, rich history, and a sense of this place as a cradle of humanity, as well as central to our own Chaldean heritage. And there were a few memorable purchases for Sophie at the Grand Bazaar. The best part was: Just. Being. Together. Was it easy for me physically? No. Sometimes getting around was very difficult, but we figured out how to manage it. I didn't miss a thing. Having fun together filled me up. A booster shot of love that will see me through the rest of my time here. Sophie and Grant also visited the clinic and took comfort in the kind and effective treatment I was receiving. As sorry as I am that this cancer journey is part of our family story, I also know that, even now, we appreciate everything—*especially each other*—so much.

Below are some highlights from our time together. Enjoy! ●

Jackie's family during a visit to Istanbul, Turkey, December 2021

CHAPTER TWENTY ONE • JANUARY 7, 2022

Lost and Found
Reflections on Two Years of a Cancer Journey

Sculpture is my favorite form of art, so this cancer journey has been ironic. Cancer has a way of chiseling away at a person, removing what doesn't really matter, leaving behind what does.

In two years, I've gone from being a vibrant, "healthy," yoga-teaching, hands-on-parenting, working, young-ish woman with long curly hair—to being an old-and-sick-looking lady who needs a wheelchair to tour Istanbul with her family. It didn't happen right away. I put up a good fight. For the first year and a half, I managed to continue running, practicing yoga, cooking, eating, working, fighting cancer with every traditional and nontraditional means in the book...being more or less myself, while carrying the burden of advanced disease and often with a bald head. Then, things went downhill fast, as they sometimes do with high-grade cancers. In July 2021, my running slowed down. In August, I gave my last speech. In September, I was grateful I could still deliver empathy workshops virtually. By October, I struggled against pain to participate in Zoom meetings, while eating became difficult and cooking impossible. I was grateful to still be able to watch our son play soccer. By November, we realized Thanksgiving at home was not going to be a celebration and opted for one more chance to live by traveling to Istanbul for treatment. We had to leave our kids to celebrate with their extended family, without their parents. It's a family affair, these losses, including the sense that life is secure, we are immortal, and we will always have each other here on earth.

What is harder to see in the midst of the losses, is what's found. What is new. What's reorganized about people and life. In the dark moments, I cast about fishing for these insights. In the lighter times, they come easily. There is a certain symmetry to it all. For everything that is lost, something is found. Mostly, it's a transition from ego to something else...something bigger and more universal. Something beyond the self.

> "In short, Beauty is everywhere. It is not that she is lacking to our eye, but our eyes which fail to perceive her. Beauty is character and expression... The work of art is already within the blocks of marble. I just chop off what isn't needed."
> — Auguste Rodin

Here is what has come to mind two years into this journey...

Lost—figure, hair, vanity, whatever I used to think was beautiful.
Found—how gray my hair really is, appreciation for the pixie cut, and a kind of liberation from society's gaze. In a way, it's accelerated aging. This is what women in particular refer to when they say getting older is like becoming invisible. It's sad but true in American society. It hasn't been an easy transition, but I'm struck by both the shift and the upside of freedom.

Lost—the opportunity to parent our teenage children at close range, including cooking for and spoiling them on holidays and birthdays during this treatment in Istanbul.
Found—a remarkable village willing to step in and take up the slack, how much goodwill our kids have built, and how incredibly capable our young adult children are of living in this world (and traveling internationally during a pandemic!). Although I will never, ever stop wanting to cook for, love, hug, advise as needed, and pamper them, I have seen how well they can stand on their own two feet. It's good for us as parents and for them to know this now. I don't think I underestimated them, but it's simply awesome (and liberating) to see them in action.

Lost—countless chances to do work that matters in the world, much of which I was in the midst of doing when I was diagnosed.
Found—an ever more authentic voice, crystal-clear priorities, new creative outlets for pent-up energy, and the hope that work can continue in deeper and more meaningful ways when I am well. I'm grateful for colleagues who involve me when and as I can work. I'm a recovering workaholic. So this trade-off has been another struggle, which brings me to...

Lost—the frenzy of doing a lot.
Found—the good, bad, and ugly of more time. What this means is that I've had

to face down feelings, history, and the reasons behind my addiction to motion. To deal with them. To resolve them as best as I can, so that when I'm well, I live a more balanced, patient life.

Lost—the relationship I knew with my husband, between two busy, independent, peaceful, and loving people.
Found—an unexpected intimacy, new interdependence, and depth of soul-to-soul understanding that comes with the deepest conversations of all after 23 years together. We never had reason to reflect so poignantly on the life we built together, legacy, a "good passing," and what we hope for each other and our kids, even in the other's absence. We also have an appreciation for all the little things we took for granted, like the moments we're out to dinner and feel as though we're on a "normal" date night again.

Lost—a body that moves, breathes, eats, and functions easily.
Found—appreciation for all the people who suffer physically in this world as well as an understanding of my own capacity for this kind of sustained suffering (before I turn into a raging bitch!) In short, empathy for anyone struck by physical discomfort and disease, especially for the incomprehensible number of cancer victims and their families. I also gained a fierce determination to understand and expose as much of the why/how/what our culture does about cancer as I can in this lifetime. What I'm still finding, little by little, day by day, is an appreciation for things I used to consider automatic, such as eating without discomfort, walking to the store, cooking a meal again. Eventually, even returning to that headstand in yoga for a different perspective.

Lost—the days when I was the one delivering food and comfort to people who were sick or hurting.
Found—the exquisite beauty of vulnerability and how much joy others take in helping when and where they can. In many ways, vulnerability is a portal to the best of humanity, a view our family won't forget. I was a pretty extroverted and networked person before all of this went down, but we connect through our vulnerabilities. Sharing this cancer journey has exponentially multiplied the people I've heard from since, offering a poignant opportunity to be in the flow of the #currencyofempathy. As John Mellencamp sang, it, "hurts so good."

Lost—a sense that life is limitless, not just for me, but for our whole family.
Found—a realization that limits make meaning. Knowing we don't have each other forever really does make us appreciate the time we have together more. Of course, I hope it's still decades to come and there is more after this life as we know it, but the saying that you can only really live when you accept death is real for us now.

There you have it, a sample of the "lost and found" of one person's cancer journey so far. Perhaps this is just an accelerated version of what we all go through as we age. It feels like that. In the US, where ageism is real and people strive to look and be younger all the time, we'd do well to realize what we're gaining as we move along through life too. ●

CHAPTER TWENTY TWO • FEBRUARY 5, 2022

 Appreciating the Simple Things

"Happiness equals reality minus expectations." "The fundamental question" of well-being according to economists Rakesh Sarin and Manel Baucells in their book, "Engineering Happiness: A New Approach for Building a Joyful Life"

I should be dead by now. Talk about low expectations!

That was what an "expert" told me in August 2020, and later my oncologist's prognosis in October 2021. These are surreal moments, certainly as I experienced them, and even in my memory. I wasn't alone. John absorbed those blows too. We had no choice but to consider the real possibility of my death and even plan for it by engaging in hospice and learning about the drugs that might help me be comfortable (and hopefully graceful in front of our children) on the way out. Yeah, we went there. We did that. But we were also spurred into action.

In August of 2020, I was still active, but I had a plan for recovering from chemo, settling the mast cell activation that traditional treatments caused, clearing mold which took hold when my immune system was under attack, pursuing hyperthermia, hyperbaric oxygen, mistletoe, and other naturopathic remedies. I did all that and felt well for quite a while. The expert seemed pretty stupid. But ovarian cancer is wily and tough. Not finishing chemo in range leaves you vulnerable, and I'm not luckier than anyone else. By September of 2021, it had the better of me. No matter what I did, I couldn't outrun the cancer stem cells left behind by ineffective front-line treatment and was going downhill fast. In October of 2021, I was given three months to live. I wasn't supposed to make it to our son's 18th birthday.

Dinner out with my friend Jeanne at Park Fora Restaurant in Istanbul.

But I'm still here. And getting better every day.

Thanks to effective treatment in Istanbul.

Should I have to leave my home and family to pursue these well-known combinatorial therapies? No, but I've written a lot about that already. Today I'm not lamenting what I've lost or what I'm missing. I'm taking pleasure in simple things I took for granted for most of my life. Here are some of the things I've enjoyed, I look forward to, and that get me out of bed in the morning these days:

- **Quality time with friends.** My friend Jeanne has just been here and it was amazing to just be fully present, together.

- **Eating a hearty breakfast** (with pleasure and without pain), same for lunch and dinner.

- **Cooking anything and everything** I desire and can dream up. This is not just a means to an end for me, but a creative outlet that has been central to my being for as long as I can remember. Going for months in the fall without being able to stand at the counter and stove cut off a piece of me.

- **Scrolling through Instagram and following fabulous chefs** to learn (yet another new way—plant-strong keto) to heal my body through food. As much as I'd love to live without food constraints, somehow cooking with restrictions drives a certain amount of creativity...and feeds my cookbook obsession!

- **Talking/WhatsApping with our kids** about...anything. Mostly their lives. Some updates on ours. Watching their stories unfold, even as they rise to the challenge of having me and John so far away. So far so good, and I don't take for granted for a second the time we were able to spend with them growing up, so our connection can be strong even as it is more virtual than we would like. It's been wonderful to hear about the kids through John as he returned home several times during our stay.

- **Date nights** with my husband in Istanbul.

- **Discovering new restaurants, new cuisines, new dishes.** The best Ottoman food we had so far was at Zennup 1844. Their cookbook is now in English; yes, I bought it and you can too here: https://www.kitapyurdu.com/kitap/the-zennup-cookbook-amp-traditional-recipes-from-anatolia/594528.html. Jeanne and I made zucchini fritters inspired by those pages! I'll be cooking from it for a long time. Not sure if you like Turkish food? It's a mixture of Arabic, Middle Eastern, Asian, European, and Ottoman. Imagine homemade yogurt, braised lamb and/or beans, lentils, salads with pomegranate seeds and sour syrup. You can be keto, vegan, and everything else. The food is flexible. Here are the top Turkish chefs on Instagram to give you a taste: https://www.doyouknowturkey.com/the-best-13-turkish-chefs-on-instagram.

- **Exploring the city** in which I live with family and friends. Istanbul is *a magical city where the ancient and the modern live side by side.* Noting the progress my body is making here by realizing I didn't need to use a wheelchair to get to/from/through the Hagia Sophia recently. It felt good. Cleveland has its own magic, as do Chicago, Boston, Bilbao, Marbella, Detroit, Ann Arbor, wherever you live...all in their own way.

- **Grocery shopping** especially in the produce market, where I have a new friend in the purveyor there. I'm a grocer's daughter and a former produce girl. These are my people.

- **Seeing friends** in the restaurant downstairs and sharing our lives, food, and news. Our friend and the manager, Suleyman, has a son who now is ranked second in all of Turkey for age 18 and under in chess!

- **Learning and practicing Turkish** (slow going, but appreciated and fun) and other languages with the international community in the clinic. New friends Halva and Ahmet, the nurses, people in the restaurant downstairs...all teach me something new every day. I can also recommend Pimsleur audio courses, which I've used for many other languages as well. I can't sing, but trying out new languages feels like that to me.

- **Moving my body.** I used to run and plan to do so again. For now, walking to the "far away" grocery store is a triumph and gentle yoga and light weights are possible.

- **Reading.** I had stopped for a while, needing more active distraction, but can be quiet again within myself. I suppose the theme is immersion, as I'm currently loving, "Istanbul: Memories of a City" by Nobel Prize in Literature winner Orhan Pamuk. Thank you, Karel Paukert, for the recommendation!

- **Games!** John and I, understandably, weren't in the mood or habit of playing games when we arrived in November. Jeanne brought that fun back and made treatment time fly with *Quiddler* and *Words with Chums*. And yes, I wait for the new *Wordle* every day just like many of you!

- **The upside of social media.** I have a whole new appreciation for these connections now. Being far from home, having the virtual "conversation" with people who take the time to read my blogs, comment on posts, and message or video chat with me about their lives is not only encouraging but helps me stay connected to home. My feed is loaded with positive and supportive people, recipes, pictures, and messages. I'm constantly surprised to hear from people who have been following my writing for some time, then take a moment to reach out. Thank you.

- **Writing** is another creative outlet that makes me feel like myself, whether it's a blog post, an article on leadership and empathy for a journal, or emails with friends and family. I'm grateful for this channel and the inspiration that flows through it.

- **Sleeping and dreaming.** Pain is very interruptive of everything. For a while, I stopped dreaming at night. I missed it. Dreams are back, in full color with new meanings and messages. I'm listening.

- **Meditating, praying, daydreaming.** For a while, with the dark outlook and pain, I needed more constant distraction. I am ok being quiet now.

- **Movies and shows.** Mostly feel-good stuff I missed in all of those workaholic years. "Love, Actually" was fun. "From Russia with Love" is mostly set in Istanbul! So is "The Club/Kulüp," telling the story of the rise of nationalism in 1950's Turkey. "Queer Eye" is so much more than makeovers. Who wouldn't want to spend a week with those adorable guys?! When my curiosity gets the best of me, I'll check out an episode from the new season of "Ozark." How much worse can it get for Marty and his family? Don't tell me.

- **Dreaming about vacations.** Starting to plan some. "Hell, I almost died," is my mantra. Why wait?

- **Did I mention dry wine can be keto?** Oh, I know, I know. But, "Hell, I almost died." There must be pleasure—and wine on a night out to dinner is one of mine.

Am I free of all discomfort? No. Do I have to be poked many days for infusions? Yes. Am I done with chemo? Not quite. Am I assured of remission at the end of all of this? No. Do I still worry sometimes about the long-term? Yes.

So I have to come back to the simple things, both to mark progress and to live while I'm here. After all, I shouldn't be. I have to take things one day at a time. Literally.

People have talked about focusing on simplicity forever. The more modern and complex our lives, the more we need reminding. It's always in fashion, whether you like schmaltzy movies like "The Sound of Music" (how many times have we watched that one?!) or classic rock songs like Lynyrd Skynyrd's "Simple Man" (always one of my husband's favorites).

I listened to these messages but can't claim to have lived them until recently… when my expectations became so low, that I'm grateful just to be here. And without constant pain. Maybe you can appreciate such simple things in a new way without the portal of a death sentence. I bet you can do most of what I listed above.

Grant—*our youngest*—turned 18 on February 1, 2022.

I. Am. Still. Alive.

I wasn't able to be home, but wonderful friends and John made sure he had a memorable time and shared as much as they could with me by text, video, and email. It was Grant who shook off the latest prognosis and said his mom dying young did not, "feel like part of his story."

So far, the expert doctors are wrong and our son is right. His empathy helps him see clearly.

It's that simple. ●

CHAPTER TWENTY THREE • JANUARY 29, 2022

 Divine Inspiration

"All will be well."
— Reverend Jeanne Leinbach undergoing treatment for breast cancer, 2015

Growing up, I never imagined I'd have close friends who are priests (pastors rabbis/spiritual leaders). It's not that I don't like priests. The priest who married John and me, Father Brian Chabala, has been a family friend for years and showed me as a young woman that priests can have humanity and humor.

But as a young girl growing up in the Catholic Church, none of the priests were very…relatable. Men who never had children have to work hard to relate to young girls; first, they have to want to. It didn't seem to be part of the job description. I can't say I was the best catechism student either. When it came time to make my confession in fourth grade, I was at the front of the line (benefit of the name Acho). The priest seemed to be expecting something. I said, "Hi." He asked how long it had been since my last confession. I must have missed the, "Forgive me, father, for I have sinned, it has been X since my last confession…" lesson. I leaned in and whispered to him that the whole line of fourth graders behind me were newbies. I couldn't believe no one had clued him in! Then, I proceeded to unburden my soul about fighting with my brother and peeing in the Gulf of Mexico (why did I think that was a sin?), said my Hail Mary's, and was on my way. Listening to sermons didn't stir my soul either. I just. Couldn't. Relate. No offense to these men, but I wasn't one. In many ways, I was more moved in the synagogues and by the bar/bat mitzvahs of my friends growing up. One of them, Francine Green Roston, even grew up to be a rabbi!

As an adult, I tried again for the sake of our family. The miracle of our children being born was enough to bring me back to spiritual pursuits. We landed at St. Paul's Episcopal Church in Cleveland Heights, Ohio. A good compromise for a lapsed Catholic and a grown-up Southern Baptist (John), with the incomparable Carnella Peck who immediately stole all of our hearts as the preschool teacher during services, giving us that peaceful hour every week.

Also, St. Paul's struck us as a more inclusive place. I was struck by beautiful Akua Saunders during a weekend seminar and have been nourished by that friendship ever since. St. Paul's even had…wait for it…a woman priest as Associate Rector! Reverend Lisa Hackney was known for occasionally choking up during sermons, and I couldn't have loved her more for it. She talked about being a woman in a patriarchal world, a mom, and a girl growing up. Finally, sermons came alive for me. The work of holding holy scriptures in one hand and the newspaper and our daily experiences in the other—trying to make sense of it all—was real. I was *into it*.

So into it, I became a lector, a student then graduate of the 4-year Education for Ministry (EfM) program through Sewanee: The University of the South, a children's Sunday school teacher, a vestry (Board) member, and then Senior Warden (chair of the Board) for two years, among other roles.

When it was time to search for a new rector, I was on the committee. I got to see many, many priests with lots of different styles from around the country and the world. I was moved by these people who live in the place where humanity meets divine inspiration. I became aware of the challenges of leading churches and practicing spirituality in the messiness of human behavior and the reality of organizational hierarchies in which we humans find comfort, even as we

Jeanne and Jackie in front of the Bosporus Strait

strive for democracies. In all of that, we and our kids made deep and enduring friendships, many of which have sustained, comforted, and continue supplying us with endless prayers and encouragement during our journey with ovarian cancer. But I grew most from more private journeys, including my relationship with our current rector/head priest.

When we were searching for a new rector, the Rev. Tracey Lind, a friend from Trinity Cathedral in Cleveland, took me by the hand at a national conference and introduced me to Reverend Jeanne Leinbach from Chicago. "All things being equal, we'd be thrilled to call the first woman to lead St. Paul's," said one rector search committee member. And we did.

When Jeanne arrived in 2015, she let me know that she had *just* been diagnosed with breast cancer. She came anyway. She moved to Cleveland alone. An empty nester and single by then, she had no family in town. It was a brave thing to do. I accompanied her to doctors' appointments, treatments, and surgery. Not all of them, but enough to see who she was and how she walked through these challenges.

When she officially became the Rector of St. Paul's, she stood at the front of a packed church with a bald head, beaming. When she came out of surgery, she cried, not from what had just happened to her body, but because she was so moved by all of the people praying for her. When I worried, she said, "All will be well." No matter what happens. I never saw her faith waver, and it was one of the most inspiring currents to pass through my life. Her example meant so much to me then. "All will be well" applies to, well, everything, including the (in hindsight) relatively addressable challenges I was facing in my own life back then.

Fast forward to 2020, and it's my turn to go through cancer…in a pandemic. Jeanne and I are friends with lots of shared personal and professional history. Her example means even more to me now. As a flawed human who can be distracted from that higher love from time to time (especially with severe pain), I have returned to her steadfast belief that "all will be well" as a mantra that brings me back to center, time and again.

So, it was a great blessing to have her visit me in Istanbul while John spent time at home with our kids and Rocky. I'm an independent person who enjoys alone time, but the chemo plus hyperthermia combo can be as draining as it is effective. It helps to have company. We've been walking, cooking, eating meals, talking, catching up, taking in the city, praying, and enjoying a nice meal out.

The intimacy and vulnerability of going through treatment with someone other than my husband are new. My body is not the same. I don't look the same.

I don't feel the same as I did even two years ago. But some priests have the best, most comforting words—balm for the soul. I was ripe for a faith infusion. Oh, I never waiver in my belief that there is a higher power, but the day-to-day remembering that "all will be well" in the midst of the pain, discomfort, treatment, and the struggle of a difficult cancer...well, I'm only human. We all are. It's one thing to believe there is more than this life we experience daily; it's another to *feel it*. To be comforted by the love of something so much bigger. That's what enveloped Jeanne during her cancer journey. That's what I witnessed. I can still access it on my own, but sometimes I forget and have to talk myself back into it. It sure helps to have a friend who is a priest remind me. Not so much with words as with her peaceful presence. This pandemic has kept many of us from gathering to reflect together on the bigger picture of life, including me. The truth is we don't need buildings for worship so much as people. People who reflect that love.

I've always thought that G-d* speaks to me through people, if for no other reason than I'd be freaked out by a burning bush. I'm lucky to have relationships that give me glimpses of higher love and the peace of "heaven on earth," starting with my husband and kids, radiating out from there.

Still, it's special to spend time with a spiritual leader whose calling is to walk the line between humanity and that higher love. There is a lot to be learned by just resting in that example. Thanks to my friend Jeanne, I have this special calm in the eye of one of the most challenging storms of my life.

It's so comforting. The ultimate empathy. ●

---

*G-d is written this way out of respect for religions that hold this practice sacred.

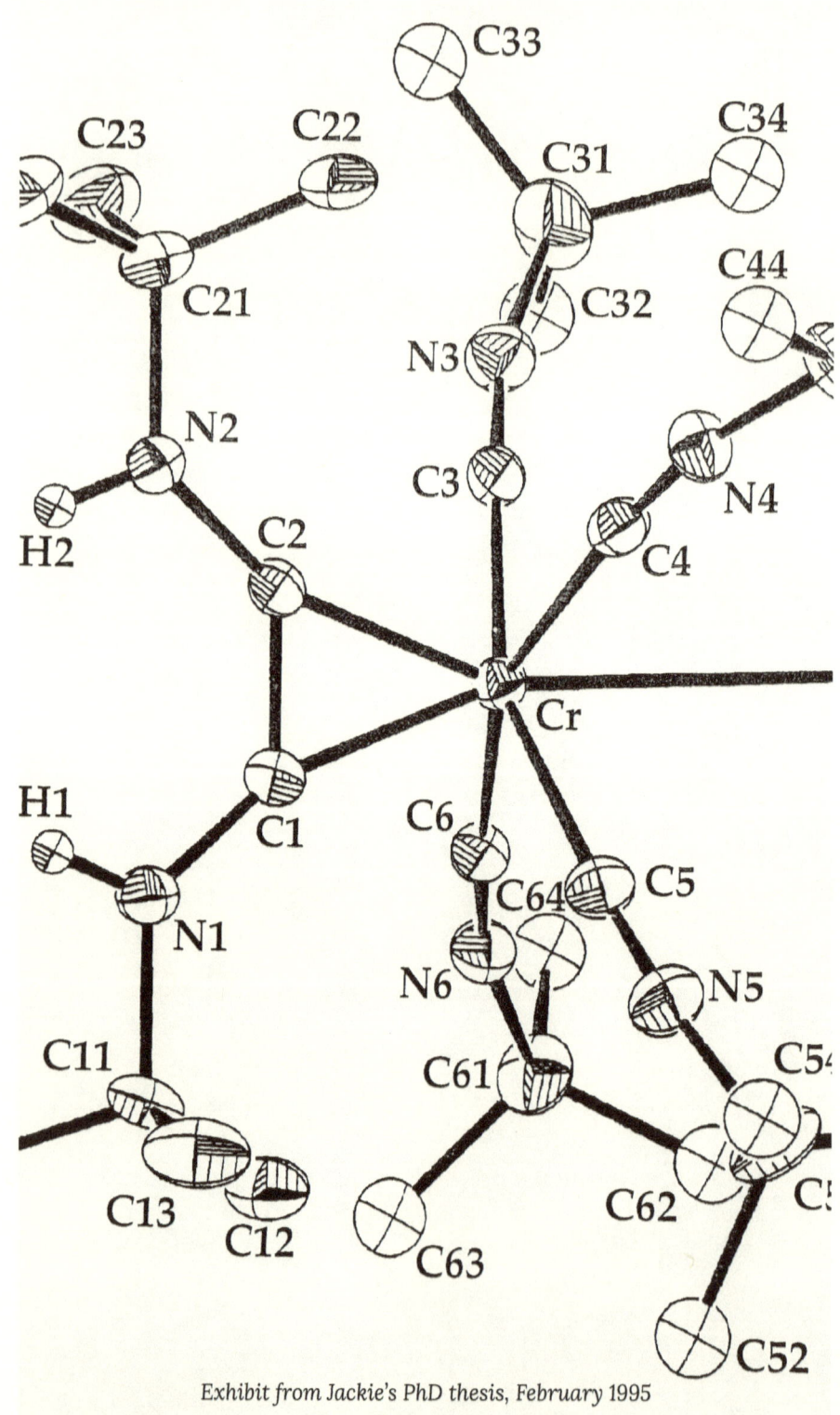

Exhibit from Jackie's PhD thesis, February 1995

CHAPTER TWENTY FOUR • JANUARY 21, 2022

 Keeping the Faith... In Science

"Failure is success in progress."
— Albert Einstein

I have always been a big believer in science. All the way to a PhD in chemistry from MIT. That's commitment. My career has also included lots of technology-related work and tech-based economic development. I believe in progress through carefully chosen science.

But my body has been something of a failed experiment in the last decade, and that's hard to swallow. In this way, despite all of my education, I can relate to why people are so fatigued with the state of the world in a pandemic, many distrustful of the scientific advice they are getting.

Experiment 1: Better Living Through Chemistry
The promise to my generation was that science and technology would save us...time, effort, aging, pain, our earth home, etc. The results haven't been so great. I've since learned—with lots of data—that my body couldn't clear all of those time/age/effort-saving chemicals, leading to increased food sensitivities, illness, and ultimately cancer. Mother Nature reminds us with ever-increasing frequency (fires, tsunamis, earthquakes, glyphosate and other toxic waste wreaking havoc in our water and food system, etc.) that we're failing to keep up with our mortgage on the earth and in our own bodies.

Experiment 2: Healing the Body Through Functional/Natural Medicine
After I woke up to the warning signs (around the age of 40), largely thanks to our daughter's health issues, we cleaned up our act at home. I worked with

experts and tried most of the diets you all might believe in. Certainly always clean. Gluten-free. Dairy-free. Sugar-free. Sometimes (two years) vegan. Many years grain-free and lectin-free. Celery juice. Smoothies. Believe it or not, with careful planning and a lot of effort, there is still plenty to eat and a way to balance meals.

Saunas. Yoga teacher certification. Meditation. Exercise. Better sleep. We did heal Sophie's hemiplegic migraines. Yay! We did ultimately learn about our sensitivity to molds and heavy metals, and how to safely clear them. Yay! I did feel better for a while. Then, I didn't. Then I got one of the more difficult cancers to heal, all while I was doing "everything you can do" to avoid the health issues that tend to come with aging, regardless of my genes. Maybe it was too late in my life to reverse that course. Maybe my body is especially sensitive. It worked for Sophie (and lots of other people), and I'd make that trade-off over and over. Heal my daughter; leave me with the work.

Experiment 3: Treating Ovarian Cancer With Traditional Medicine
February 2020 to May 2021. Surgery. Chemo. It works sometimes—20% to be exact. I'm not particularly lucky in this case. I relied on science and a gifted nutritionist to fare well through that whole onslaught, continuing to eat, run, practice yoga, parent, work, and have a life. But when I finished chemo with my cancer marker out of range, I was told to go into palliative care. That wasn't my fault. The chemo was ineffective against my cancer, as it is the majority of the time. Why do they use it? It's the "gold standard" despite 30 years of bad results. I believed it would work because my oncologist was encouraged about "how well I was doing." I believed it would be a blip before I could begin healing again. This lab mouse's hopes were dashed again but, knowing all I did, I leaned back into my faith.

Experiment 4: Naturopathic Medicine/Metabolic Approach to Cancer
May to October 2021. The marker went down with mistletoe, ketogenic diet, hyperthermia, hyperbaric oxygen, targeted foods, and supplements...until it went up. A lot. Fast. No matter how hard or fast I worked. It turns out that unless those cancer stem cells are squashed with chemo, it's hard to fight the tidal wave of high-grade serous ovarian carcinoma naturally, at least in my body. And I haven't met anyone else who's managed that particular trick (akin to a triple lutz with a half twist and five backflips) either.

So, there I was in Istanbul, taking on **Experiment 5:** Let's call this, **"Hit It With All We've Got."** Everything above worked, some. Just not enough. So now, here I am upgrading and combining all of it (chemo that's been tested in vitro against my cells, whole body and local hyperthermia, HBOT, nutritional infusions, keto, metabolic approach, and more) with hopes that the combo will be powerful enough to get after the stem cells and finally put me in a stable place. That I'll still be able to look back on these past two and a half years as a (long) blip in an otherwise reasonably long life of logical, intuitive approaches to health and healing. I have good, scientific reasons to believe again: the current chemo protocol has been tested and found effective against my cells, all of those methods worked somewhat, just not enough alone—hopefully, the combo is at least additive, if not multiplicative. Full-body hyperthermia alone is a regular two and a half hour sauna. I suspect it keeps the mold (which featured prominently in dysregulating my immune system prior to cancer and after frontline treatment) at bay/cleared, as do the antioxidant and Vitamin C infusions and HBOT. This integrative approach should leave me less vulnerable than I was after traditional (and ineffective, as it turned out) chemotherapy. Finally, they've healed people with even later stage and more difficult cancers than I have, including ovarian.

But can I admit that it's hard sometimes to keep the faith in medical science? That's a lot of disappointment, right? The truth is that science is always an ongoing experiment. I'm a scientist at heart and an entrepreneur, so the unknown doesn't usually bother me. But it's a different experience *when you are the lab mouse*. And when you've watched other healthy, positive, well-supported people "doing cancer just right" succumb to it. No need to cheerlead; I find simply listening to be the biggest help when I occasionally, understandably feel discouraged. Also, mindset is a great tool, but so is discernment and deep, honest, two-way conversation with (hopefully entrepreneurial and smart) doctors about how the experiment is going. Because science is experimental. No one has all the answers. If someone is doing well, it's a combo of luck (chemo worked, yay!) and effort. These stories—hopefully including mine someday—can inspire, but the science around many kinds of cancer is still pretty raw and nascent, even after decades of investment. I say all of this from a well-educated, inside-out view.

So, I'm not going to tell you to drink juice, make smoothies, avoid fruit, eat berries, take chemo or not take chemo, "stay positive," or any of the other formulae that are out there. The pieces and parts may or may not help you heal or avoid cancer. It's best to find out what works for your individual health challenges at any given time. Certainly eating clean, avoiding toxins, getting good sleep, managing stress/mental health, discerning and receiving effective treatments, and getting smart bio-individualized approaches and nutritional support whether you are trying to stay healthy or bear the onslaught of treatments...all of that is good. Most of which, your grandmother could have told you.

So what's the lesson from my story? I think it's this...

Be the first author in your story. Be the head scientist. I've been the first author on scientific papers, so I know what that feels like. It was natural to approach cancer this way. *Be the first author is the one thing I can tell you that I know will always be true.* It's not a fad or marketing gimmick. Part of how you know this is true is it's not about me. It's about you. Especially for cancers with bad outcomes, the results show the researchers and doctors do not have everything, or even much, figured out. Be in that conversation. Get information from multiple sources and angles and then do what makes you feel good. Listen to your body—the *real* expert, from whom we were often disconnected during the "better living through science" phase. Be ready to pivot. Forgive people who don't have all the answers, because that's just where we are. Science is always an experiment. That anyone ever presents it as done, known, or finished...is great for marketing programs and personal brands, but it has done a tremendous disservice to both science and all of us, especially the people who didn't survive. Because when those methods don't work, it causes us to lose faith in science and scientists, or blame ourselves for not trying hard enough. Conversation stops. Priorities get decided by a few, with only a few in mind, whether it's climate change or individual cancer treatment. The power in the experiment is including all voices, especially the intuitive and divine ones like our bodies, other sentient beings, and the natural world.

I still have faith in science, but I'm a realistic optimist about what we know and don't know. At this point, I've done an unlimited amount of the experiments from every side of the lab bench. I know the outcomes and limitations. What occurs to me is not that science is bad or flawed, but that living systems are miracles we will *never* fully understand. In many ways, my faith in higher powers has always risen in parallel with my scientific education. The more I've looked into the night sky or at molecules through x-ray crystallography, the more I've realized that this astonishingly beautiful world is not something we could create or recreate. The symmetry. The thoughtful design. It's something we can only ever approximately understand. It's awe-inspiring.

I'm still very much in this cancer healing experiment. I'm most definitely the first author...with a litany of partners...in the story of my health. Results TBD. What I know for sure is this...I'm still here, and I haven't lost faith. ◉

CHAPTER TWENTY FIVE • JANUARY 18, 2022

Dreams Instead of Resolutions

I've never been much into New Year's resolutions, and I'm even less interested in "should" these days. "Should" is probably one of the worst habits I needed to break, actually. I did a lot of things I should have done, including eating healthy, exercising, and living a clean lifestyle for the last decade. Not that those things are bad and didn't help me be healthy longer, but I got cancer anyway. I did the work I should, hosted celebrations I should, took care of others as I should, volunteered as I should. I did too many "shoulds" and didn't seek as much joy as would have been good for me. In the busyness of "should," I lost the dreams. I lost the play.

> "But it's a low low road you've gotta roll down before you find your way, my friend
> And it's a high, high hill you've gotta climb up before you get to the top again"
> —Grace Potter and Mark Batson, from Grace Potter and the Nocturnals' Low Road

I should be dead by now. That's the last "should" I'll ever need. I am done with "should." My dreams orient my days. I will do what's naturally needed to realize my dreams. What got me through treatment far from home was dreams of more normal times and vibrant life. I sit through chemo and hyperthermia dreaming of little and bigger things that I'll enjoy when I heal. In that way, I put one foot in front of the other in terms of the things I must do. It's the dreams that pull me into the future through the daily grind. They orient me without chastising or dictating or yelling too loudly. Dreams are more like good friends, rather than bullies.

My dreams involve simple things like cooking in my own kitchen and shopping at the grocery store myself. Taking a warm bath. Being able to run around the track and lead another yoga class or even do a regular Vinyasa flow for myself. I dream of trying out a Hammam (communal bathhouse) in Turkey when I feel better. Wearing more normal clothes that don't have to accommodate a swollen abdomen, as recommended by my ever-stylish friend Kathryn. Learning from Shelby how to wear whatever ends up being my hair again. Adding the make-up and earrings to feel pretty because that still sounds like fun. Trying out the air fryer I bought for Grant for Christmas. Hugging my dog. Walking my dog. Sitting in the backyard with the Lacks and other neighbors. Perfecting keto pizza. The sun on my shoulders and the sand between my toes. Many more spectacular sunsets and breathtaking sunrises. Ongoing date nights with my husband. I dream of walking in the Cleveland Metroparks South Chagrin Reservation—*being strong enough to cover the whole trail*—with my friend Sharon again.

Bigger, longer-term dreams include watching my kids flourish in college and beyond. Being on beaches, frolicking in the water, and vacationing with my family for years to come. Empty nesting and retirement travel with my husband. I've wanted to experience Iceland, Australia, Africa...and anyplace John would like to see. And Michigan and Florida from time to time, where we have friends and family I'd like to hug, including my cousin's daughter Aria. I dream of live music like seeing Grace Potter and the Nocturnals again at the House of Blues.

It's still incredible to me that my cancer has overlapped completely with a pandemic, for good and bad. I dream of the normalcy of traveling to board meetings in New York City, and the novelty of finding a keto restaurant where I can eat *everything on the menu including dessert!* I dream of hiking in Colorado and dancing with abandon at our niece Sarah's wedding. I dream of swimming in any body of water whether it's Lisa and David's pool, the Gulf of Mexico, any ocean or sea, or Lake Michigan. Beaches feature prominently in my dreams. Any and all. I dream of connecting with and having fun with friends old and new.

My heart dreams of soaring as I watch my son graduate from high school. I dream of the melancholy but "it's-all-good-really" feeling of moving him into his dorm for college later this summer. I can hardly wait to see my daughter enjoy a semester abroad this fall while remembering my own experiences as a student in foreign countries. I want to see what she makes of these experiences and what good our kids will do in the world. I dream that our kids orient from joy rather than "should" because I finally learned how to model that.

I dream that they won't have to learn these lessons the hard way because I did that work while they watched.

I dream of continuing to work in whatever ways make sense, feel good, and make the world a better place...including this book...not because I should but because I *can't keep it in*, as was true for my first book. I dream of the joy and satisfaction of creative flow. I dream of learning new ways "to channel cosmos into the chaos" as author Madeleine L'Engle alluded to. I dream of seeing and realizing more beauty, not because it's new, but because my eyes and soul are more attuned to it. Or maybe because the veil of adulthood is pulled back and I can remember what I used to see as a child.

In many ways, I dream of the life I had but with much more presence and appreciation. That's what I've heard from people who go so low as I've been physically and climb back up again. The physical transformation mirrors the emotional and spiritual.

I'm done with "shoulds." What I'm not done with is life.

I have dreams. I wonder, what are yours? ●

CHAPTER TWENTY SIX • MARCH 20, 2022

Treat Yourself Well "Kendine Iyi Davran"

While living in Istanbul, I'm learning Turkish. It's not an easy language to pick up, but it's a fun, rhythmic, and poetic language to practice. It's also succinct. A few words say a lot. People appreciate that I try and teach me phrases all the time. A very common parting saying is "kendine iyi bak" or "take care of yourself."

During a recent conversation with my oncologists here, we were celebrating all things moving in the right direction (numbers, how I feel, scan results). Although taking chemo—*even integratively, with nutritional infusions and naturopathic treatments*—is never easy, and I miss home, that was a moment for celebration. One of the docs speaks mostly Turkish, but we've managed to communicate through translation and the little bit I know. So, I proudly said, "Kendine iyi bak" as he was leaving. He turned back with a smile and said he would rather that I "kendine iyi davran" vs. "taking care of myself." I should know that the treatments are working, have patience, and meanwhile, "treat myself well!" I've come to realize there is a subtle but important difference while opting to do exactly that, over and over since.

"Taking care" is freighted with responsibility, especially if you are fighting illness. It connotes eating the right foods, getting your exercise, adhering to a sleep schedule, drinking enough water, figuring out how to adjust treatments to optimize effectiveness, etc. These are all important, but not so much fun. The idea of "taking care" is also something of a patriarchal notion, whether you are taking care of someone else or yourself. It contains the idea that there is a right way, out there, and that these rules somehow guide our ability to care for ourselves.

"Treating yourself well" takes all that goes into caring for yourself and makes it more fun. It's like being a guest in a five-star hotel where the concierge knows exactly what you enjoy most because *you* are the concierge and nobody knows you better. It also means being in conversation with your body and soul to realize what feels best at that moment, because we change and grow. It admits that the right answers aren't always known or clear, especially where the body is concerned and healthcare isn't always true to its name. It's more of-the-moment and evolving.

"Treating yourself well" is more empathetic than "taking care." So, *what's the difference*?

Here's what "kendine iyi davran" (treat yourself well) has come to mean to me…

Rather than simply eating the right foods, you take the opportunity to dream about what would be the tastiest, healthy thing you can eat and make that. You indulge in dinner out with a wonderful friend like Sharon Sobol Jordan who was visiting for the week, if that's something that brings you great joy (it does). As my dad used to say, "You gotta eat," so we might as well make it celebratory. It means you get to know the produce guy well because it's always worth the walk to get the fresh strawberries. It also means enjoying that glass of organic wine with your meal from time to time (which only has a few carbs). It doesn't mean going crazy eating foods that would make you ultimately feel bad, because "treating yourself well" must include empathy for your body now and into the future.

Getting exercise might still include boring reps with those five-pound weights to build muscle, but it also means that taking the long walk to the park with your friend, sitting on the bench with a coffee, and watching the kids play might be enough of an accomplishment for a particular day. Getting enough sleep may include the luxury of a nap without any guilt during the middle of the day, especially if your main job for this period of time is to heal your body of cancer. It may also mean that you don't accept Zoom meetings that take place at 10 p.m. in your time zone, just because that's when the famous oncology team that wants to learn more about what you're doing happens to have their meetings. You are helping them; they can adjust too.

"Treating yourself well" means setting boundaries and protecting your time to heal, work, play and do the things that are nourishing for you. It means staying connected to home, friends, and family in the way and at the times that synchronize with your life and needs. It means sharing what feels right and holding private what's your business, which other people might find triggering and hard to hold in any helpful way. If you have some options, it means saying yes to work that brings you joy but leaving for later work that is...more like work. That doesn't mean the work you do is without challenge; it means the juice is worth the squeeze. Having a voice in the world is part of living and growing, so the chance to continue to do that even during a period that typically necessitates more hibernation to heal is oxygen for our souls.

"Treating yourself well" means doing what you have to do (e.g., truly yucky chemo days) but thoroughly enjoying a day exploring Istanbul with a friend and leaving cancer behind. I had a chance to do just that this past Thursday while Sharon was here. We had a magical day that will stay with me and rounds out what could be a full-time slog into a part-time adventure. John and I take the time to do these adventures too because we both love them. It also means indulging in *two* movies on a snowy day because today is a day of rest, or playing games because fun is nourishing too. Sharon took the week mostly off as well, which was good for her soul too. We both have a history of working hard alone and well together, so to just relax and have fun was a conscious choice more than an old habit for both of us. You don't have to be sick to treat yourself well.

"Treating yourself well" means letting others take care of you sometimes, when you have to conserve your energy just to survive. I'm not being dramatic. This is the reality of cancer. It means letting someone fan you or get you water during hyperthermia, cooking together, and not feeling guilty if that cooking uses up all of your energy so someone else cleans up. It means relaxing with a healing massage if that's one of your favorite things to do, even if you are a little embarrassed about the current state of your body vs. what it used to be.

"Treating yourself well" means continuing to grow and learn because that feels good and keeps you connected to people, near and far. Learning Turkish is not always fun in the moment, but the return is getting to use it over and over, and connecting with kind people and a rich and storied culture. It feels like singing a song I've learned. Treating myself well also means continuing to reflect and share in writing and speaking because I love being in conversation with people about things that matter.

"Treating yourself well" means understanding your body, pushing the boundaries of treatment for difficult health issues, and advocating for yourself, but not perseverating or worrying once decisions have been made. It means finding medical partners you can trust, including them in your care where they best fit, and falling back into their arms, so you can finally rest in some faith that the best choices possible are being made and executed for you at any given time. The energy of fighting a system that isn't empathic to your body and soul is exhausting; I know this from too much experience. Here in Istanbul, it's been easier to treat myself well.

"Treating yourself well" means not dwelling on things you might have done differently once you've learned that lesson and not being anxious about a future you can't control. It means giving yourself the grace to know that you did the best you could with what you knew every step of the way, even if you know better now. It's even congratulating yourself for a difficult job well done, even when it's always inherently imperfect. It means continuing to do your best but not overthinking, so you can rest in that empathy for your past self, going forward. It means accepting the present for the present that it is, especially after you've outlived expert expectations and experienced a time when you couldn't imagine being out of pain. It means letting go of the fear of dying as much as you can because you already did the hard work of entering hospice and planning for (not just imagining) that transition. It means reaping the benefits of living further beyond that fear than you did before all that arduous work.

These are some of the small but meaningful shifts my Turkish doctor instigated with one small phrase. I wonder what it means for you.

Kendine Iyi Davran! ⦿

Galata Tower steps, Istanbul

CHAPTER TWENTY SEVEN • APRIL 8, 2022

Chronic Illness
A Master Class in Appreciating the Gift of the Present

Living in the present can be a challenge. We replay the past, fantasizing about what we'd tell our younger selves to make life easier. We imagine enjoying the future if we do everything "right" and catch some breaks...or we imagine adjusting to a different future, again, if we don't. Is this all bad? I don't think so. We would do well to learn from history and change behaviors so we don't repeat mistakes, but hang onto the good stuff. We do well to dream and do what we can to live into those dreams. Culturally, we're rewarded for having and achieving goals and all the busyness that entails. But sometimes, life is passing us by while we do all that.

Add a chronic illness with debilitating symptoms to the picture and the urge to escape the present becomes an even bigger challenge. How could we have avoided this suffering? If only we didn't eat this, do that, allow so much stress... How much more will there be? Maybe someday we can plan a vacation like we see others enjoying on social media, will have hair again, can go for months (dare we hope, years?) without treatments? How can we get out of this cycle?

Given the impacts of the illness on our everyday life, our dreamtime is sometimes better than our awake time. We go anywhere, see everyone (including ancestors who have passed), and eat anything. Oh, the feasts I've had in my dreams lately. Tuscan food features prominently, especially pasta. Celebrity chefs sometimes preside. My body is whole. My head is covered with long, curly hair that requires washing (such high maintenance)! I move as freely and easily as I did a few years ago before cancer was a reality in our lives. I've heard this from other friends too. In our dreams, we are whole. I guess a couple of years of being "sick" cannot overwhelm decades of identifying otherwise.

So, it can be a challenge to accept the present, much less live in it. We have to remember to be grateful for progress. Not being in pain is huge. Knowing the cancer is backing down is also encouraging. Being able to cook, eat, and digest food is better than not, even if pasta isn't on the menu these days. Getting a little stronger every day and walking farther—even uphill—is possible. Still, somehow, it's hard to accept these are big wins when I was "so healthy" just a few years ago. Measuring progress versus "I should be dead by now" feels like cheating somehow, even if it's the truth. It's remarkable what cancer and its treatments will do to a human body in a short period of time.

Everything physical takes more effort than it used to. There is a tendency to focus on current symptoms, wishing them away. I nap like a champion because I'm tired. I take breaks when I'm cooking because I need to. I still remember moving more easily in my own body. I still identify as that person. So, part of the challenge of the present is not being disappointed with how I move, how I feel, and what my body can and cannot do these days. I've had to learn to live in a new lane and et the old one go.

Spiritually, cancer is not breaking me but making me stronger...so far. Life beyond the physical is easier in some ways. Mentally, words flow ever more easily. Work is especially rewarding, as is the idea that I have made a positive impact. Emotionally, I'm more comfortable with quiet. My dreams are vivid and my internal life, rich. When I'm out and about, I'm both proud and fascinated—like when I was kid—seeing things anew. Spring has sprung in Istanbul.

When I talk to our kids, I thoroughly appreciate every detail of their lives and how they are moving through them. My husband and I communicate easily, with or without words. Maybe this is what happens when busyness gives way to a kind of forced quiet. Everything important is in graphic relief like one of those pop-up books we read as children.

Living in the present is also forced on those of us with chronic illnesses, in many ways. So much is unknown about cancer (and so many other illnesses) that there is only so much utility in rehashing what we did/didn't do. I've done as much of that as is useful, to some good ends.

For the rest, I look forward to answers flowing in after my consciousness transitions off this earthly plane (hopefully many years from now). That's my version of heaven. All of our questions get answered. The internet is great, but there are so many answers Google will never be able to provide. Similarly, there is only so much planning for the future we can do because...there are so many unknowns about cancer. What we know and can do, we are doing. Beyond that, there are hopes, prayers, dreams, and then just resting in some faith that we do the best we can. Of course, we have plan Bs and Cs just in case, knowing that the only thing we can control is our reaction to what happens.

So, we have some special perspectives on the persistent but difficult advice to "live in the present." It's an extra challenge, but also a necessity for those of us with chronic illness. Doing otherwise is unwise, unhealthy, not empathetic to ourselves, and kind of impossible. Our bodies keep pulling us into the present. I was still learning to accept the gift of the present before I got sick. Having kids helped a lot, especially when they were younger and demanded more attention. That time too, was a mixture of acceptance and frustration—enjoying the moment with them and imagining a life with more time and freedom. Little did I know the experiences and lessons on accepting the present awaiting me as our kids got older...and I got sick. Living with a chronic illness is like a masterclass in being present.

Maybe if I get it right this time, my soul can take a rest and just enjoy the present, with a dash of learning from the past and dreaming about the future. Just enough, but not too much. Like salt and pepper in one of those dishes in my dreams.

Maybe my lessons about living in the present will finally be done, and I can live with the gift beyond the struggle. Maybe you can learn the same lessons without getting sick. That would be a wonderful gift. ●

John and Jackie at Kadiköy Market

CHAPTER TWENTY EIGHT • APRIL 15, 2022

 I am Still That Girl... Integrating Our Lives

Integrating life experiences can be tricky. People come and go. Locations change. We grow up and out of certain mindsets. We move on from relationships, sometimes necessarily.

Perhaps one of the hardest things of all is to remember who you were and are before and after trauma. Cancer is one such traumatic journey that can rob us of our innocence and ignorance of mortality. Of course, it also deepens our appreciation for so many things. But can we sometimes recapture the carefree side of ourselves...the person who was able to have fun...on the other side of cancer, or even in the middle of it all?

It's not always easy, but today, I say yes.

We finished a beautiful tour of Kadiköy on the Asian side of Istanbul. Our "work" (chemo, daily life, Zoom calls) happens on the European side in the health district, and these tours take us to the places more carefree visitors enjoy when they come to Istanbul. I find any and all glimpses of the water especially healing. Just crossing the bridges is breathtaking. Like all Istanbullular, I'm pretty obsessed with the Bosporus. The Golden Horn and the Sea of Marmara are special too.

Kadiköy is a seaside town with one of the most vibrant fresh markets in Istanbul. It's easy to get lost in the sights, smells, and tastes of fruit and vegetable stands; fresh fishmongers (with fish swimming in barrels in front—it doesn't get much fresher than that); specialty stores with olives, cheese, fresh grape leaves for dolma; nut and dried fruit purveyors; Turkish delight and candy stores; kahve (coffee) shops; backgammon and game shops; cafes and bars.

My mind wandered to markets I've walked through in other countries, as well as Detroit's Eastern Market which I visited with my dad and where my grandpa used to buy goods to sell at his grocery store years ago. More recently, I have special memories of the North Union Farmers Market in Shaker Square where we enjoy shopping at home. Our daughter and her friend sold homemade natural beauty products there one summer.

Kadiköy has residential areas as well, around all of this activity. In that way, it reminded John and me of our early days of dating in Lincoln Park, Chicago. Stopping to have a beer and a glass of wine (in the middle of the day!) was reminiscent of a time before cancer, before kids, before marriage even...when we had few cares and more free time. The sun was shining. People were passing. The whole scene was brimming with life. I was transported to being a young adult, newly in love, looking forward to a bright future.

A dear friend is expecting a baby this summer! So, our conversation often turns to the feelings of impending parenthood—all of the excitement and responsibility. Some of it one can imagine ahead of time. Most of it, one cannot. It reminds me of those early days when Sophie and Grant were twinkles in our eyes before they became people that blossom over and over in ways that make our hearts full. I remember that time when they were very young too, with such tenderness...even as we recount with clarity the bleary-eyed exhaustion of parenting newborns and toddlers. Despite the challenges, the miracle of it all was never lost on us.

Kadiköy Market

Driving back to the European side, realizing it was a week "off" of chemo and I was back on next week...I'd been forced to integrate my current experiences into this crazy, nonlinear life as well. Our plan was to retire and travel, not to travel just to stay alive. But here we are, living on borrowed time since I've been told more than once I would be dead before now. While I hate the work of chemo and being far away from our kids, I love the adventures, big and small, I have in Istanbul together with John and with friends. Nothing is really worth having to go through chemotherapy, but if I have to do it (and since the US system left me for dead after round one), I may as well be here, integrating my Middle Eastern heritage with my American-born self.

I can feel a certain integration across life, even with all of the physical and emotional trauma of the last two years. Thank goodness (Mashallah, as the Turkish say) our kids are managing well with the help of friends and family, and our relationships are more than intact. They are stronger. Those relationships are crucial to integration. It's that love and empathy that forms the unbreakable thread running through the various facets of who I am and who I've been.

I'm the same girl who loved perusing markets with her dad, traveling the world, learning languages, trying new foods, drinking up local culture, enjoying a lazy afternoon beverage with her boyfriend while people-watching in a vibrant city, and preparing together to parent two kids who would constantly amaze us. That John and our kids haven't looked at me differently (honestly, I can't understand it) since I lost my hair, my figure, and almost my life, is certainly a big part of why I can still connect to those other parts of my life. They feel both far away and like yesterday. Time is magical like that. Their empathy is the river that runs through it all. I don't take any of that emotional support for granted. Sometimes I think about what it would be like to be on this cancer journey alone, and I can't tolerate more than a millisecond. It's hard enough as it is.

It certainly helps to remember. To re-member, meaning to pull all my selves together into an integrated whole—one that might even be more than the fragments when I am living, G-d willing (Inshallah as the Turkish say), beyond cancer. There can be a temptation to shut off one part if it was too painful, but it will just come back to bite us subconsciously if we don't transform the trauma. Or maybe it's too hard to remember the good times because the losses are too many and so profound. But those good times are also part of the fabric of our lives, important to remember or we might become bitter. In some ways, life feels like a big quilt to which we keep adding pieces. Some are neat and colorful. Some are more bleak and messy. They are all true. Or maybe life is the stew you make from all of the beautiful ingredients you find in a fresh market.

In any case, the whole is something creative, new, and more than the sum of the parts. A kind of alchemy.

Integration is important if we hope to live a whole life. Living a whole life is important if we want to keep growing our souls. Growing our souls...is why we're here. So, integration seems to be part of our work.

In that case, it's a gift to have a day when I can so clearly remember being "that girl" all along the way. I hope you have these opportunities to re-member, as well as steady, true, empathetic relationships that help you feel integrated too. We all need them. ⚫

Jackie and Susan in Istanbul

CHAPTER TWENTY NINE • APRIL 28, 2022

The Healing Power of Good Friends Is Empathy
Getting Your Own Triggers Out of the Way

I'm lucky. Oh, yeah, not so fortunate to have cancer, but...

I have friends who are willing to travel around the world—*literally*—to be with me. Susan Colby, a longtime, dear friend whom I first met in the early days of working with McKinsey & Company, visited me in Turkey. The best part of that prior work at McKinsey was the legacy of wonderful people, and Susan is no exception.

She was the first and one of the only women I worked with at McKinsey. She was also a mom and breast cancer survivor when we met. She was senior to me and inspiring in the way she integrated work and life. She's had her priorities in order. Working with Susan was the first time I looked ahead in my career and thought, yeah, I'd like to be that person. No offense to all the men I worked with at McKinsey, but balancing work and family just wasn't usually done at the same level.

Susan and her wonderful husband Peter and adorable daughters, Rachel and Rebecca...well, that was a model I could embrace and get excited about. Susan put tight boundaries around her work hours so they could cook and have family dinners, read books, and do the things that families do. She insisted on working part-time when hardly anyone did, so she could work around being there for her family. Investing in life made her work even better, more centered, and wiser than it would have been otherwise. We became fast friends and enthusiastic co-workers. For a time, after she left McKinsey to join a company, she was even a client of mine...a truly effective, co-creative experience. She knew me when I first started dating John. I remember being so glad to see her face in the church when we got married.

You know how you have some friends that don't live near you, but you stay together even though you're apart? You don't have to be together to be together. Susan has lived in Washington DC, and San Francisco, while I've been in Chicago and Cleveland. We made time to connect through the years, including some fun travel. When she had a recurrence of cancer, I was part of her life and did what I could to be supportive from afar. When cancer struck me, she was a nurturing ninja, knowing just what to say, sending uplifting notes and little gifts, and generally just-right empathizing with the horrible nature of the disease and the treatments.

The week Susan arrived brought it to a whole new level. Susan *took over my kitchen!!!!!* There is something special about coming home from chemo day, lying on the couch, listening to cooking sounds, watching her expertly dance around a foreign and small kitchen, and smelling the most amazing chicken piccata a la Susan. Now that is mothering in the best way. I had not two but three plates...one at midnight because I couldn't stop thinking about it. I can still use some more weight, so this is goooooood. I'm no dummy, so I gratefully requested more meals. Beef tips and veggies au Susan and chicken Provencal were also on the menu. Yummmmmmm.

We enjoyed some beautiful fresh fish and iskender out as well. So nourished, it was somehow not so hard to walk all the way from my apartment through Macka Park to the Bosporus to enjoy a Turkish coffee. Ahhh, sea breeze.

We had a wonderful day with tour guide extraordinaire and friend Hakan Gurger, enjoying Galata Port, Balat, Fener, crossing the Galata Bridge, and wandering the spice bazaar. It's a good feeling to forget why I'm here sometimes and imagine we're just enjoying another girls' trip. Life with treatment interrupting as opposed to treatments with a dash of life.

I've also slept well this week, no doubt because of her caring. Susan also, despite her own traumatic experiences with cancer herself and in her family, kept me company in all the best ways through chemo day.

What I hate about chemo day is chemo. Even nutritional infusion days are frustrating. It's hard to be poked and hooked up for hours, unable to leave. But there is an upside to that...time. Without tight deadlines and plenty of time to fill, we talk, we laugh, we remember things we've done together, we share stories about family and other times in our lives. This luxury of time with such a longtime and dear friend who doesn't live nearby can't be underestimated. The whole Colby family is here with her in spirit. Rachel has inspired me by gracefully managing her own journey with breast cancer way too young. Susan got me through hyperthermia by reading a funny article about #vanlife sent by Rebecca and playing and dancing to music (I danced inside). The rest of the family sent supportive notes and texts. Susan set up the food, the fan, brought water, applied cold compresses, and brought a coloring book and markers (not just any coloring book!)

It's not easy work and certainly could be triggering for someone who has been through this kind of dance before, and not just once, as a patient and a mom. That's the biggest gift of all and what's so hard—Susan managed to get her own triggers out of the way to be with me. That's pure empathy. It's so simple but so hard to do. Susan is a survivor who retained her humanity and empathy.

That's the secret. That's the key. That's the healing power underneath the cooking, company, and nurturing. That compass of empathy is a guiding force that brings the best out of us, even in difficult circumstances. Metabolizing your own trauma is certainly one path to liberating that power. I can say that receiving this kind of nurturing from Susan, John, and my other friends and caregivers here in Turkey has also tempered the trauma of this experience for me. That helps too.

So, I hope when you are faced with trauma, you find empathetic nurturing, and I hope when you have the chance to help others, you can get your own triggers out of the way. I hope you have such good friends, who would nurture you and vice versa.

It's simple. It's not easy.

But it's powerfully healing. ◉

Rocky

CHAPTER THIRTY • APRIL 20, 2022

 Home With a Capital H

Home is where the heart is...held safely, lovingly, and earnestly. Home is where empathy and love flow.

One month from today, I will be home for the first time in six months. I dreamed of returning fully well, triumphant, and free from the burden of future treatment. I won't get all that, but...I am still alive, and I've earned and can afford a break.

There is also fun to have and work to do! And I'm still here, even though I was predicted to be dead months ago. Our son will graduate from high school on June 8, 2022. I'll have the honor of delivering John Carroll University's commencement address on May 22, 2022. Our daughter will be preparing for a semester abroad next fall, and our son will move into college. I'll be here for that too. John and I will officially become empty-nesters in September, something we both dreamed about and kind of dreaded, the way most people do. But what is the "nest," really? What is home?

I think a lot about home. Sometimes, I'm grateful to feel like a global citizen with "home inside." I've always loved to travel and incorporate myself into other cultures. Home is wherever I am, from Detroit to Bilbao to Boston to Chicago to Shaker Heights, Ohio. Lately, family and friends have visited Istanbul, connecting me to my American home, and we've made new Turkish friends we won't ever forget.

Sometimes, I'm simply homesick for our kids, friends, house, kitchen, bed, and dog that have surrounded me for the better part of the last two decades. Always, I'm grateful to feel virtually held by friends and family that connect me/us to that home at every turn. Photos and videos from a college visit or track meet we couldn't attend. WhatsApp videos with our kids, sharing the details of their lives and occasionally pretending they still need our advice. Calls with Carnella, who is staying at our house, giving me the scoop on our son and the dog too. I'd like to think we were involved in our kids' lives in the right way before I had to move to Istanbul, and that as much as I fantasize about family dinners, our son would be living his life very much as he is now...leaving us in the dust a lot of the time. It's only natural at 18.

In May of 2021, our little family (and dog) were all together, on the other side of one round of surgery/chemo and hoping I could keep this cancer at bay with natural treatments. Being altogether was, and continues to be, all I really need. What I dream most about being home is just being present with whoever is home, whenever they are. Family meals when we can. Just cooking favorite foods for the kids, John, and/or myself when we can't. Being there for big events like graduation and also casual conversations that take place easily, without having to operate across a 7 to 8 hour time difference. Not just hearing about but also seeing our kids in action in their summer jobs and the fun they have planned with friends. I can tell a lot just by the way they walk in the door. That's what I miss.

John, Sophie, Grant, and Jackie, May 2021

And the dog, Rocky! Will he even remember me after six months? I think so. How does he make sense of such a long absence? I'm pretty sure I'll be forgiven (or it maybe will be forgotten). The good news is I can walk him around the block again...I couldn't before we left. He'll enjoy food scraps again...I couldn't stand at the stove to cook before I left. Those little victories matter. I must count them, even as my body isn't "fixed" yet. In any case, he sure is handsome, and I miss him a lot!

But, of course, I'd like to be...done.

I'd like to throw an "I'm-free-of-cancer-no-need-to-worry-about-me-anymore!" party and see everyone who supported us near and far. The truth is I can't. Even though the pandemic is over for most everyone, I'm still immunocompromised, receiving chemo, and masked, and we're not sure how much time I'll really have at home. That will all be determined as I leave Istanbul, after getting scanned and measured in every way. Maybe I'll have 20 days at home, then have to come back. Maybe we can manage some bridging care in the US (a euphemism for fractionated IP chemo that mimics what I have been getting here). In any case, my carefree time at home is limited. That makes it both more enjoyable and urgent. Limits make meaning, but they can also be stressful. Living in the present, hoping for a future without limits will continue to be my work. Time is precious.

Luckily, I love international travel. I just don't love being away from my family. Thank goodness our kids are old enough to have busy lives of their own now. I don't take that for granted for a second. If I could just rest at home, maybe they'd be too busy for us anyway...

What's surprising perhaps is that I will also miss Turkey because my hands and heart have been held here. Sure I've taken 18 chemos and as many full-body hyperthermia treatments, 44 local hyperthermia and hyperbaric oxygen treatments, sat through countless hours of nutritional infusions, been poked more days than not over six months (for a total of 100 times, not counting the occasional double and triple redos). I've been in and, thank goodness mostly, out of pain, occupied an unrecognizable body with a swollen abdomen and worn dresses I hope I'll not need someday.

I've struggled up and down Istanbul's hills trying to build back my strength and my glutes. But I've also enjoyed delightful Turkish food, ancient sites, and breathtaking views. I have learned the culture from the inside out, including some beautiful language, and made real friends along the way. From the people who work in our hotel and are caring friends, especially Suleyman and family, to the amazing people at Chemothermia (Dr. Slocum, Sirin, Noor, Halva, Ilena, Omar, Aran, Furkan, Ahmet, Eray, and Seren), it will be strange not to see them every day. Dr. Slocum likes to encourage me by saying, "You'll miss me!" when I get to remission. He's right. I will. I won't miss the treatments, but I'll miss the people.

I've had unforgettable times with friends visiting Istanbul and conversations/e-mails/notes/messages with others rooting for me from afar. This little apartment is home too and, in many ways, all the space I really need. We cooked and ate here, worked here, talked, and watched too much Netflix. John and I have a lot of shared memories here too now. I'll especially remember the fun times we were able to have on weeks off of chemo.

What's not here always though...what is central to my idea of home...always, is our family: John, Sophie, and Grant. My heart is always with them. **They are Home with a capital H.** It's time to reincorporate myself into their usual lives in the way I used to enjoy, at close range and uninterrupted by IVs and difficult chemo days, at least for a while. It's time to remember something about what my own "usual life" was and imagine what it might be again. I hope someday for that life to resume, in whatever form it will take.

For now, I have to be satisfied with...and am quite excited by...the idea that I'll be home, at least for a while. ●

Part 4
More Empathetic Cancer Care

CHAPTERS

31. Is It Empathetic To Treat Cancer as a Chronic Condition?	161
32. Will Western Medicine Change and How?	167
33. If Only Cancer Science Were as Brave as Cancer Patients	173
34. Dear Aspiring Oncologist	181
35. Looking Cancer in the Face, We Find Hope	185
36. Choosing Life Over Fear	191
37. Working Towards Checkmate – A More Empathetic and Strategic View of the Cancer Long Game	197
38. The Rhythm of Home	201
39. We Shouldn't Have to Choose Between Living and a Life	205
40. Immunotherapy Is the Answer	209

CHAPTER THIRTY ONE • MARCH 4, 2022

 Is It Empathetic To Treat Cancer as a Chronic Condition?

M aybe.

At the beginning, those of us with difficult cancer diagnoses hope to do the unlikely: survive the treatment, ring the bell, and be in "remission." We imagine all the ways and reasons we might beat the odds. Statistically, most of us don't. Even people with "treatable" cancers sometimes don't get that ending.

Cancer cells are smarter than we are. They adapt to the crude chemotherapies we've used for decades and keep multiplying sometimes. Continuing with treatment too often means compromising a patient's immune system and overall health. We die from the treatments, not just the cancers. At some point, usually pretty early on with difficult cancers, doctors give up. My doctor in the US did. I should be dead already according to him.

But there are some different ways of thinking about cancer prevention and treatment, more like chronic conditions to be managed through diet, supplements, pharmaceuticals, and when necessary, medicines that are strong enough to turn the situation around.

I worked hard in my adult life to stay in shape, eat well, take my vitamins, hydrate, etc., so I could avoid pharmaceuticals. In fact, I did. I didn't regularly take any drugs (not even Advil or Tylenol) at the time I was diagnosed with cancer. My body is vulnerable to toxicity in many ways I didn't realize, so cancer was growing just the same. Although that's some pretty bad luck, it did put me in shape to tolerate the first round of chemotherapy very well. I ran. I ate. I kept my weight up. Parented. Worked. Wrote. All good. That's not so unusual. I can't tell you how many of my cancer warrior friends were "so healthy" no one could believe they had cancer. We who are vulnerable were working hard to get ahead of the health curve. Intuitively, maybe we knew we were trying to outrun something. In hindsight, I did.

But the chemo for my ovarian cancer didn't really work. I rang the bell knowing I wasn't having a real "remission." My marker never came into range. That's not so unusual either.

With ovarian cancer, recurrence happens to most of us over time. Multiple rounds of chemotherapy are common. Even if we eat perfectly and do everything we can to support the treatments and maintain our health. It's not all in our control. I hate it when that happens. Don't you?

So what happens next? Well, taking conventional chemotherapy without supplemental support and protection, the treatments become intolerable and/or ineffective. It's like sending us into war with a BB gun. All the positivity in the world won't help us win. Obviously, we need better and braver cancer science, preferably that does not include injecting poison into our already challenged bodies as well as radioactive materials (stored in lead boxes before they mainline it into our veins) to measure progress in PET/CT scans. Seriously.

But maybe there is a middle ground, right now. Maybe treating cancer as a chronic condition is the right kind of guerrilla warfare to keep us in the fight, for now, and ultimately win. It's not for the fainthearted. The end is not clearly in sight. There is no bell. There are no promises. The illusion of control went up in smoke months or years ago.

But there is hope. Not of life as we imagined it before we were diagnosed, but life, nonetheless. More time to love. More time to create. I suppose it's a form of settling—or we can call it non-attachment—but it truly sounds better to us than the painful dying process we shook hands with more than once on this journey.

What does it even mean, to treat cancer as a chronic condition? You can think of it on a spectrum really, and pretty much every cancer patient does it in one way or another. None of us is the same after we get diagnosed and go through whatever treatment is required. Even people with stage 1, treatable, cancers worry about recurrence and mark anniversaries. Those of you who accompanied friends or family with cancer are never the same either. We change our diet. We avoid toxins. We focus on emotional well-being. We take up yoga and become a teacher. We take supplements or pharmaceuticals that are recommended to prevent or interrupt the process of cancering. We all do *at least something* to ensure our bodies are not a hospitable environment for cancer cells. No one wants to be in an acute relationship with cancer.

If chemo was never part of the picture for your cancer, you were fortunate. If it was a one-time deal, that's also pretty darn good in my book. For many of us, chemo is a bad boy/girlfriend we just can't shake without dire consequences in the not-so-long term. Our cancer cells are that smart and powerful, compared to what they've figured out to treat us.

This is where combinatorial therapies come in. Although there may not be a silver bullet, there is plenty of evidence that people can continue with a high quality of life by addressing cancer cells and their body terrain with approved therapies, given all at once. Protective measures (e.g., hyperbaric oxygen, nutritional infusions, antioxidant infusions, supplements) and cancer-toxic therapies (e.g., chemo, pro-oxidant iron, IV vitamin C, hyperthermia, ketogenic diet, a handful of targeted and effective pharmaceuticals) are given together *to kill cancer and improve health at the same time.*

The *and* is very important, and what is missing in conventional therapy.

Continuing to give traditional chemotherapy without supportive measures compromises patients' bodies no matter how strong, positive, or brave they are. In fact, these patients are the bravest of all; how they face their transitions without anger is a marvel to me. Of course, cancer can also kill. When there are no options for conventional treatments, strong, positive, brave patients also face a transition none of us wants to take. We'd all like to die peacefully in our sleep at 100 years old, preferably after a nice vacation and family meal.

Istanbul Street near our apartment

What does my experience have to say about treating cancer as a chronic condition? In the case of effective combinatorial therapies, it is an empathetic way to go. It's not my dream, to be clear. I hoped for remission the first time. I hoped for remission the second time. My imagined timelines are irrelevant. My imagined lives (focusing on work after the kids are grown and flown, empty nesting, retirement, etc.) also don't seem to have much bearing on the reality I'm meant to live.

But, I'm still here. Loving. Creating. And I'm both healthier and freer of cancer than I was in the fall. The combinatorial therapies are working. I'm better on three dimensions that make the doctors happy: clinically, biochemically/markers, and scan-wise. Did I finish these treatments in Istanbul "in range" and out of danger? No. Will I need ongoing treatment? Definitely. Is it killing me? Not today. Are treatments helping me? Most definitely. Are there other experimental options we're still exploring? Yes, which we will pursue if/when the benefits outweigh the costs to my body.

We built a life in Istanbul. The city is magical. The people are kind. We have made real friends. We cook. We walk. We have Turkish residency, and I may just apply for dual citizenship to make this all easier. I'm doing my best to become fluent in Turkish. It's fun. People appreciate and like to teach when you try to speak.

The truth is that I love international travel, immersing myself in other cultures, and being a global citizen.

Always have. Always will. I even love flying, remembering all the trips, all the souls who have passed through my life, grateful for the ways we've touched each other. I was an exchange student in Spain the summer of my 16th year, studied French in Switzerland when I was 19, and deliberately chose work that took me across the US and Hawaii, through Europe, to Brazil, and Moscow, among other places. I book a window seat and look out at the clouds. I still get excited about meal delivery. (I may or may not indulge in wine over international waters.) Going back and forth for a while isn't the worst thing to imagine (and I really do *intimately know* lots of worse things at this point.) Our son will be enjoying college, probably not wanting us in his business too much. Our daughter will likely be abroad in the fall. She'll probably be a short jump from Istanbul, which has excellent coverage of Europe with direct flights. I'm so very fortunate to have a life partner in John who has a similar sense of adventure.

I missed home. I missed our kids. I missed our friends. I missed our dog. Thank goodness, they have been well in all the ways that really matter. I'm eternally grateful I was there for our kids during the years they needed me most, and

I'm still here on earth for the smaller ways they still do. I missed my kitchen and the chance to cook for them. It's so good to be back home for the summer. It will take adjustment for everyone, but if there is one thing I've learned to count on, it's our resilience as individuals and as a family. I can't predict the future, but what I know is that we can face it together.

Sure, I'd rather not be in this fight (at all, much less still after two years), but I never wanted to golf in Florida anyway. The whole idea of "retirement" is kind of weird anyway and shifting in seismic ways for all of us. Maybe an apartment overlooking the Bosporus is part of the deal for John and me, with side trips here and there around the world. I can work flexibly from anywhere and appreciate the opportunities people have given me to do so. There is likely some sacred sharing still to be done, bearing witness to this crazy experience, and I won't stop until cancer is not a threat to anyone anymore...which will certainly take my lifetime. Yes, I still hope my time here on earth includes some kind of "remission." Some kind of break. Yes, I'm tired. Yes, the world feels unstable. But we watched a pancreatic cancer patient go home to Switzerland—alive, well, and having earned his respite from treatment. An unusual and hopeful example of success with a difficult cancer.

As for me...

- I've been fighting cancer entirely through a pandemic.
- I've been sentenced to death twice.
- Today is not that day. Tomorrow won't be either.
- We literally moved around the world, while our kids and friends and family held down the fort at home (some of them joined me in Istanbul so John could go back and forth!)

And I'm still here.

So, is it empathetic to treat cancer as a chronic condition? Yes. In fact, I think that's always the case if we look at it in the right way.

The idea of remission is just one more paradigm holding doctors back from helping patients. Cancer is a chronic and epidemic condition, individually and societally. Seeing it as such is the only way we'll help people survive, now and in the future. ●

CHAPTER THIRTY TWO • MARCH 27, 2022

 Will Western Medicine Change and How?

Yes, one nanometer at a time.

I had an encouraging Zoom meeting with a University of Chicago oncology team and a brave friend who ultimately lost her oh-so-healthy-until-he-got-cancer husband last year. He put up an amazing fight, within the boundaries of Western medicine. He had access to "the best" care and trusted his doctors. He lived with enormous pain and under very difficult physical circumstances following multiple surgeries and harsh chemotherapies for appendiceal cancer. He hung on for the sake of his young family, waiting for the next cure or idea until he couldn't anymore. Traditional care took its toll on his body, one that would be the envy of any young dad before that all began.

So what was encouraging? The team asked to hear my story and learn about integrative care and what they might do in a new cancer center they are building. Why? They want financial contributions, of course, but now people who are making these donations, like our friend, demand more from these doctors. They've seen what cancer treatments do to their loved ones, and they want a better way. This is part of how Western medicine will change.

There are conversations happening at the Cleveland Clinic as well. Parents still advocating for their kids, whose care was bungled in practical ways that can and should be avoided for others. Patients who are watching friends receive alternative care are taking those stories to their doctors. I have another conversation scheduled with the head of oncology from the Cleveland Clinic. Will he listen? I don't know, but I remember him to be an empathetic guy when he treated my friends several years ago. Hopefully, that compass remains.

In having these conversations, two "barriers" to integrative care seem to come up over and over.

1. The need for "evidence-based medicine"

2. Cost

Let's dispel these myths right now.

The Illusion of Evidence-Based Medicine
Evidence-based medicine was probably constructed to protect patients initially, under the banner of doing no harm. Doctors are bound by their oath and their hospital systems (especially the legal and compliance groups) to only offer to patients that which has been proven through research to have positive results. The problem is that research is a human endeavor with a variety of purposes, starting with profit for pharmaceutical companies, including funding for academic laboratories, and ending with new drugs for hospitals to use with patients. The aims are patentable products that confer an advantage, but it's acceptable and common that the product is a me-too drug, and the advantage is a few more weeks of low-quality life to patients who are already suffering greatly. That's an all too common experience for us, despite the large-scale, multiphase, and multiyear research to get these chemicals to market—meaning, into our compromised bodies.

Even research professionals are acknowledging the illusion of evidence-based medicine now. Read Richard Sears article, "How Evidence Based Medicine Became an Illusion," online at https://www.madinamerica.com/2022/03/evidence-based-medicine-became-illusion/

As a published PhD scientist, cancer patient, former McKinsey partner/businesswoman focused on helping large organizations change, and successful entrepreneur, I agree with and have written similar arguments for why cancer research and treatments aren't as brave as they need to be. If there is any sense in a "healthy woman like me" getting this cancer, it's to bear witness from the inside-out with all of that expertise.

The authors of "The illusion of evidence-based medicine," originally published in the British Medical Journal hit the nail on the head, pointing to, "*three significant issues currently destroying the integrity of evidence-based medicine: corporate interests, failed regulation, and the commercialism of academia.*"

Yes, yes, and yes. The bottom line is that evidence-based research did not save our friends and was not saving me. Toward the end of my time in Western medicine, I would have opted out of the few weeks of painful time conferred by this or that drug in favor of a peaceful passing in front of our children. Their definition of success was not mine, at all.

On the other hand, there is plenty of evidence—*which is way more than anecdotal because of the volume of us having to go elsewhere rather than die badly*—for integrative oncology conferring meaningful quality of life and a chance to live despite cancers that are typically death sentences. The reason it's not included in the conversation of "evidence-based medicine" is that the pharmaceutical companies cannot fund large studies without the outcome of patenting a particular me-too molecule they want to sell as a new drug. The integrative studies are published, however, and the integrative oncologists have been trying to talk about them for years, in the literature and at conferences. Dr. Slocum in Istanbul has produced some of this research and shared remarkable remissions of stage 4 patients with difficult cancers (pancreatic, metastatic breast, etc.) for whom traditional oncologists had left for dead.

The truth is that people in Western medicine are hiding behind the moniker of "evidence-based medicine" because:

- change is difficult,
- their training doesn't support any other way,
- the system doesn't allow for innovation,
- and in some cases, to protect the cancer industrial complex which is profitable.

The True Costs of Integrative Care
It costs less per cycle to treat me in Istanbul than it did in Cleveland. Not all insurance companies pay for integrative treatments, but they should. The important question is, "What is the difference between the cost of traditional treatment and integrative care?" In addition to the chemotherapies, which are standard, here are the therapies which make the treatments more effective and protect my healthy tissue:

- **Nutritional advice** = very low cost. Here, the conversation with the doctor was short and focused on clean, healthy, plant-strong keto, on which I'm well informed through prior experience and the wonders of the internet.

- **Supplemental and off-label pharmaceutical support** = much less costly than patented pharmaceuticals

- **Nutritional infusions** = vitamins, antioxidants, both of which are standard, not patented and so certainly less expensive than the next greatest me-too pharma concoction

- **Hyperbaric oxygen** = soft shell or hard shell chambers; there are approximately four at the clinic in Istanbul, the cost of which is amortized over hundreds of patients and many years of use

- **Local and full-body hyperthermia** = basically hot pads and soft shell saunas, there are four of these at the same clinic, the cost of which is amortized over hundreds of patients and many years. Many people, including us, have saunas at home for reasonable prices. Sauna Space makes a nice one, if you're interested. It's not cheap for an individual, but they last for many years and confer great health benefits to the entire family. Certainly, this is not out of range for a "world-class cancer center."

- **Terrain blood testing** = a handful of smart add-ons to a complete blood count (CBC) to help patients achieve precise support and results

The truth is that none of this is terribly expensive and is certainly in reach of a "world-class cancer center" soliciting large contributions to honor patients who have passed. All of these therapies are used in a variety of ways elsewhere, and none does harm. Can we treat cancer with just these and no surgery/radiation/chemo? Not usually. Not yet, but do these therapies confer a significant advantage for quality of life for anyone going through those more traditional treatments? Absolutely. Positively. Yes.

The True and Larger Costs are Mental and Emotional
When doctors bring up costs, they are right, but it's not about monetary currency. It's about the currency of empathy, actually, of which there are mental and emotional components in this case. Mental, because it requires a re-education of MDs and an overhaul of the medical school curriculum, focusing from the patient backward again rather than the market for pharmaceuticals. Emotional, because it requires admitting that the way we've been waging the "war on cancer" has not worked to prevent or treat this epidemic affecting increasing numbers of us and our families.

Having these conversations has sharpened my own sense of the challenges doctors face as they even consider generative changes to the medical system. Even when—especially when—they are in charge, these barriers loom large.

But, the fact that these conversations are taking place at all is a positive sign and reminder that even as we feel most vulnerable, we patients and families have power. Change will happen. People will vote with their feet. The centers that truly help patients will emerge winners, and with the flow of information being swift and transparent now, we will know who they are.

It takes a lot to change large systems, but they will either change or die of their own weight. As a patient, I'm not nearly alone. There are many more people seeking and cobbling together integrative care right now. I hear from them all the time. Our stories are not anecdotes anymore. They are becoming common sense, and we are building evidence, not sponsored by Pfizer or Merck, whose intentions we are starting to question anyway. My professional career has been focused on helping organizations, often large ones, make big positive changes. I know from decades of experience how hard it is. I am hopeful but realistic.

Change is coming, but only one nanometer at a time. ●

CHAPTER THIRTY THREE • FEBRUARY 25, 2022

If Only Cancer Science Were as Brave as Cancer Patients

As an ovarian cancer warrior/survivor/patient/victim/thriver for more than two years, I've been told countless times to: **Be brave! Be strong! Be positive!**

Here's what I can tell you from this side of the fight:

- If only the scientists and executives controlling our Western institutionalized medical system were as brave as the patients, we would have upended a system that is often not serving patients but rather profiting insurance companies and big pharma while enabling careerism. This is true of all diseases, but cancer patients too often pay the ultimate price.

- If only oncologists were as strong as the patients, all doctors would have the courage to admit what they don't know or can't do and sit with us in that devastating reality rather than awkwardly tousling their hair and making a quick exit after announcing nothing can be done and she has three months to live...only to be so wrong countless months later when the patient is very much alive.

- If only cancer caregivers were as uniformly positive as the patients, no one would bluntly tell a patient dressed for a run that it was time for palliative care based on a poorly understood marker...and be so very wrong two years later when that woman is still alive!

Thanks to Brandt, Naomi, and the Butze family for sharing Jacob's stories and photo. If you are so inspired, please go to butzefoundation.org to learn more about Jacob and donate to the Jacob Butze Memorial Fund.

There are bright lights, such as integrative and intuitive nutritionists who put patients first, entrepreneurial clinics that operate outside the constraints of the mainstream system, and smart and curious doctors who never stop learning. But these are not the norm that most patients encounter.

We put a lot on patients—*to do, to be, to feel, to try, to work*—when the truth is that most of us have sensitive genes that make us especially vulnerable in this toxic world. Cancer is an epidemic for a reason. That reason is not that we are mutants or didn't take care of ourselves. I say this as a trained chemist, a mom/daughter/wife who helped heal family members naturally, a successful entrepreneur, and now someone with way too much experience inside the machine of cancer treatment.

The reason cancer is an epidemic is that the *system* of research, treatment, and prevention of cancer (what I'll call here "cancer science") doesn't measure up to the patients.

*If it did...*cancer science would be hardworking and courageous.
- We would never ever give up, like Jacob who was doing leg lifts hours after being told he had days to live. Leg lifts, so he would be in shape, because that's how this outstanding scholar-athlete rolled, even in the aftermath of the most devastating news a person can hear. How many of us would do that? Slowly but surely, I ran around a track all the way through the first round of chemotherapy. These days exercise is harder, but I feel better when I do it because I'm still here...and Jacob did leg lifts until the end. I'm also inspired by Carrie who has been living with active stage 4 ovarian cancer for years, searching, seeking, working in every way imaginable to survive for her daughters. She took up yoga. She changed her diet. There isn't a book she hasn't read, a podcast she hasn't heard, or an idea she hasn't considered.
- We would have the courage to do whatever it takes, such as lie in full-body hyperthermia with chemo dripping into our veins, get on a plane to Turkey when the US system fails you, move to Atlanta for integrative treatment, or subject your body to countless surgeries and maintenance chemo just to be around for your young children, as our friend Jack did until he couldn't anymore. Cancer science would push boundaries, take calculated risks, and seek exponential benefits with multifactorial and combinatorial therapies. Most of these therapies aren't even risky and are approved for other uses. They are well known in many parts of the world and safe but have never been incorporated into Western care (e.g., plantstrong ketogenic diet, supplements, proven techniques for emotional well-being and trauma healing, hyperbaric oxygen, and mistletoe therapy).

- We could look in the eyes of children and honestly say we are doing the best we can to fight a disease that is growing significantly. Those of us surviving cancer with and for our kids do this every day. If that kind of bravery were the gold standard of cancer science, we'd have more true cures and fewer copycat drugs or conference backslapping that advances careers but leaves statistics unchanged for literally five decades.

- Cancer science would focus on what matters, driving for meaningful differences in survival.

- At the end of life, things get very clear. My friend Michele shared the realization that we're here to create and to love in her final weeks. It doesn't get much simpler or clearer than that. I've been far enough down this path to gain a new appreciation of the simple things too, most of which revolve around love and creation, just as Michele said. Cancer science should simplify as well, rather than hiding in complex nomenclature and what pretends to be science when it's more like throwing spaghetti against the wall to see what sticks. (That pretending may earn a patent and more money even if it doesn't confer any meaningful time or health to patients). Cancer science should be laser-focused on meaningful survival and high quality of life. Current survival statistics and a false belief that a growing number of humans are somehow unlucky mutants are unacceptable. Cancer patient bodies know better. We took good care of ourselves, sometimes increasingly so, becoming sicker when we couldn't get ahead of the toxic assault. We have convinced ourselves that the problem of cancer is so hard to solve, but are we really always focused on the right questions? Research is only as good as the questions we ask.

- So many patients manage to focus on love and stay present for their families through the assault and pain of treatments and increasing disease burden. I remember the final days of my Uncle Ray who died of pancreatic cancer. I was too young and inexperienced then to know the strength it took for him to say goodbye to all of us. I marvel at it now. I still remember how my cousin Brian, dying of brain cancer way too young in his early twenties, reassured his mom he would, "be ok, no matter what." The people who die with grace seem even more heroic to me now than the people for whom the treatment works, enjoying remission for years to come. Jacob spent some of his final time writing letters to his family. Can you imagine what it takes to actually do that? I can. I've been scared to death multiple times now and written two versions of those letters. I cried through all of the writing but simply had to let my family know the depth of my love. Again. It matters. Jacob's last words to his family were, "Thank you."

- Cancer science would drive for big rather than incremental change because we would all be irate and motivated to reverse the epidemic of cancer touching all of us in some way, whether it's you, someone in your family, or a friend.

- We'd insist on a cleaner world. Our kids have an inkling of this challenge, and it scares them. Cancer patients' bodies are leading that rebellion. Screaming, in fact. If only cancer science would listen.

- We would upend the healthcare pyramid so that it would serve the patient rather than the obscene inversion happening now. Pharmaceutical companies, insurance, hospitals, doctors, and careerist scientists all benefit at the top of the current pyramid while too many cancer patients still die, crushed at the bottom. Cancer victims face this truth head-on, every day.

- Cancer science would be entrepreneurial, like the patients who are willing to do treatments "unproven" in our Western system but showing promise nonetheless. There is no new data without meaningful experiments. Most clinical trials in the West confer a few weeks or months of low quality of life. Experimenting outside of these constraints is the only way to make the kind of serious improvements we need. Entrepreneurial doctors have to do this in private clinics nowadays. Thank goodness there are, at least, these options, but it's not enough to help the tsunami of cancer patients now and in the future. I'm all for protecting patients, but we need to question whether that's what the FDA, CDC, and other government agencies are really doing for us versus hemming researchers into incremental science. The evidence suggests not. We are sicker than ever without breakthroughs in sight.

- Cancer science would measure what matters and truly understand it, not leaving us terrorized by markers that literally rise and fall by a thousand from one week to the next with few people even questioning why. Even more important, measuring upstream terrain markers before anyone ever gets cancer would be part of mainstream healthcare (rather than waiting for us all to get sick). That would truly be healthcare.

- Cancer science would be creative, curious, humble, and empathetic because that's part of our purpose here on earth.

- Patients heed this yearning to create, as do the music and art therapists who work so hard to help us feel that spark no matter how we are doing physically. Hollis wrote music and sang until he died of pancreatic cancer, with Tori's help. Jacob kept playing the guitar. Kim made beautiful art right up until she passed from gallbladder cancer, with the materials and gentle directions Barbara and her team so thoughtfully shared. If they can create in the midst of those realities, surely we can all do better in more "normal" circumstances. I tried my hand at music and art, neither of which are my gifts, but both of which kept my pilot light on. I continue to write because that's what I can do.

- Patients are curious. We try all the healing modalities, special diets, emotional and spiritual exploration. If you haven't been on this kind of journey, you may have no idea how many there are and how hard we work. We leave no stone unturned and no question unasked. Cancer survival is currently a function of having a popular (=bigger market like, e.g., breast, prostate) cancer caught early on that fits the research paradigm (=consistent with the 5% mutations identified through the Human Genome Project). What about the rest of us? What's driving the other 95%? Why can't we move the other statistics? Ovarian cancer survival has been dismally the same for 50 years. What about prevention? These questions beg an answer. Curious cancer science would start with that big picture, grabbing hold and not letting go, like a cat with a ball of yarn.

- Patients are humbled daily, often facing the reality of difficult cancers and knowing remission is not a typical reality but searching for clues from their bodies nonetheless. There's a lot—too much—we don't know. The body is complex and we must honor and marvel at that design, realizing we're only chipping away at a surface understanding. But there are clues in synchronizing with the natural world in ways we've failed to do because of arrogance.

- Patients get deep lessons in giving and receiving empathy, including from the old souls who keep us company on this brutal journey, no matter what. They are able to process news, keep their own triggers and biases at bay, and sit in our reality rather than separating themselves with platitudes. Cancer science should not be about patented drugs that don't really help, iterative publications and career progression, or profiting from our body's disease. It should be the optimal combination of realism and caring, taking patient outcomes and physical and emotional experiences into account.

- Being empathetic means listening to our bodies and honoring that design, the way Michele did in her journey, and even on her way out of this world. She let her body and soul guide her and her family through that transition, accessing the mystery and beauty of it all. There is so much we don't understand, spiritually as well as medically. One of many things we don't understand is the role of mold and other inflammatory issues in cancer. My body gave us some clues about mold and cancer earlier on, if only cancer science would pay attention.

Patients are **all that**, especially the ones who faced death with grace.
The truth is that cancer science is **not all that**.
We don't need to tell patients to be strong or brave or positive.
Our lives require it.
Every. Minute.
Every. Day.
We need earnest company more than advice.

Attitude matters but it's not just ours. It's all of us. We should all be dissatisfied and motivated to do the right work around cancer so that *none of us* has to suffer anymore. I sit in special admiration of those who have braved the biggest transition of all, in more painful circumstances than most people can imagine. I never think of cancer patients who don't survive as losers; I imagine their soul was fully evolved somehow. Perhaps they had nothing more to learn, even as they had so much more to contribute. What about the rest of us?

As for me, I'm still here so there must be more work to do. More creating. More loving. I've felt and continue to feel compelled to bear witness, with empathy and scientific knowledge and curiosity, to the system that's failing so many of us so that it might be changed someday. I'm not alone. My friends and family who face/have faced cancer—alive and dead—make up too big of an army. Maybe the challenges we faced until now were just part of our preparation for this fight. It takes a lot of bravery, strength, and all of the characteristics above to turn this whole system around. Collectively, we have what it takes. But, there is no time to lose. ◉

Our Turkish team, led by Dr. Slocum (back center, in the suit), who is one example of a wonderful oncologist

CHAPTER THIRTY FOUR • JULY 23, 2022

 Dear Aspiring Oncologist

In the two and a half years since I was diagnosed with ovarian cancer, John and I have experienced a range of medical, oncological, naturopathic, and healing support. Oncology is fascinating in the way it attracts certain personalities, some wonderfully empathetic and some, very much not. I've had the privilege to hear from other patients about their experiences along the way as well. The stories are not great. To that end, here are some thoughts...

Dear Aspiring Oncologist,

IF...
- You are going into medicine to make your parents proud, don't. Just don't.

- Memorization is your strong suit and if creative solutions elude you, don't choose oncology. Certainly don't work with more difficult cancers and later-stage patients for whom the gold standard of care fails. Parroting the usual plan, or worse yet, the one we had to design ourselves, doesn't give us any comfort in your ability to care for us.

- Not having answers to difficult questions is an affront to your ego, stay out of oncology. The important questions are really hard, and nobody has good answers. You don't either. Pretending with us doesn't help, especially when we have more experience than you do, inside-out, dealing with cancer.

- Fear of dying is a trigger for you, run the other way. We don't need any more fear. The situation provides plenty. We can't help you with your fears, and blaming our bodies or mutant genes is out-of-date and wrong.

- You're empathically hindered by prior wounds, get therapy before you go into medicine. Some issues are intractable, so some of you just won't cut it.

- You have to be the one with all the answers, choose a less complex profession with better-known solutions. The truth of healing cancer requires a multi-factorial approach and the best answers are coming across and outside of medical silos now.

- Your own insecurities make it difficult to admit what you don't know, stay out of oncology. It's complex. Experienced patients can spot a phony as quickly as small children. The conversation won't go well and your triggers are big, bright, and shiny.

- Competition jazzes you more than empathizing with other people, maybe surgery is your jam. Oncology is not. As medicine evolves to what it should be (effective, preventive, patient-centered healthcare), that won't suit you either.

- You have a g-d complex and really need patients to look up to you as an all-powerful healer rather than collaborate on their care, that's another good thing to explore in therapy before or rather than working with people (in any way, medicine included).

- To that end, if it's tempting to point to or even start fires (i.e., stating worst-case scenarios such as "sepsis and death" from a treatment we've had 18 times before with no problems) just so you can be the hero. Well, we're not sure what profession needs that. None. Head back to therapy. Good luck.

However, IF...

- You are both fascinated and humbled by the natural design of the human body (and the world at large) and want to be part of healthcare of the future, medicine needs you.

- You are keen to change solutions and systems that may drive GDP but don't work for patients, keep on.

- You can deal with fellow humans in their full lifespan, healthy, sick, or even dying with dignity, please continue because that's all part of your job description.

- You have both the practicality and imagination to provide vision and hope to people for whom the gold standard of care failed, oncology is a great choice.

- You know that patients and behavioral choices are keys to healthcare, and collaboration is exciting to you, stay the course.

- Your self-awareness and emotional stability are exceptional, leaving you in a steady place for dealing with difficult diagnoses, ground yourself and stay here with us.

- You are cool with knowing what you don't know and admitting that...getting answers elsewhere when they exist...and lamenting with us when they don't. Stay awhile.

- You have the maturity to sit with people in good or dark places, with good and bad results, you could do this job.

- Empathy is the secret sauce to how you move through the world, making work with people natural and endlessly productive, then we need more people like you in oncology.

A lot of this comes down to healthy empathic capacity, which can be evaluated and developed, both individually and at the system level. Wouldn't it be great if medicine really understood empathy, rather than gave it lip service, wrapped in snazzy marketing campaigns? Patients know the truth. We see and feel the reality way too often, and we're sorry to say, many of you are getting C's, D's, or just plain failing. Ouch. It's not really your fault though. Probably, no one told you what the job really was.

Well, now you know. Choose wisely. ●

Jackie on left with active ovarian cancer, January 2020–three weeks prior to diagnosis

CHAPTER THIRTY FIVE • SEPTEMBER 10, 2020

 Looking Cancer in the Face, We Find Hope

"Embrace uncertainty. Some of the most beautiful chapters in our lives won't have a title until much later."
—Bob Goff

Do you know someone who has battled cancer? I hope it's not you or a loved one, but it may be. I hope they're still with us. I won't bore you with statistics and graphs. What those numbers say is that we all know someone with cancer now, and it feels hard to make sense of who and why...

- Ovarian cancer rocks a bikini at 51 (humor me please, it will be a minute before I wear a bikini again...)

- Colon cancer comes in superheroes like actor Chadwick Boseman and superheroic authors like Ibram X. Kendi.

- Brain cancers hitch a ride with resilient young men who rock climb and paint amazing murals

You have your stories too. I know you do. Statistically, you must. I've been sharing my story from inside the belly of the beast of cancer, as seen through the eye of a scientist/business person/author/mom. Diagnosed with ovarian cancer in February 2020. Surgery on March 2, 2020. Seven cycles of chemo (carboplatin and taxol from March–August 2020). All in the midst of a pandemic. The more intense the journey, the more revealing is the lens of empathy. It's been eye-opening in so many ways.

Here are three things I know for sure:
- **We are not mutants.**

- Empathy in MEDICINE is required for cures and prevention
- Empathy in RESEARCH is required for cures and prevention

We are Not Mutants
Most cancer research, drugs, and treatments are based on the theory that we are an unlucky few, riding in a body that is somehow broken. We are not just a few anymore, and many of us don't have the usual cancer mutations. I'm like that. I'm not mad at my body or even my cancer. My body reacted in perfectly logical ways to the toxicity I lived with unknowingly in my first four decades. I confess I believed in "better living through chemistry" until a decade ago. I didn't realize how much I needed to protect myself from ubiquitous pesticides, additives, preservatives, pathogens, molds...on and on...which were terrible food for my cells. I thought nighttime was a vast reservoir of time I could use to balance work and raising young children—sleep was optional. Emotional toxicity was something I thought I could absorb, unharmed. My immune system reacted just as it's designed to do, screaming, "Danger!" with every emotional and physical assault. In particular, that's the job of mast cells—positioned like sentries at the environmental interfaces of our bodies—and they did it well. They were so overworked that a few random mutations went unnoticed. Then a few more. And so on. I know how I tilted into cancer, and I believe I'm not especially unusual.

The old way of cancer research hasn't yielded the miracles we need because it can't. We will prevent the onslaught of cancer by making the environment our bodies experience friendlier to vibrant life, not by presuming we can design something better than life...on a lab bench. Drugs have s***ty trade-offs (aka side effects) because the body is smarter about its interconnections than we are. The game of scientific design, experiment, publish, or perish forces researchers into narrow playgrounds. As a friend in drug discovery for cancer treatments recently said, "Most of what I do every day fails." That's why I left research and went into business. Most nights, I left the lab feeling like I hadn't done a good day's work. (Watch my TEDx talk, *A Good Day's Work Requires Empathy*, online at https://youtu.be/x6dyrmHIjao)

I went into scientific research to help people, but my own work in organo-metallic chemistry was too far removed from humanity. Ironically, this work of curing my own cancer from the inside-out fulfills some part of the dream of my 22-year-old self. The difference now is that I have empathy for the patient. I am she. I know and love too many more like me.

Empathy in MEDICINE is required for cures and prevention
I'm not talking about slick institutional marketing ads with actors pretending to read the minds of people passing by. I'm talking about real-life doctors

who listen. They have the emotional resilience to be bothered by the fact that too many people die on their watch with the same treatments used for 50 years. These special doctors metabolize grief rather than become numb to it. They walk in sacred spaces with their patients and families, hoping, praying, and working for new options. They don't have all the answers and admit it. They realize patient intuition is powerful and they incorporate those insights into treatment plans, balanced by hard-earned perspective from decades of practice. They learn and express gratitude for new ideas that are logical and seem to be working. They offer hope, respect, and empathy, over and over. They do all of this despite the inhuman constraints imposed on doctors by hospital systems.

Other doctors get burned out. It's understandable. They start conversations with, "I'm not going to sugarcoat this..." before reciting commonly available statistics. Uhm. Please *do* sugarcoat. And, we can Google too; information is not your superpower anymore, ma'am. Some docs convey more arrogance and power than the statistics support. They present themselves as our only salvation, and our fear is their fuel. If only they had a miraculously different record to back up that bluster. Unfortunately, they don't. "Standard of care" is a kind of factory model, when you strip away the humanity. Sometimes doctors forget to ask, "How are you today?" opting for, "You must be feeling awful after all that chemo, so here's my advice..." Actually, I'm heading out for a run. Are we done yet?!

A cancer diagnosis is a vulnerable thing. It's hard to walk away from the fear and find empathy. But it's possible. Only a doctor who works with us and our bodies can bring about the cures we need. Doctors who retain empathy are heroes...and rebels in a system that too often saps humanity.

Empathy in RESEARCH is required for cures and prevention
You might not think empathy and scientific research are compatible at all. Independence. Logic. Data. Cold, hard facts. That's what we've been taught wins in research. All that. Yeah, sure, but to what end? In what context? Asking and answering which big questions that really *matter*? And what are the *real* motivations of the human being doing the work? Independence is as much of a myth in science as in any other human endeavor. Pretending cold hard facts add themselves up without the help of human interpretation and theories is naïve. Being honest about the humanity of science would help people trust it more.

Most of us go into research to do something meaningful and useful. I did. As I gained experience, I found that the reductionist nature of research pushes us time and again into a very narrow box. We settle for solving small problems instead of big ones. We design. We experiment. We publish papers. The first few are exhilarating. Then the niggling voice asks, "To what end?" Maybe it quietly asks, "When was your last good day's work?" We try to build on each other's work, but too often, it adds up to less than we hoped. We lose touch with our original motivations, creativity, curiosity, and imagination. The game becomes more about looking smart at a conference, publishing enough, getting that coveted professorship, earning a named chair position, filing a patent...just making a living. People scramble to test pharmaceuticals—often old drugs that might find new uses. Sometimes it's like throwing spaghetti against the wall. We celebrate when drugs and treatments confer a few more months of survival, even though a lifetime is what we all want. All the while, cancer becomes an epidemic.

Empathy would make all the difference. Looking into the faces of young kids whose dad is bedridden by years of cancer treatments would remind us to stay focused on the big problems and develop more holistic and integrative solutions. Patients who are listening to their bodies offer clues from the inside-out which we should heed, co-creating research design with what works in human bodies. Let our bodies tell us what the lab bench cannot. The internet can be a source of confusion, but also a *system-smashing, model-busting* way for patients to connect, share their journeys, and excavate hope from cross-functional studies and metadata when burned-out experts toss tired old statistics our way. Researchers who are guided by empathy are heroes...and rebels with a good cause.

Those are three lessons so far from my perch in the belly of the beast of ovarian cancer. We kissed some frogs along the way, but were fortunate to have landed with a team of local and virtual healers, who combine empathy, intellect, curiosity, and imagination. We are also fortunate to live in a time when information flows freely. It's a blessing to have the tools we do. I hope and pray that cancer research and treatment is upended and improved in ways similar to other systems that serve the almighty dollar before people. It's time.

It's funny. In the last yoga class I taught, I used inspiration cards to help students with their intention for practice. The one I was dealt said, "entrepreneurship." What?! I was heading into surgery and so much more; my entrepreneurial business was definitely going to take a back seat. Now, I understand. Many times in life, I've walked through traditional experiences only to come out the other side knowing change must come, with ideas about how. Research. Business. Work/family balance The traditional models have their merits but all left me wanting. This cancer journey has been no different.

Combining old and new into a retro-futuristic art form has a name: steampunk. For the first seven months, I took traditional "standard of care" surgery and chemotherapy, which did some good work. Integrative supports helped me live well in the midst of that assault. Those treatments hit the reset button so that healing can begin, unwinding the cascade of events that led to cancer in the first place and making my body's terrain inhospitable to cancer again. At heart, I'm an entrepreneur and a rebel. Ask my dad. He fired me from our family's grocery store when I was 13 for insubordination! But innovation and entrepreneurship have their place when the outcomes of the usual way aren't ideal. Healing from ovarian cancer and sustaining remission requires steampunk.

Steampunk as imagined in art therapy

In many ways, this next part of the cancer journey puts me in touch with my 22-year-old self, who was excited to walk into MIT. Back then, all I wanted was to make a difference and help people through scientific inquiry and discovery. Such was the audacity of youth. Luckily, that girl is still here. She has more tools than ever...and she's hanging onto the bikini for later. ●

CHAPTER THIRTY SIX • JULY 21, 2020

 Choosing Life Over Fear

"Courage is not the absence of fear, but the triumph over it."
— Nelson Mandela

Do you easily remember quotes? I usually don't, but some version of that one has been on the tip of my tongue for decades. I've been afraid many times. Stepping onto a plane alone as an exchange student to Spain at 16 in 1985 (cellphone?! Not a thing yet). Showing up for my first day at MIT...so scared I suddenly couldn't remember my social security number. Taking a left turn after grad school to work with McKinsey & Company in Chicago, knowing little more than profits = revenues - costs. Stepping out onto a TEDx stage to deliver 18-minutes straight from the heart...and from memory (gulp). Conducting research by going on a ride-along with the Cleveland Police on a Friday night in the most statistically violent district of the city. Yeah, I was scared all of those times. But in every case, I knew the risk was worth it. I knew I would grow in ways I wanted. I *chose* those challenges and many more.

Getting diagnosed with ovarian cancer at 51 wasn't like that. It was...well, devastating. I didn't choose it. I didn't want it. The challenge dawned on me more slowly than my husband. To be honest, I absorbed the truth watching him spring into action. Our response to fear is similar. We get to work...preparing, solving problems, making plans, etc. It's a useful adaptation most of the time. With cancer in *my own body*, I needed some time for the shock to wear off. He carried me through that time. Back then and many times since, I would gladly have passed on this particular opportunity for growth.

Since then, I won't pretend I haven't been afraid or would rather not have cancer. Of course, I am. Of course, I would rather not. What I have come to appreciate, mostly in hindsight, is the way we humans have the capacity for moving through, over, and beyond fear. Over and over. It's like surfing. Falling off. Kicking to the surface. Climbing back onto the board, and for some time—often too short, especially for us amateurs—riding the wave instead of drowning in it. That ride is a fun prize, resulting from hard work.

Like at the end of what I've come to call "vacation week." No chemo. No side effects. No new tests to understand. Looking back, we spent the first couple of chemo cycles figuring out how to manage that assault without the worst side effects. The next couple of cycles revealed why I got cancer and what will be important to sustaining my immune system and healing. All along, we have experienced life-affirming waves of love and support for our family and the sharing of new, powerful ways to heal. Spiritual growth in this journey is possible and profound.

We are encouraged by the progress of my body's response to treatments, and we couldn't be better supported by our healing team and their empathetic, encouraging comments. "You are the boss of chemo." "You are already winning." "You are making me a better doctor." We know how rare it can be to have this kind of partnership, and we hang on all of these words. Because the tricky thing about cancer is that "remission" can be hard to sustain. "Recovery" feels like a more accurate description of what lies ahead. For many, chemo is more of a reset than a cure, and regular scans and tests become part of the rest of our lives. CA125 (the typical marker for ovarian cancer) is notorious for false positives. More reassuring are leading indicators/terrain markers/measures of the body's underlying health, strength of the immune system, and anticancer activity. There's a lot we can do to recover or prevent cancer in the first place. Start with the book, "Life Over Cancer" by Keith Block, MD.

Even as I sit on the positive "long tail of the distribution" of statistics for ovarian cancer so far, what we have learned from friends with cancer is that they do life differently after treatment. Recovery doesn't end with a certain infusion, drug, test, or date. It's a lifelong endeavor. And, just to put a big exclamation point on that truth, there is still an ongoing pandemic, political unrest, and racial awakening underscoring a big shift to something new which none of us can fully picture yet. Most of the time, I can see *that's all ok*. It's even better than ok.

I've been asking friends who went through cancer how they live without fear. You know what? They don't. Fear is there, but they *choose life*. They make plans, anyway. They do work that is meaningful. They don't put off taking vacations. They take better care of themselves physically and emotionally than before. They prioritize better how and with whom they spend time. Some of them even talk about yearning to recapture the quiet...of the cancer journey. The focus. The clarity about what is really important. The beautiful love and empathy offered all along the way. I have loved all of that too, and I don't want to lose it either.

So at the end of "vacation week," I look forward to stringing together more of these weeks at some point in the future. I may be the boss of chemo, but it's still a beast! After my next chemo treatment, there will be scans, tests, and plans for "recovery." My body will tell us what else it needs. Who knows, maybe the ongoing clinical-experiment-of-me might contribute to the knowledge of what some of the tests and scans really mean and how to stay in remission for decades. I hope so. What I know for sure is that recovery will be my focus for the rest of my life. Maybe it's like alcoholism in that way. Similar to friends in Alcoholics Anonymous, I've been buoyed time and again by the support and encouragement of understanding people near and far. The work is to be ever vigilant but not paralyzed. In many ways, focusing on recovery is liberating and one of the most important things we can practice whether faced with a cancer diagnosis, a pandemic, or anything that makes us afraid...including more ordinary changes at work and at home.

Recovering from cancer is a chance to choose life over fear, again and again.

No doubt, there will be fear. Life is vulnerable and living can be traumatic, whether cancer is ever a part of it or not. But, once you find you can kick up to the surface of the water, get back on the surfboard, and ride again and again, there is also fun, appreciation, exhilaration, and joy. Chemo cycles have been a strange but constant practice of just that. That kind of resilience resides inside all of us, but don't fool yourself into thinking we do all of that alone. Resilience is powered by empathy. Empathy helps us move through the fear of change together, whether it's a devastating diagnosis or loss that marks life before and life after, or something less dramatic. Empathic connection is a lifesaver when the water is too choppy to swim on your own...and you feel as if you're drowning. Empathy provides oxygen when your own supply runs short. Then, you kick. You get to the surface and take a sweet breath. You move through the fear and choose life, again.

That's exactly what I'll do. I'm grateful for smart, empathetic, and kind doctors/healers/nutritionists who practice whole-body science and trust their patients' intuition. I'm grateful for the broad and deep support of friends and family, near and far. I'm grateful to ovarian cancer survivors who reassure and inspire. Most of all, I'm grateful for the bottomless pitch-perfect empathy and love of John, Sophie, and Grant LeMay (Rocky too) with whom I look forward to sharing many more "vacation weeks," fun, and joy in the years to come. And thanks to all of you for throwing me the lifesavers of prayer, encouragement, and more. I'll be kicking up to the surface, over and over...working for the chance to ride the waves. ⚬

"Swim"
by Jack's Mannequin

You gotta swim
Swim for your life
Swim for the music
That saves you
When you're not so sure you'll survive
You gotta swim
Swim when it hurts
The whole world is watching
You haven't come this far
To fall off the earth
The currents will pull you
Away from your love
Just keep your head above
I found a tidal wave
Begging to tear down the door
Memories like bullets
They fired at me from a gun
Cracking me open now
I swim to brighter days
Despite the absence of sun
Choking on saltwater
I'm not giving in
You gotta swim, You gotta swim
For nights that won't end
Swim for your family
Your lovers your sisters
Your brothers your friends
You gotta swim
For wars without cause
Swim for these lost politicians...

Who don't see their greed is a flaw
The currents will pull us
Away from our love
Just keep your head above
I found a tidal wave
Begging to tear down the door
Memories like bullets
They fired at me from a gun
Cracking me open now
I swim to brighter days
In spite of the absence of sun
Choking on saltwater
I'm not giving in, I'm not giving in
Swim
You gotta swim
Swim in the dark
There's an ocean to drift in
Feel the tide shifting away from this war
Yeah you gotta swim
Don't let yourself sink
Just follow the horizon
I promise you it's not as far as you think
Currents will drag us away from our love
Just keep your head above, Just keep your head above
Swim, Just keep your head above
Swim, Just keep your head above
Swim

Songwriter: Andrew Ross McMahon
Copyright: Lyrics © Kobalt Music Publishing Ltd.
Source: www.lyricfind.com

"Corny as it sounds, what I'm really interested in is the human spirit—in how people react to stress and adversity. I'm fascinated by the way people fight back, by how they keep fighting their way to the surface."

—Dr. Mark Renneker, family-practice physician, MCAS-cancer expert, and serious surfer

CHAPTER THIRTY SEVEN • MAY 2, 2022

Working Towards Checkmate
A More Empathetic and Strategic View of the Cancer Long Game

I'm no champion, but I do like chess, ever since Uncle Jack taught me to play as a kid. It's a strategic game, in which you can think your way out of a fix, picture several moves ahead, and revel in beating a worthy opponent. Lately, it's been helping me to think of cancer as a chess game.

Remission is a wonderful word and a nice dream to which those of us with cancer aspire. That's what the traditional oncology world teaches us. The reality is different. Many of us live with cancer. We don't get to ring the bell unfettered, declare chemo a success, and get back to "normal life," whatever that is post-cancer.

But that doesn't mean you can't have a life.

There is such a thing as thriving with stage 4 difficult cancers, keeping tumors in checkmate, unable to move and metastasize throughout the body. So, what does that really mean?

In every body, even yours, there are cancer cells forming and dying all the time. When your immune system is strong and undistracted, it takes care of those cells and cancer never creates a ruckus capable of causing symptoms or disrupting bodily functions. For those of us "with a cancer diagnosis," the game is well underway, and the immune system is losing, distracted by a variety of triggers that are both somewhat and very poorly understood (e.g., modern toxicity beyond our genetic capacity to clear it, stress, nutritional deficiencies). Cancer has us in check.

That's the situation I was in when I went to Istanbul in November 2021. My body and immune system were overwhelmed by cancer, more than ever. That's a nice way of saying I was dying, in pain, unable to eat and digest, committed to hospice by my oncologist, and given three months to live. That's just a few more, painful, rounds of chess in which your moves are few and resources limited, with seemingly no way to win.

The surprising thing is that we turned the game around after six months of treatment in Turkey. I'm still here, stronger than before, with improved clinical presentation, markers, and scans. I missed home and my kids, but I also built a life there. I have friends who are near and who come from afar. I eat. I enjoy. I'm pain-free. I've gained muscle and weight. I'm able to walk for miles and explore Istanbul's neighborhoods and treasures. The side effects from my treatments have been almost none, save another chic minimalist hairdo. I'm not free of all symptoms or visible cancer, but the cancer is on the run. These treatments have been the reinforcement my immune system needed to put the cancer in check. I am not free of treatments since I returned home in May 2022. The game is not over, but the tables have turned. I hope the cancer cells are feeling as defeated as I did last November.

When I started fighting ovarian cancer in February of 2020, of course, I hoped for a speedy remission. Like so many people, I never got it. Even the people who get remission from ovarian and other difficult cancers often have a recurrence so quickly that you wonder what the word remission really means. Traditional oncology presents remission as the goal. Take your chemo. Ring that bell. You are cured. Enjoy remission. Resume life as usual. We humans like black and white answers. Winners and losers. It's not really empathetic to patients, because traditional treatments are limited. The reality is much messier and more of a spectrum.

The earlier the stage, the less aggressive the cancer, the more effective the current treatments, the more likely you'll get cancer on the run to the point that it's indiscernible on a scan and below certain "safe" numbers in the simplistic markers we've figured out how to measure. Many times this means it's better to get a more popular cancer with a larger market. The word remission is accurate (i.e., "a temporary diminution of the severity of disease or pain") but the way I was thinking about it was wrong. Cancer-free. Cured. Those are Holy Grail words for cancer patients like me, but I've come to believe there isn't such a thing really. It's really helped to pivot into thinking about a game of chess.

There is "check"
(the immune system is winning; cancer is on the run)
and "checkmate"
(the immune system has won; cancer can't move or hurt you anymore).

What does "checkmate" look like on the outside? No more chemo. Hair growing back. Bothersome symptoms are gone. Living a thriving life despite a few spots on a scan or a marker that runs high, so long as the cancer is contained. How? Through mothering ourselves just right, which may include ongoing nontoxic anticancer care (e.g., mistletoe therapy; hyperbaric oxygen; clean eating; minimizing stress; safe, slow and ongoing detoxification; continuing to envision a vibrant future). In other words, the rook still needs to stand guard. The knight must stealthily protect against moving into the empty squares. And the queen (in all of us) must use all of her skills and varied powers to keep cancer boxed in. Cancer may have knocked out some pawns and other pieces, but our immune systems are well-equipped so long as we know how to liberate and support them and so long as the treatments empathize with our bodies and don't destroy them (i.e., integrative with nontoxic support for your healthy cells).

Just as in chess, it helps to have a strategy. To know something about why cancer got the upper hand, and what that means for what to do differently going forward. It's a worthy opponent. After all, it's us. Our own cells. Cancer cells are just trying to do what they are biologically programmed to do...replicate. Playing against cancer can take our game of life up a notch. It feels that way for me. Most lessons are things I wouldn't have learned—at least not as quickly—without being in this game. It has felt like a fast track to certain kinds of soul evolution. At some point, it's enough. In many ways, I feel I'm there.

Oh, yes, there is always much more to learn. Many more ways to evolve. But there is nothing like almost dying to sharpen priorities, clarify whether and how we still want to be here on this planet, put relationships in context, and force us to seek and find joy in the simple things.

But in this dramatic game of my immune system versus cancer, I've moved to having the cancer in check, working toward checkmate.

Cheers to that. ●

Grant's high school graduation, June 8 2022

CHAPTER THIRTY EIGHT • JUNE 20, 2022

The Rhythm of Home

I am home, much of the time, these days.

John and I packed up in Istanbul and flew home on May 20, 2022. On May 22, I rallied to give a commencement address at John Carroll University. On May 23, I felt the weight of the moving, the seven-hour time difference, the ongoing cancer battle and treatments...and exhaustion. In many ways, I'm still recovering from all that. So, I've been quietly reintegrating into life at home.

I'm trying to be patient with low energy, satisfied with walks around the block (instead of runs around the track), and nourished by being a central touchpoint of our kids' busy lives: graduation celebrations, working, a summer class, an internship, enjoying friends, family dinners, a boys' trip to Florida, and Father's Day. They haven't missed a beat, and it makes me happy. Oh, and there is the dog. How is it that Rocky is even cuter than before? By all accounts, he's had an emotional year and seems so much better with his family altogether now. I'm happy to be back in my kitchen, cooking for myself and our family, and eating their delicious food too. (Well done on the keto-friendly eggs benedict and berry cobbler for Father's Day, Grant and Sophie!)

It's been a big adjustment being home, and also as if I never left. Time can be strange in that way. At first, I wondered how I fit...but that quickly became clear. Our kids lead the way. They have kept their s**t together throughout this whole journey. In many ways, they are mature beyond their years. They don't need oversight so much as love and support. That, I can give in spades. And admiration. I admire both of them so much and revel in the adults they are already. I really like this parenting moment.

I have my own lifeforce here too. This book is a result of that. Interest in other work on empathy, with the police and personally, continues via podcasts and invitations to tell my story (e.g. the City Club of Cleveland).

Of course, too much of my time is still spent fighting, mentally, emotionally, and physically, late-stage cancer. Anyone who has been there knows, it's a full-time job all by itself. Nutrition. Supplements. Treatments. Tests. Meditation. Exercise. Prayer. Absorbing new results. Reconciling ourselves to the present work and traumas and accepting an uncertain future. And so on…I am not always gracious. It helps that this work is broken up by occasional fun visits, walks, and outdoor lunches with friends and extended family who keep us company along the way, although there is energy to conserve and still a pandemic to consider.

My life in Istanbul feels like a dream. I'm still in touch with friends there, though, so I know it was real. I also know they saved my life, because my memories of home before I left are painful, physically and emotionally…that was real too. The toxic mold issue that dogged me before/during/after diagnosis and the first round of treatment is gone, gone, gone, remarkably. Turkey gets credit for that too.

Time at home now feels old and new at the same time. I still mourn the things that are more difficult than before cancer…I can't seem to shake 51 years of healthy body memories even by acknowledging two and a half years of struggle. When I dream, I am well and whole. Awake, I feel the loss of life as it might have been…and as it seems to continue for our friends and family because it's apparent here. It's all around us. John and I (and Sophie and Grant) have jumped lanes, and we don't get to go back.

We do get to be home and together though, most of the time. Our solution for the summer is integrative oncology via the Block Center for Integrative Cancer Treatment in Chicago—i.e., safer chemo—every two weeks out of three. They are old friends on this journey. Via supplements and nutritional advice, the Block Center helped keep me feeling well and without side effects throughout the first round of chemo from April to September 2020. As in Istanbul, they deliver chemotherapy drugs along with nutritional infusions and hyperbaric oxygen to protect healthy cells and ward off side effects. So far, so good. As important as it was initially, it's crucial to have integrative oncology when you consider how much and how long my body has endured these treatments. This is true for anyone with a difficult cancer. Full-body hyperthermia is not part of the deal here as it was in Turkey; it's not legal in the US. It was effective, but I do not miss it. Brutal. Truly. I challenge anyone not to turn into a raging bitch in that chamber!

We are following cancer and terrain markers to see how effective these treatments in Chicago are. Soon, we will know. At the very least, we hope I remain stable so we can have this time all together before the kids go off to their various adventures in the fall. There are some new tricks (e.g., curcumin and other nutritional infusions) that bode well for addressing the one cancer gene I, and anyone who gets cancer, have (TP53), which may "up the anticancer game" at this point. We hope so.

Also, being home and in the midst of our family has benefits that can't be quantified...or can they? Before I even took more chemo in the US, my cancer marker went down by about 30 percent. Maybe that's the "empathy factor" at work? In any case, we will know how these treatments are working and have the data to make adjustments that might help keep us home, most of the time.

So, for now, we travel to Chicago to get chemo sandwiched between nutritional infusions. I wish it weren't so often. I wish it weren't so necessary. It is our reality for now.

The funny thing is...

Chicago is where John and I met and fell in love.

Chicago is where we thought we might live out our married life, or maybe some part of retirement.

So here we are, on another adventure...engaging in an alternate future (regular residents in Skokie, dinner out in Winnetka, appreciating the beauty of Lake Michigan in the summer, the chance to see dear friends) with a similar twist (Jackie getting pummeled with kinder, gentler chemo as part of the deal). Oh, to have retirement without that price! Is that too much to ask?!

I so often wondered what life would've been like for us if we stayed in Chicago. For now, I can say, we love Shaker Heights. It's a special bubble in this country. We would've loved Chicago too, but it's hard to imagine how life might have been better, especially for our kids. So, there's that. I can stop that particular kind of wondering now.

For our kids, adventures await. Grant will move to Villanova for college in mid-August. Sophie will move to Granada, Espana(!) for a semester abroad in September. Oh, the places they'll go, with their able bodies, thank goodness. I couldn't be more excited for them and am so glad to be here to help them get ready. We will be empty nesters, but what it means is so different from what I used to imagine. For now, I'm thrilled to see them living their best lives and relieved that our adventures in health don't seem to slow them down much.

No matter where our kids go or what they do now and always, the rhythm of home keeps beating inside. I know, because it was with me in Istanbul and resumed at a closer range/higher volume here at home. It continues to sustain me through brutal cancer treatments in Chicago and tests, etc., here at home. That rhythm is what we've built together and the legacy we all carry, across time and space.

It never stops. Like a dance. Like a heartbeat.

Maybe this is what's meant by "home is where the heart is"...it's comforting to know you can take it with you.

It's right there, inside. Always. ●

CHAPTER THIRTY NINE • JUNE 7, 2022

 We Shouldn't Have to Choose Between Living and a Life

Shaker Heights is my home. My people are here. John, Sophie, Grant, Rocky (he's a person too, really). Our friends. My colleagues. My kitchen. My bed. My life is here.

Istanbul was a great adventure...enough of one to see me through six months of brutal cancer treatments for the majority of days I lived there. It was a temporary home, made all the better by John's company most of the time, Turkish friends, and American friends who came to visit and help me get through chemo.

The place has a special magic. The people are uniformly kind and gracious. The language, culture, history, and food were fun to learn and experience. I threw myself into all of it. I had a life there, but it was meant to be a short-term assignment to get me to a more stable place. Mission accomplished. Did I get to remission as we'd hoped? No. For some reason, like many women with difficult ovarian cancer, chemotherapy isn't all-powerful and healing. Did I return safer and healthier than when I left? Well, I was in hospice then, so, definitely yes. In Turkey and when I returned, I was able to eat. I didn't have pain. I could walk for miles. For anyone who questions whether we in the US have something to learn from other ways of approaching cancer, my case shouts a loud, clear yes.

The treatments in Chicago are not working as well as the treatments in

Istanbul did. We know because the cancer marker is rising again, even though I've had three chemo treatments since we returned to the US on May 18, 2022. Heeding US standard of care advice as an experiment, we agreed to back off some of the drugs I was given in Turkey to protect my bone marrow. Even though chemo given in an integrative way is tolerable, bone marrow keeps the score with increasing difficulty producing the red and white blood cells we need to survive. It was a bet. We lost. Badly. So far.

It's now clear there was more wisdom in the Turkish protocol, which the Block Center has agreed to follow more carefully and as completely as possible. (Full-body hyperthermia is not legal in the US...for good reasons? Nah, but it was brutal. I hope it's not crucial.) Will it stabilize my marker/condition? We hope so. Can I chemo my way into remission here or anywhere? Not clear. How long would that take? Not clear. Would I have gotten to remission by now if I'd stayed in Turkey? Would I achieve remission in another six months if I went back? The math doesn't support those ideas. Am I sorry I came home? Definitely not. My life is here.

I have less energy. I'm exhausted by this fight, and it is a fight...with ongoing poking, prodding, cutting (I finally got the port), and poisoning, at this point with no definitive end in sight. My body is keeping the score, and we're doing our best to handicap the outcomes with nutrition, supplements, etc., but we don't have control over the endgame.

What I do have control over...what remains a choice...is how I live my life, even now. I might have questioned the decision to continue to receive treatment at a discouraging point like this in a cancer journey before it was me, now. It's incredible how we adjust to new normals, so long as living seems incrementally better than dying.

Although I was buying time and living an adventure in Turkey, my life is here. The work that remains for me is here. I'm working to get another book out. As a parent, I have adult kids—although 18 and 20 are not that old—to admire and help prepare for their own adventures in college and study abroad, and more. My joy is here. Cooking and eating meals together. Snuggling with the dog, Helping one kid with her chemistry, and the other order dorm supplies. Relaxing with John over the latest show in the evening (have you seen the drama series "The Bear?" Highly recommended).

I've traded the hills of Istanbul for the tree-lined streets of our block in Shaker Heights, sometimes with friends when I'm feeling up to it. Our life here is interrupted every two weeks with three days of treatment in Chicago, but this is our life. It's better than participating via FaceTime. I know. I've done it both ways.

And there are conversations we can have in person that would have been hard...maybe impossible...virtually. Conversations I wouldn't have thought to have without facing mortality. A chance to talk about the most important things in life, which we put off, sometimes until it's too late. What I hope for John, Sophie, and Grant. That they live, no matter what. That we find fun and joy together for as long as we can. That they continue with their plans with no regrets. Go to college. Go to Spain. I want what I've always wanted: what's best for them. I've made clear that their adventures, fun, and work in the world bring me more joy than anything they can do for me here. Their bodies are healthy. Their worlds are big. I believe I'll be able to participate in some way, no matter what. I love them completely. I'm not afraid of dying, but I do hope to manage the pain better than the last time I was given over to hospice.

Grant thinks I should try meth or _____ (insert powerful legal drugs that make being in a body more bearable). I can't disagree. To be clear, I feel I've been training for the next phases of life and will feel pretty ripped off if I don't get to live them. Watching our kids become who they will be. Traveling with John. Dancing at weddings. Holding grandbabies while cooking for their new parents.

My husband and children are loved. They should live in full color, now and always. John too. Let's not forget him. If we've learned anything in all of this, it's that life is precious and short (hopefully not too short). Living in full color is the only reasonable choice.

I shouldn't have to choose between life and living, don't you think? Thank goodness we went to Turkey in the first place where I was put on a protocol that worked and probably would not have been considered in the US. Why not? Well, I've written plenty about this...which comes down, time and again, to a failure of courage, imagination, and empathy for patients. For this reason, I write. For this reason, I've put it all into this book. This story must be told and told again so that it is heard and might make a difference someday for someone else.

As for my health, let's just hope we can get back on track. And resume life with the promise of living, as abnormal and imperfect as it is these days. ●

Jackie and John

CHAPTER FORTY • AUGUST 26, 2022

Immunotherapy Is the Answer
Co-written with John LeMay

We have long believed that immunotherapy is the answer to cancer for many people, and certainly for me. I'm not one of the lucky minority with late-stage ovarian cancer for whom chemo catalyzes remission. We've known this would be the case since early in my first round (of what has become three) of chemotherapy two years ago. I tolerate the chemo well, through diet and nutritional supplements, but it doesn't really work.

Why? Maybe because my immune system was dysregulated by mold toxicity and mass cell activation in the first place. Maybe something else in my particular genes makes it difficult to stop the cancering process once it begins. Maybe because chemo is truly poison, not really a medicine, and shouldn't be mainlined into human bodies. Yet, it buys time for me and others, so we abide it. It's an old solution, often considered the "gold standard of care" in the US, even when it doesn't work. Knowing all of this, it's a struggle to sit in a chemo infusion chair.

The hope has always been to somehow right my immune system so that it can fight cancer on its own. Once we got through chemo round one, I tried to do this naturally, with all of the nontoxic anticancer therapies that work (e.g., hyperbaric oxygen, mistletoe shots, plant strong clean ketogenic nutrition, immune boosting supplements, hyperthermia). Like blanket chemo solutions, these often effective therapies, even when conscientiously applied in combination, were no match for my particular cancer. I bought some time, but not a lifetime. Combining chemo with nontoxic therapies in Istanbul (e.g., whole body hyperthermia, hyperbaric oxygen, nutritional infusion) saved my life, but didn't give me a remission. Similar treatments closer to home in Chicago have been less effective for reasons that flummox all the doctors. My cancer is very, very smart.

So, it's time to pivot, hard. Immunotherapy for ovarian cancer is relatively nascent, and it's clear that not all ovarian cancers are the same. Personalized immunotherapy would give us the best chance, but that's not how the research is usually done. So, it's tricky, and yet again, experimental...in which I am the lab rat. We have some leads, and we have some guides, but John and I are hard at work again trying to sort out options and discern the best way forward. To find the true "gold standard" of care, for me.

Certainly, immunotherapy will be a big part of the future of more empathic cancer treatments (and perhaps even prevention). Immunotherapies work with our bodies, rather than against them. They support natural functions versus kill indiscriminately the way chemo does. Here are the basics:

- Cancer immunotherapy treatments seek to both increase the level of immune system activity and also overcome cancer's ability to hide from the immune system.

- Cancers can take hold in the body for many reasons but the immune system is always part of the story—cancers can progress if the immune system is compromised in some fashion or if cancer finds a way to hide from the immune system.

- Cancer hides from the immune system by presenting itself in a way that the immune system doesn't recognize as a foreign body—once it achieves that condition it is able to grow uninhibited by our normal immune response.

There are several types of immunotherapy treatments in use and under development:

- **Monoclonal antibodies and checkpoint inhibitors**—Made in a lab, these antibodies slow or stop the growth of abnormal proteins in cancer cells. The goal is to alter the cancer cells so they are no longer able to "trick" the body into thinking they're healthy cells so they can keep growing. This is the most commonly approved type of immunotherapy at this time.

- **T-cell therapy (CAR T-cell therapy)**—The patient's own T-cells (immune system cells that fight infection) are removed from the blood. Next, a lab-created receptor is added to the T-cells, which are put back in the body. The receptors are able to identify cancer cells and destroy them.

- **Cancer vaccines**—Treatment vaccines are still mostly in the research phase to see how they can use the body's immune system to identify and destroy specific types of cancer cells. A common approach is a dendritic cell vaccine. Here a patient's dendritic cells are loaded with a tumor-specific antigen (a toxin or other foreign substance which induces an immune response) and reintroduced to the body, which allows the body to recognize and attack tumor cells. The same mRNA technology used in Pfizer/BioNTech's Covid vaccine is now also being used to develop cancer vaccines.

- **Oncolytic virus therapy**—Oncolytic viruses are those that are non-pathogenic to healthy cells but infect cancer cells, prompting a broader immune reaction.

The field of immunotherapy has exploded over the last decade, and these emerging therapies are the most promising treatments to come out of cancer research in a very long time. Some people are calling this explosion of immunotherapy research and treatment options cancer's "penicillin moment." They don't work for everyone with cancer, and there is much more work needed, but supporting immune system function makes intuitive sense.

There are many things we can do to support a healthy immune system on our own. Sleep. Exercise. Eat clean, healthy food. Drink pure water. Take additional vitamins/supplements as needed (e.g., C, D, A...get a great functional doctor to help you understand what your body needs). Laugh! Yes, laughter increases natural killer cells. Not so easy to do once the cancering process has begun, so try to get your laughs in while you're not in a health crisis.

Once the cancering process is in motion, we need more. We need effective, empathetic (working with the body) medical interventions to restore immune system function. That is our hope with immunotherapy for everyone, including me.

We're back to work, excavating options. We'll let you know what we find. Immunotherapy is the answer for the future of cancer treatment...hopefully in time for me. ●

Part 5

Finding Peace at the End of the Journey

CHAPTERS

41. I Am Done	213
42. The Biggest Trip	217

CHAPTER FORTY ONE • OCTOBER 2, 2022

 I Am Done

I am done being poked, prodded, cut, and poisoned.

Somehow, it seems I am finished with my work here on earth as well.

Chicago treatments aren't working. Why?

They were not able to replicate what I was receiving in Istanbul closely enough.

Should I have stayed in Turkey? Maybe, but I was not near remission there either…my body couldn't hold onto the progress I'd made there through so many brutal treatments. I've lost approximately six months of hard work.

I've loved being home with John, Sophie, and Grant and would have made this trade-off to come home with full knowledge of what would happen.

At some point, even with integrated chemotherapy, the bone marrow gives out. I'm nearly there, and nowhere near remission.

There are no effective immunotherapies that seem to be ready for me now either.

It has become hard to eat and drink, with cancer disrupting all of that.

My body is done. It's time to find peace and pass as painlessly as possible.

We are initiating hospice. A few last thoughts…

I'm glad I learned...
- How much I love my family. John, Sophie, and Grant are my favorite people. Rocky too. Being with all of them has been comforting.

- How liberating it is to dissociate from emotional toxicity...better late than never.

- How much I've enjoyed being alive for as long as I have been.

- How to navigate cancer, with John's constant partnership, to be alive and mostly out of pain this long...not without complaint, mind you. This whole thing is obscene. Courage amounted to going through these treatments, anyway.

I wish...
- CA125 testing were standard for perimenopausal women (Note: you can ask for this and order it yourself through any number of lab services, e.g., requestatest.com); there are many false positives but secondary imaging will let you know if you need to take action (which could be as simple as having your fallopian tubes removed).

- Gynecologists listened to women coming in with unusual symptoms (bloating, UTI's, post-menopausal bleeding) the first time.

- Integrative care I received in Turkey were fully available in the US.

- Effective treatments were available for the majority of ovarian cancer patients—chemo simply doesn't work most of the time.

- Chemotherapy for all cancers is ultimately replaced by immunotherapies that don't damage our bodies.

- Preventive cancer care, including clean nutrition and environments, becomes normal from birth on. This would be the "gold standard of care."

- I could stick around for the fun part with John, Sophie, and Grant.

- I had more time to live, love, work, enjoy.

I hope...
- Sophie, Grant, and John can remember me when I was well, forgive me for not being able to stay that way, and live fully without me.

- That you will help them do that and keep them company; there is never a good time to leave.

- That their memories of me provide comfort as they navigate a new normal without the wife and mom they knew until now.

- That my words provided some inspiration along the way, and they might continue to do so (*Currency of Empathy* holds true).

- That life in some form continues so I can keep my family company somehow...I believe this is true...I just don't know how. Soon, I'll find out. It's a big adventure, really. I'm not afraid of death, just the painful part before the transition.

- That I get all the answers to the questions I have about health, life, the point of everything...my version of heaven. Even Google can't do all that.

- That my dad meets me on the other side.

- That in the life after this time on earth, I again experience the kind of wholeness and joy which has been hard to access while accepting cancer treatments, dealing with many constraints, and living with constant discomfort (who knows how it works, but maybe pizza and wine come back on the celestial menu...Minna's dumplings and peach cobbler, Aunt Rusty's spaghetti, Grandma Acho's tacrathas and dolma).

- That you who get to carry on here with life on earth, enjoy retirement, have fun with your spouse, travel as much as you'd like, watch your kids graduate, become adults, get married and have kids (if they so choose).

- That you get to rock your grandkids...that maybe you'll even rock mine and somehow let them know how much I love them already.

I'm grateful...
- For the unfettered love I've experienced in my life.

- For the partnership and family John LeMay and I have built; may it sustain him even in my absence...as I've told him, he's so loveable and deserving of partnership in his life still, but I get first dibs in heaven.

- For the work I've been able to do in the world.

- For a healthy body that supported all of that for approximately 50 years, with hardly a thought about time limits.

Maybe we always want more time. I bet we do. I know I do.

But it's time to rest, and I've earned it.

Thank you for your company, love, and prayers.

Much love back to you. ●

CHAPTER FORTY TWO • NOVEMBER 10, 2022

The Biggest Trip

What do you do "in hospice" when you have an upcoming expiration date but still a clear mind? I've never done this before and am no expert, but life and death are so fascinating...and mysterious...that one person's experience might be interesting. So, I'll share.

I'm planning for the biggest trip of all.

It's a different kind of work than I was used to doing, so it took me a beat to see that's what I was doing. I'm used to being busy with too much to do and lots of company in this world, not quiet and contemplative with the urge to hunker down with John (and the kids when they're home). Hunkering down isn't my nature, but when you think about it, it makes sense, doesn't it? If you have the flu, do you feel like seeing people when you're at your most sick? I'm not in great pain (thank goodness) but cannot eat much and am growing weaker every day. Our hospice team is ready and willing to help in every way possible, but in many ways, this is a waiting game. I can't control it. That's hard. I can only control my reaction. Hunkering down feels right.

I spend much of my days now learning about this last, great adventure which we will all take. I learn from people who died and came back, psychologists who hypnotize patients and are surprised to learn about past lives, and hospice caregivers who have been part of this sacred dance, many, many times over decades. By the way, thank goodness for hospice and the work of Elizabeth Kübler-Ross and others. Dying in the modern medical age, before hospice, was often just plain cruel. Our ancestors knew better, but, as with so much, we separated ourselves from the reality of death and forgot how to do it.

I have always thought there is too much evidence of a higher power to ignore the idea. (Just try to make even a single leaf without raw materials, much less a rainbow; we can't.) The glimpses we get of higher love, even amongst ourselves, bear even more witness to whatever source power you choose to believe in and whatever you want to call it. I was glad to find there is similarly lots of evidence of a soul life after our physical bodies can't sustain life on earth anymore due to cancer, terminal illness, an accident...or if you're really lucky, old age. Raymond Moody's "Life After Life" was a groundbreaking book when it first came out. Now, there is a whole genre of books about the experiences of patients, caregivers, and families at the end of life. Most of the stories have at least a dozen elements in common (the bright light, floating above your body, meeting soul mates, etc.). This is not my first reading of these books, but it's certainly the most focused. Can they all be wrong? No way. It's a mystery but not without clues.

So, I read. I meditate. (Confession: I don't love it and forget about sitting on a cushion.) I dream and pay attention to those dreams, hoping for visits from souls who can comfort me. I'm looking for my dad, who passed away in August 2022, my beloved grandmother, my aunt, my cousin, his dad...I'm looking for guidance because they are the people who actually know what this transition is like. They've done it. They are our mentors. My dreams have always been wild, so following them sometimes feels like hanging onto a mechanical bull. At times, they are peaceful. Jesus sat with our little family in a light blue robe a month or so ago. He was there for my soul, but he comforted John, Sophie, and Grant. We didn't say much (anything?), but it was nice...and consistent with my Catholic and Episcopalian roots.

We all grieve what might have been, also. That's real. I'd rather be preparing to visit Sophie in Spain or Grant at college, dancing at Sarah's and Chelsea's weddings, prepping for that big trip to Australia with John or Namibia with Susan. It feels as if that's what should be, but this is what we have. Our kids are bravely carrying on with life as well. It took a lot of balls for them to hug their mom goodbye, then get on planes to Granada and Philadelphia. We are left with "empty nesting" in hospice. I hope you are enjoying the weddings, the travel, and even just the dinners out that John and I imagined at this stage. What do we do? John and I spoil Rocky even more. I take some pleasure in the leaves changing, the sun on my face, and the little bit I can eat. With John's help, I still cook some, mostly for nostalgia (e.g., Chaldean hamuth kibbeh, tortilla Espanola, anything Minna made), whatever the kids want when they're home, and because that's one of my creative expressions and love languages. It's hard to stop a lifetime habit. I'm still a foodie, just a hungry one. I gathered our favorite family recipes, so they will be handy later. I play word games because I still can. I made our family photo album again this year and bought some Christmas presents. It's hard to stop doing the things of life if you don't have to yet. It's liberating to know that I can be done when needed. When I need to rest.

Nothing has been left unsaid to anyone. I've had extraordinary conversations with both of our kids, who are learning to face their mother's mortality so much younger than most these days. I hope it somehow helps them live more fully, with less fear...eventually. John and I have had almost three years of meaningful conversations; we don't need many words now. There are letters waiting for John and our kids, some for specific milestones I'll miss on earth (good idea, Sophie). I've gotten my metaphorical, and in some sense physical, house in order. This has been the benefit of a long goodbye rather than an abrupt ending. John and I have discussed my cremation and burial. How's that for surreal? Our priest, Jeanne, has been by to share blessings and plans; I'm lucky she's a friend. We've planned a memorial for later when kids and friends will be home (and I'm likely to be gone). I hope it gives you what you need, and that you love each other and surround my family.

We watch shows at night. Documentaries. Series. Nothing dark anymore; I just can't. Mostly it's just John, Rocky, and me. I still love to share what we think about these shows. John's my favorite conversation buddy. He gives good foot rubs too.

I treasure the goodnight hug, thinking of a time when I may not be able to make my presence so known, so solid.

I'm still sad that medicine didn't work for me…all of the kinds we tried, but I don't spend so much time perseverating on all that now. It's all in this book. I hope that will make a difference for someone else, even just not to feel so lonely.

I reminisce. I can look through old pictures and family movies with more sweetness than sadness. I've had a good life. I don't feel as though I wasted time. I don't have many regrets. I just wanted more of this particular assignment, with these people.

And I imagine…
What it will feel like in the end.

Who will come to meet me. What happens next.

How I'll feel at the "review" of this life.

Whether I'll get more chances at embodied life on earth, or maybe a cleaner planet where there is no cancer.

If so, will I level up to help others? Is that even a thing? Some people and ancient texts swear by it.

Will I get to flit to Spain to see Sophie, Philly to see Grant, and back to Shaker Heights to make sure Rocky is giving John as much love as he can, all in an instant?

I know the basics of what will happen to my physical body. That part interests me less (and sure, scares me more) than what will happen to my soul. Still, it's good to be educated. To make choices while I still can. It helps to move through the fear.

I have always loved to travel. How could I not embrace this biggest trip of all? There are a lot of upsides…no packing, no worries about passports/ID/TSA, and leaving behind a body that did its best but has been challenged to the brink. It's been strange eating solely for pleasure, leaving most of the supplements behind, and not pushing myself to walk/run/practice yoga/keep up my muscles. Been there. Done that. Now is a time of rest. This trip requires peace, not last-minute leg-shaving, lists, and snacks. If we've been paying attention, we've had lots of invitations to prepare, all along the way. It's a lifelong process. The biggest obstacle is fear. I don't claim to be fearless, but I don't spend all day crying or shaking in my boots. Hospice is here to help. I look forward to relief. There's more evidence that this biggest trip of all is a beautiful one rather than a tortuous one (even if we weren't all saints on earth).

So, I'm taking care of my soul. I'm getting ready for the trip. Not just on Sunday. Not just in prayer or meditation, but as my day job now. It's quiet work but it's not boring.

It's the biggest adventure of all. ●

Part 6

Acknowledgments	223
Afterword	227
About the Author	234
Appendix One: Cancer Treatment Information and Resources	236
Appendix Two: Eulogies from Jackie's Memorial Service, January 7, 2023	241

Acknowledgments

I was grateful to live as long as I did. That was not a given, and is true in large part due to the following people...

My husband and children did not give up on me at a time I almost did. Their love has been the inspiration and motivation I needed to stick around, tolerating difficult days and treatments. My husband, John LeMay, and I have grown into an even more intimate partnership, in researching, talking about what really matters, and considering all options. I fancied myself a pretty independent person prior to getting sick, but I would be dead without him. He would be very sad without me. I've come to see that mutual interdependence as a beautiful thing, one of the highest and best containers for empathy that I know. Our children Sophie and Grant have been unwavering in their support and faith, and kept their s**t together as teenagers throughout this ordeal. I'm both grateful and amazed by them, constantly.

Entrepreneurial and integrative doctors and healers steered us into treatments my body needed to stay alive. Dr. Abdul Slocum of Chemothermia in Istanbul, Turkey, has been chief among them, as well as Dr. Nasha Winters, Dr. Laura Mourino, and Dr. Jessica Hutchins. The care team at Chemothermia became friends, including Sirin, Noor, Elena, Halva, Aran, Omar, Furkan, Ahmet, and Eray. Dr. Mark Dabagia never ceased supporting us with his knowledge and friendship.

Friends and family continued to communicate with and support us throughout two things that might have left our family isolated: the Covid pandemic and six months of remote care in Istanbul. I'm endlessly grateful for the practical companionship and empathy they have shown to our family, especially our son who spent a good part of his senior year of high school without his parents at home. They cooked, organized food deliveries, showed love to our kids and us, sent us videos, kept us in the loop by e-mail/phone/WhatsApp/Messenger/Signal, accompanied Grant on a college visit, and even picked out clothes that would accommodate my changing body and needs. Thanks to my parents, Peter and Barbara Acho for their love and prayers, and my brother Mike Acho for taking care of them when I could not physically be there.

So many people have kept us company throughout this cancer journey, especially Kathryn Passov Edelman, Hallie Stuart, Brant Butze, Lisa and David Levine, the O'Brien/Landever Family, Rebecca Schanberg Polsky, the Hofner and Ashley families, Brett Wessler, the LeMay siblings (Elaine, Jim, and Jeff), Liz Duffett, and Heather Weingart. I'm endlessly grateful for our kids' friends and teachers/professors, who have been incredibly supportive. One of the biggest blessings in our lives has been and continues to be Carnella Peck. She is pure empathy and love, and we all feel it, including Rocky the dog.

We're also grateful for friends who were willing to literally travel halfway around the world to keep me company while John was at home, including: Reverend Jeanne Leinbach, Sharon Sobol Jordan, Dan and Monica Lacks, Susan Colby, and Rhonda, Nick and Hope Laurencelle. I've been the recipient of weekly healing prayer for, incredibly, over two years thanks to Akua Saunders, Leslie Amadhi, Eleanor Hooks, Jane Reynolds, Rachel Robinson, and Elizabeth Welch.

Turkey came alive for us through tour guide extraordinaire Hakan Gurger, a portal to past, present and future. Sulyman Ekinci and his family made us feel at home from day one in Istanbul, as did many of the staff at TZL Suites.

I'm grateful that empathy proved a true and steadfast window to make meaning of this cancer journey. It's been a blessing to continue to write, blog, work, and speak on the multifaceted topic of empathy throughout. I appreciate the people and places that continued to value my work, giving me one more reason to stick around. In particular, this includes the Cleveland Police, Katie Tercek of Cleveland 19 News, Hyperion Materials & Technologies (a KKR company), Jessica Lindberg, Lila Lazarus, Danita Harris, Daniel Stid, Minter Dial, and the handful of traditional oncologists at University of Chicago and the Cleveland Clinic who have been open to hearing my story of alternative, integrative care for cancer. I hope such connections will contribute to longer lives and better days for all of us who suffer with difficult cancers. I also hope that together, we can focus on more effective cancer prevention, so that all of our children will never know what it feels like to take chemo. Thanks to Matt Ewalt, Lauren Fine, and the Chautauqua Institution, as well as Barbara Brown, Al Miciak, and John Carroll University for the special opportunities to speak to those audiences.

Finally, I'm grateful for the dear friends and colleagues who brought this book to life in the most generative way possible: Jeffrey Bauer, an empathic friend and creator of this book, and Andrea C. Turner, trusted friend and editor. For my words to be safe in their hands means a lot. ●

Afterword

Empathy is Your Compass to an Inspired Future

Editor's Note: The following text is the commencement address Jackie delivered at John Carroll University on May 22, 2022, days after returning from treatment in Istanbul, Turkey.

Good morning and congratulations! What a beautiful day and a profound moment. It's awesome and humbling to be part of this day, looking at you and thinking of all of the amazing people who have launched from John Carroll University. A day like this can feel overwhelming, but as comedian Andy Samberg said, "You are graduating from college. That means that this is the first day of the last day of your life. No, that's wrong. This is the last day of the first day of school. Nope, that's worse. This is a day."

I thank you for letting me be part of *that day*, so I can tell you about an internal compass you have *to achieve an inspired future*, no matter what life throws at you. You already have it inside, and you always will. It's just up to you to remember. It's simple but not always easy because the world sometimes makes us forget. It's your human superpower of empathy, your sacred inheritance.

Now, take a minute to reflect on what it took for you to get to this moment. What hard things did you overcome? How did you do it? Did anyone help you or did you do it on your own, through grit and resilience? Only you know *exactly* what it took for you to get here. From here on, I hope that when you face difficulty, you sometimes have empathetic people to keep you company. *I have found, especially recently, that just knowing you're not alone can make a big difference.*

**I should have been dead months ago,
so it's something of a miracle that
I stand before you.**

I was diagnosed with late-stage ovarian cancer in February of 2020, so I was fighting for my life as we were all navigating through a global pandemic. I feel for you students because our kids are college students now too. You've had to adjust in so many ways in the last two years. So have I. I was otherwise very healthy and strong going into the cancer journey so I fared well through traditional treatment of surgery and chemotherapy. I worked. I cared for my family. I ran—slowly, but I did—I lifted weights, practiced yoga, and ate clean and healthy food. But, for this cancer like many other difficult ones, traditional treatments don't usually work. By October 2021, the cancer was growing again and my oncologist gave me three months to live and put me in hospice. That's why I should be dead already, but I'm still here, in no small part because I used my internal compass of empathy and sought integrative care in Istanbul, Turkey for the last six months. I'm fresh off the plane and *so utterly joyful* to be home and with you today. The other key to surviving for me? Empathy and love from family and friends. I was never alone.

**I share all of that to say that even if life throws
you that kind of curveball, you can continue to live
into an inspired future by staying in touch with
your internal compass of empathy.**

What do I mean by empathy? *The ability to understand the feelings of another and have an appropriate emotional response.* That last part is really important and often forgotten. In many ways, empathy is the foundation of so many spiritual teachings, because it's the gateway to love.

You heard my background, so you already know that empathy was not my starting point! It wasn't part of the chemistry curriculum at MIT. It was not the focus of business or McKinsey. What woke me up to remembering empathy were two people very much like you were years ago—our kids, Sophie and Grant. It turns out that hands-on parenting increases empathy in the brain. It doesn't mean you have to have kids to be empathetic, but parenting and early childhood are both times when our empathic circuits can grow like crazy.

Sometimes the world works to sap our empathy, getting in the way of our inspired futures. Competition in work and school pits us against each other. Our work/life balance challenges our ability to take care of ourselves, much less anyone else. The news—including what we absorb through constant social media—is so negative—or worse, falsely positive, making our lives look boring by comparison—that it can make us numb. And that's why you have to work to *remember* your empathy.

The good news is that you can do three simple things to live into an inspired future while growing your superpower of empathy:

1. **Find meaning,**
2. **Keep growing, personally and professionally, and**
3. **Focus on being whole. You are built for all of these things.**

They feel good. I'm not sure *exactly* how each of you will do it, but I can tell you some of what I've done so you have some ideas.

Inspired Future Secret Number 1: Find meaning. It's an active sport. I remember struggling with, "What should be my mission in life?" when I graduated college and beyond. Maybe you can relate? What I came to understand is that it wasn't so much about what I did as *how I did it*. No matter where you work, if you can help at least one person, you are making the world a better place. You'll likely have several jobs or even careers. I have. I've been a scientific researcher, a businesswoman, an entrepreneur, an author, a speaker, a wife, and a mom.

Frederick Buechner said, "Your vocation in life is where your greatest joy meets the world's greatest need." The world has many great needs now. Solving climate change. Making business more human. Eradicating war and disease. Feeding a hungry planet healthier food. But let me be clear—while I'm hopeful about what you'll all do, it's on us, the generations before you to clean up these messes while we're still here too. I'm not *counting* on you. I'm *with* you.

The older I've become, the more I've been zeroing in on what I can uniquely do. First, I made molecules that were new to the world and might help clean up the planet. I helped companies grow, trying to focus on the ones that were doing more good than harm. Eventually, I started digging into the power of empathy—redefining leadership and helping organizations become more human. Like the Cleveland police, in a time when people think police and empathy don't overlap. Oh, *but they do*, and it matters. Cleveland is leading the way. Right here in our backyard, we've decreased the use of force by 29%, citizen complaints by 45%, and helped officers find more meaning in serving people. That's how you weed out psychopathy and reform policing. Since I was thrown the cancer card, I've used all my scientific, business, and personal experience to advocate for integrative care that will help others beat the odds as I've been doing.

You will evolve into many missions too, because of the world's many evolving needs and your many gifts. You don't have to spend them all at once, and you'll develop more over time. I hope you'll spend less time stressing about *what* you do and more time marveling at the mystery of *all that is possible* for you and how it will be revealed. That you'll be open to the gift of the "present." Try to be patient. Your mission in life will come and come again. I promise. Wherever you can, in the work you do and the way you live, *choose as much meaning* as possible. You'll know because it will resonate with your soul. You'll be excited.

Inspired Future Secret Number 2: Never stop growing. College can be such a time of growth. Here at John Carroll that growth is often guided by deep, timeless values and shepherded by professors. As you go out into the world, you'll find that your growth is more of your own responsibility and not always the priority of places or people of work. My advice to you is, whenever possible, **choose to put yourself in organizations where growing people is a priority.**

They exist and you deserve that. Where they care about whether and how you learn. Hopefully, you'll have good partnerships, as I did at McKinsey and with the hundreds of clients with whom I worked then and after. So much of learning is personal too. I've dug into many passions throughout the years. Some benefited our family, such as cooking, nutrition, and early childhood development. Some turned into work in the world, like understanding how to grow empathy. Whatever your passions are—whether they include singing, philosophy, sports, or anything else—dig into all that life has to offer. You are in charge of your "curriculum" from here on out, and you get to fill it with fun stuff. Enjoy that!

Inspired Future Secret Number 3: Live a whole life. Here is where we Americans often fall down, out of cultural habit. It starts early with the worst parental leave of any developed country and continues with some of the worst work/life balance. We put up with all of that, *but your generation knows better.* Your empathy *depends* on you staying connected to your core and that requires time to *care*, for yourself and others. Caring for yourself starts with honoring who you are inside. Not contorting yourself to fit someplace or someone that doesn't deserve you. Actually, do more than take care. There is a beautiful Turkish saying, "Kendine iyi devran." Treat yourself well! Enjoy beautiful food. Get out in nature. Be with your friends or by yourself, as you need. Listen to music. Dance! Wear the fun shoes! Do the things that bring you joy and bring all of that—all of **you**—to work and to life. We need that. We need **you**. The only way to build heaven on earth is *to include everyone as we really are*. So do what *you* need to get in touch with that inner soul, regularly, and let it shine out. The world can be loud—telling you to do this, wear that, be like them—but tune yourself to the whispers of your own divine spirit. It's in each and every one of us, connected in ways we sometimes glimpse when our eyes and hearts are open.

So, preserving your compass of internal empathy and living into an inspired future requires 1. *Finding meaning.* 2. *Growing.* 3. *Being whole.* It's simple but not always easy. The world may work against you, but you always have *choices* in how you react. Sometimes, you can hit it on all cylinders.

At 50, I became a certified yoga teacher so I could teach the police—what meaningful time that is. Plus, it's kind of fun to tell the people capable of giving you a ticket to get into downward dog! In all of it, I had the chance to grow and learn through a new discipline and found more wholeness in my life, spiritually and physically.

Now, at 53, cancer has thrust me into a whole new search. I'm finding meaning in understanding and reversing the epidemic of cancer so our kids and everyone in your generation **will never know what it feels like to take chemo**. I'm also advocating for integrative care so other patients with difficult diagnoses might thrive instead of die. To be clear, this is nothing I wanted, but apparently, I was built for it, and all of my experiences until now are useful.

There is another benefit of coming face to face with your mortality. Sometimes letting go is the hardest part of growing, but it's so important. I've learned a lot about letting go while nearly dying. Of what I thought life would be versus what it is now. It's not all bad. It's often good. Cancer has a way of chiseling away at a person, removing what doesn't really matter, leaving behind what does. Like a sculptor with marble. I've lost my hair and vanity, my identity as a healthy working parent, the busyness of life as it was…but I've found freedom from society's gaze, empathy for people with illness, a willingness to be vulnerable, and an ever more authentic voice. Once you've faced dying, what's left to be afraid of?! And that helps me be whole—here or anywhere. I've realized that limits make meaning. Knowing we don't have each other forever really does make us appreciate the time we have together more. There's nothing I'd rather do than spend precious time with my husband and kids, and other souls who allow me to be authentic…including our dog, Rocky. He may not be the smartest or best-behaved dog but, he gets by on his good looks!

My priorities have gotten clearer and clearer. There's nothing like cancer to give you the excuse you need to say no to all of that stuff and/or people you thought you *should* accommodate but you don't really have to, and yes to what brings you joy. Don't wait for an illness! Just do it.

Because what is an inspired future after all? You can think about it as your *art*. I don't necessarily mean painting or singing, although if you're talented in those ways, go for it! Madeleine L'Engle, who wrote, "A Wrinkle in Time," said that all true art is "channeling cosmos into the chaos." No matter what work you do, you can think of it as channeling a bit of heaven into life on earth. Doing that would be inspired, don't you think? Making it clear that actually, heaven *can be* right here on earth and creating your corner of it for yourself and others—personally and professionally. You will always be aligned with your mission in life if you do that. It's hard to do it alone though. So connect with each other to co-create a better world whenever you can.

In closing, there are three simple though not always easy ways to live an inspired life. Learning to say no helps make room for when you should say yes. And your internal compass of empathy is your guide. *That's the best news of all. You already have the superpower of empathy inside.* You just need to remember to keep growing it. In doing that, no matter what, your future will be inspired!

Thank you, congratulations again, and G-d bless you! ●

About the Author

Jackie Acho was President of The Acho Group, a strategy and leadership consulting firm. Prior to founding her business in 2005, she was a partner of McKinsey & Company. For more than 25 years she has worked with clients on a variety of issues, with particular focus on innovation, strategy, cultural transformation, and leadership development.

Jackie wrote and spoke about creating a Currency of Empathy®. In 2014, she gave the TEDx talk: "A Good Day's Work Requires Empathy." In 2020, she authored her first book, "Currency of Empathy: The Secret to Thriving in Business & Life."

Jackie received her master's degree and PhD in inorganic chemistry from the Massachusetts Institute of Technology, and a BS in chemistry with highest honors from the University of Michigan in Ann Arbor. Jackie was named one of the "top 40 under 40" by Crain's Cleveland Business magazine, "one of the 500 most influential women in Northeast Ohio" by Northern Ohio Live magazine, and a 2019 Women Living STEM Honoree.

Jackie served on the Board of Hyperion Materials & Technologies, a KKR Company. She has also served on the Boards of Jumpstart, Inc., the National Inventors Hall of Fame, the.

Urban League of Greater Cleveland, the Research and Technology Commercialization Visiting Committee of Case Western Reserve University (CWRU), and St. Paul's Episcopal Church in Cleveland Heights, Ohio, among others. Jackie is a graduate of the Leadership Cleveland class of 2012. She taught "Finance in the Real World" at CWRU's Weatherhead School of Management, and was a speaker in the Massively Open Online Course (MOOC) "Beyond Silicon Valley: Growing Entrepreneurship in Transitioning Economies."

Jackie was a certified yoga teacher specializing in trauma-informed yoga for police and other first responders. She is also a graduate of Sewanee University's Education for Ministry program. Jackie was diagnosed with stage 3, high grade serous ovarian cancer in February 2020.

She lived in Shaker Heights, Ohio, with her husband and children, but also enjoyed residence in Istanbul, Turkey while receiving care for cancer from 2021-2022. Jackie passed away at home under hospice care on December 22, 2022. ●

www.jackieacho.com • www.currencyofempathy.com

APPENDIX ONE

Cancer Treatment Information and Resources

The world of cancer research can be overwhelming. The information below is not comprehensive or authoritative and should not be read as medical advice. It is simply a compendium of the treatment options and resources that we found to be valuable during Jackie's cancer journey. We hope you find it helpful in some way.

Integrative Cancer Treatment Reading/Consultants

1. Ralph Moss publications — Dr. Moss was one of the earliest adopters of integrative philosophy and his website and publications are comprehensive and helpful. He will also do personal consultations. https://www.themossreport.com

2. Cancer Choices — An independent, science-informed resource helping you make sense of your choices in integrative cancer care. Offers information on natural products, off-label drugs, mind-body therapies, diets and metabolic therapies and others. https://cancerchoices.org

3. Michelle Gerencser — Nutritional Solutions Consulting Group – Excellent advice regarding diet and supplements to help the body during chemotherapy treatments. www.nutritional-solutions.net

4. Dr. Keith Block — His book, "Life Over Cancer," is now somewhat dated (published 2009) but provides a helpful, comprehensive view of integrative care. https://www.amazon.com/Life-Over-Cancer-Integrative-Treatment/dp/0553801147

5. Nasha Winters, ND — "The Metabolic Approach to Cancer." https://www.amazon.com/Metabolic-Approach-Cancer-Integrating-Bio-Individualized/dp/1603586865

6. Mark Renneker, MD — Medical Advocacy for Cancer Patients — Offers an array of leading edge/integrative testing and treatment ideas. Mark.Renneker@ucsf.edu

Non-Chemo Treatment Options

1. Terrain assessment/supportive supplements and diet. Your body terrain is the state of your inner environment. It includes your nutritional status, metabolism, immune function, microbiome, environmental exposures, and other factors. Your terrain can affect how a tumor grows and spreads. This is assessed through a much broader blood panel that looks to determine some of the conditions in your body that might be supporting cancer growth and then recommend interventions through diet and supplements.

2. Off Label Pharma — there are a variety of off-label (used for something other than originally approved/intended use) pharmaceuticals that have been shown to have beneficial effects in the treatment of cancer, often in concert with chemotherapy. Examples include low-dose naltrexone, doxycycline, metformin, statins, bisphosphonates, ivermectin, itraconazole and ritonavir.

3. Toxin Cleanup — mold, heavy metals and other toxins can distract the immune system, reducing its focus on fighting cancer. There are a variety of tests to determine if you have toxin overload and binders that can help remove the toxins from your system.

4. IV treatments — e.g. Vitamin C, resveratrol, quercetin, phosphatidylcholine, and many others.

5. Modified Ketogenic type diet – There is significant research that suggests glucose is the most efficient fuel for cancer growth and should be limited. A ketogenic diet primarily consists of high fats, moderate proteins, and very low carbohydrates.

6. Hyperthermia
   - Full body only available outside the US
   - Local available at some integrative clinics in US

7. Oxygenation
   - Hyperbaric oxygen
   - EWOT (Exercise With Oxygen Therapy) exercise while breathing oxygen through a mask.

8. Ferroptosis – An intracellular iron-dependent form of cell death that is distinct from apoptosis, necrosis, and autophagy. Studies suggest that ferroptosis can play a pivotal role in tumor suppression, thus providing new opportunities for cancer therapy.

9. Plant based Helleborus, Mistletoe, Oleander

10. Low voltage electric field therapy—emerging treatment that is thought to selectively disrupt multiple cancer cell processes while sparing healthy cells.

Immunotherapy

1. Ralph Moss one—hour film-history of immunotherapy/review of current alternative clinics administering immunotherapy. https://www.themossreport.com/immunotherapy-the-battle-within-a-film-by-the-moss-report/

2. Cancer Research Institute — Mission is to "Save more lives by fueling the discovery and development of powerful immunotherapies for all cancers." https://www.cancerresearch.org/ Site has a clinical trial finder: https://cri.careboxhealth.com

3. Most common categories of immunotherapy treatments:

   - Monoclonal antibodies and checkpoint inhibitors — Made in a lab, these antibodies slow or stop the growth of abnormal proteins in cancer cells. The goal is to alter the cancer cells so they are no longer able to "trick" the body into thinking they're healthy cells so they can keep growing. This is the most commonly approved type of immunotherapy at this time.

- T-cell therapy (CAR T-cell therapy) — The patient's own T-cells (immune system cells that fight infection) are removed from the blood. Next, a lab-created receptor is added to the T-cells, which are put back in the body. The receptors are able to identify cancer cells and destroy them.

- Cancer vaccines — Treatment vaccines are still mostly in the research phase to see how they can use the body's immune system to identify and destroy specific types of cancer cells. A common approach is a dendritic cell vaccine. Here a patient's dendritic cells are loaded with a tumor-specific antigen (a toxin or other foreign substance which induces an immune response) and reintroduced to the body, which allows the body to recognize and attack tumor cells. The same mRNA technology used in Pfizer/BionTech's Covid vaccine is now also being used to develop cancer vaccines.

- Oncolytic virus therapy — Oncolytic viruses are those that are nonpathogenic to healthy cells but infect cancer cells, prompting a broader immune reaction.

Integrative Clinics/Treatment Options

1. Moss Report has extensive evaluation of a global selection of clinics. https://www.themossreport.com/category/doctors-and-clinics/choosing-a-clinic/

2. Chemothermia — Istanbul, Turkey. This is the Clinic Jackie used for six months and had good success. https://chemothermia.com

3. The Block Center – Chicago, IL. https://blockmd.com

4. Cancer Center for Healing – Irvine, CA. https://cancercenterforhealing.com/cancer-care/

5. The Center for Advanced Medicine – Atlanta, GA. https://tcfam.com/

6. Advanced Medical Therapeutics – Boca Raton, FL. https://www.amtcare.com/

Testing

1. RGCC — This blood test analyzes circulating tumor cells and cancer stem cells to determine which chemo and non-chemo treatments will be most effective for a given cancer profile. https://rgcc-international.com/

2. Nagourney Cancer Institute — Offers testing of cancer cells to identify the most effective chemotherapy treatments. www.nagourneycancerinstitute.com

3. Consultative Proteomics — Evaluates tumor biology to determine most effective treatments. https://med.uth.edu/pathology/clinical-services/consultative-proteomics/ Dr. Robert Brown: Robert.Brown@uth.tmc.edu

4. Guardant — Blood (liquid biopsy) test that analyzes circulating tumor DNA (ctDNA) to provide comprehensive genomic profiling, or tumor mutation profiling, for all solid tumors. It is used by healthcare professionals to detect actionable cancer biomarkers in a patient's blood that may help inform their therapy selection. https://guardanthealth.com/

APPENDIX TWO

Eulogies from Jackie's Memorial Service, January 7, 2023

Rhonda George Laurencelle

My name is Rhonda George Laurencelle, and Jackie and I were cousins. Our fathers were related, and our mothers are close friends. I'm honored to speak about her today and share a little about the imprint she left on me and on this world.

As kids, we are often defined by numbers. Homeroom numbers, soccer jersey numbers...then eventually GPA numbers, class ranking numbers, SAT numbers, number of published articles, number of social media followers, number of clients or number of dollars.

It was impossible to think about Jackie in this way...she always topped the numbers! Highest GPA, top of her class ranking, near perfect SAT scores, scientist, successful business developer, prolific writer, client manager. And...so beautiful...inside and out. And kind. And inclusive. And *funny*. **I mean, she just wasn't like us.** And as kids, you could see...she was special...that girl was going places...and she did.

Jackie and I spent time together in Boston when we were in grad school. She was so determined and focused. I'd try to get her to come to the bar with us and hang out, but she never did. We ate together often—that shouldn't surprise many of you. We were both foodies. Sometimes I'd try to bring the party to her by inviting friends to dinner or playing little tricks on her. We laughed a lot and had fun, but her life was definitely more work than play.

Over the years, I watched Jackie's focus shift from all *studies and work* to being all about *love and acceptance*. Sophie and Grant, *you did that*. You changed your mom's life and her entire perspective on living. I know for sure she is sitting right next to you.

For all of your days, she will flank your side. Be open to the signs because she is already sending them. She is fiercely protecting you, especially at this very moment. She has the ability to guide you more now that she ever did on this earth—after losing my father and my brother, I can say this with 100% certainty and confidence. Make no mistake, your mom is right here.

And for you John, several people commented over the past couple of years how Jackie taught us how to live and also how to die. I agree. But what I also believe, is that you taught us *how to be a true partner and how to love*. Watching the way you cared for each other was a gift. Thank you for that.

Jackie and I were relatives, we spent time in Boston together, we shared a cancer diagnosis, and similar careers. But setting all of that aside, our real bond was based on the fact that we just "got" each other. I don't know how to describe it, other than I just really loved her feistiness. She was SASSY. And when I think of Jackie, that's the first thing that comes to mind. She was just so real.

As a woman so accomplished and so mature, with an extensive vocabulary, it was fascinating that she just couldn't find a word more fitting at times than the "F" word. It was so funny to hear her speak like that! And honestly just like everything else in her life, she was actually really good at cursing. I loved that about her, and I'm pretty sure I egged her on. We would complain about the rigid and outdated medical industry or the archaic treatment of cancer, or physicians who think they know better...really anyone who wasn't using logic and who got in the way of common-sense health. There were a lot of "WTFs" in our texts, "dumb - - s," and telling people to go to "H - - -," a certain place I probably shouldn't be mentioning in a church. **But in all seriousness, Jackie was more inter-**

ested in being honest and real, than in being a good little girl. And I loved that about her most of all.

She wasn't afraid to speak the truth. And she was just so darned transparent about it. When people wanted to visit her last fall, she said to me, "Rhonda, do you want visitors when you have the flu? No. So why do people think you want visitors when you're dying?" Yeah—we totally get that. And we needed that reminder. Thanks, Jackie.

Jackie had her priorities straight. Her heart was huge, and she understood the most important lessons in life. Knowing her, she is already at the top of her class. Jackie will always be a great source of guidance, support, and strength for each one of us. My heart is warmed to know that she will forever be in our lives. I feel so blessed to have had the opportunity to walk with her. ◉

Susan Colby

John, Sophie, Grant, Jackie's mother Barbara, and brother Michael, family, and friends,

My name is Susan Colby. I am absolutely honored to stand here today to help remember and celebrate the most wonderful, the most beautiful, the most brilliant, Jackie.

Jackie was an extraordinary woman, leader, teacher, wife, mother, daughter, sister and friend.

I remember the day at work when Jackie and I first met...around 25 years ago. Have you ever met someone and said: I just need to know this person? How can I find a way to share time with her while we are both on this planet?

Jackie had that energy, that mind, that smile, and...oh that laugh. Recently, she reminisced about a time together many years ago. We were departing from a client dinner and I said, "Jackie, you were effervescent this evening." And she really was. She told me that she tried to remember that moment on some of her tougher days. And isn't that Jackie? Enthusiastic, bubbly, brilliant. And holding on to all that strength and energy, even when she has the biggest battles to fight.

Jackie lived fully—ideas and hope were abundant. I think of her when I hear the beautiful Tracy Chapman lyrics from the song, "Dreaming On a World."

We must always be thinking of a world as a place of infinite possibilities. Toss our coins in the fountain. Look for clovers in grassy lawns. Search for shooting stars in the night. Cross our fingers and dream on.

That's Jackie.

Jackie and I were lucky enough to be part of each other's professional journeys for the past 25 years...and maybe even more fortunate to have been present for so many of each other's important life events. I remember when Jackie met John and "tested" him by playing golf together (and besting him on the course...of course). It was all by design—to see how he would handle losing (and to a girl, no less)! As you all know, John passed the test...with flying colors!

I was fortunate to witness John and Jackie's wedding. I had a wonderful visit to Cleveland after the birth of Jackie and John's first child, Sophie, and a full family Covid-safe backyard visit with Jackie, John, Sophie, Grant and Rocky during pre-vaccine Covid days. Jackie attended our daughter's bat mitzvah in California...and visited our home on a work trip, when our girls were little. We will never forget Jackie jumping on the trampoline in her full-on professional attire—a dress and hose!

As I suspect most of you know, Jackie's work on empathy is extraordinary, ahead of its time, and will last. Ditto for her work on empathetic cancer treatment. It is deep and thoughtful, with no holds barred. Her efforts have changed, and will continue to change, individual lives, institutions, and communities.

John, you and Jackie have created and nourished the most beautiful family and a strong and durable foundation for Sophie and Grant. All of us are here for you during this unbearable time and in the future. We love you and will do everything to remember Jackie well and keep her spirit alive.

Jackie, for a moment, I'm going to speak directly to you, as you sit with your dad on the other side. We did not leave anything unsaid. We had beautiful and honest time together. I know that you will always be with me, just floating above my right shoulder. Our time together in Istanbul was extraordinary. As you said, it was not the girls' trip we were imagining, but we were together all day, for days on end.

And I cherished our time together: I can see us sipping Turkish coffee and eating that sweet chocolate marshmallow on the banks of the Bosporus in Istanbul...and I remember simpler times walking on the beach in Santa Monica. We will take that trip to Namibia and bounce down the exquisite sand dunes on our bottoms. Know that I will always be here for John, Sophie and Grant. I love you so much and that will never end. Love and peace, Jackie. Thank you for all you have given me and so many others. There is a hole in my heart today, but so much of me is bigger and better because of you. ●

Kathryn Edelman

Good afternoon. I'm Kathryn Edelman and I am fortunate to have called Jackie my friend. Lucky to have had a front row seat to her brilliance for so many years.

As the incomparable Winston Churchill once said, "Courage is what it takes to both stand up and speak; courage is also what it takes to sit down and listen."

Jackie Acho did just that. She lived every aspect of her life with courage.

She was never afraid to stand up and speak. With her brilliant mind, brave heart, and incomprehensible ability to process information, Jackie was a true trailblazer filled with a passion for justice and teaching us a kinder, gentler way to right the many wrongs in today's world.

Be it the failure of Western medicine to cure her cancer, corporate leadership gone awry, or even bad soccer refereeing, Jackie would be the first to stand up and question, sit down and listen, dig deeper than anyone could ever dig on the subject and then, in the way only Jackie could—she'd pen an exceptional blog post, letter, or even more impressively, an entire book guiding us to implement positive change on the subject.

I am certain even Churchill would be impressed.

How could anyone not be impressed with Jackie Acho?

Strong, tenacious, inspiring, wise, intelligent, eloquent—just a handful of the literally hundreds of ways people described Jackie in the comments on her blog posts.

All true and fitting yet cannot even begin to adequately express each person's feelings behind their words—because that's what Jackie was so good at: making us feel—often in ways we didn't even know we were capable of.

Jackie and I met through our kids—way back when they all rode Mr. Taylor's bus 64 to Onaway Elementary School. And much like our kids, we connected quickly and bonded over the many things we had in common—namely our devotion to family, our soccer-geek husbands, our surprising ability to swear like sailors, and most importantly, our appetites for mouthwatering food and great cooking.

The cooking was a huge part of our love language—as we often prepared meals for each other when we needed it most—mastering delicious, nutritious and comforting recipes—even when we'd have to eliminate entire food groups. Honestly, until I met Jackie, I'd never met anyone who could match my enthusiasm for the simple perfection of a late-summer, salted tomato!

Jackie's energy was magnetic—whether we were discussing a book, shopping for the perfect dress, lamenting over politics, or dancing in the pouring rain at a summer party, she emanated joy and intensity.

But it was always Jackie's courage, with a drive to accompany it, that impressed me the most. It was simple immeasurable. She was never afraid to take the road less traveled. She could accomplish more in a day than most of us could in a month.

And even as her body began to betray her, her mind continued to fuel her with the energy to write—she was determined to finish the last chapters and edits of her new book—using her personal experience to promote change in the toxic culture of traditional cancer treatment.

Jackie's writing was cathartic for her, but her brave, willingness to share her story so that others might benefit was truly courage in action and certainly my definition of a superhero.

It doesn't seem possible to say goodbye to such a force, and it is truly my belief that Jackie's radiant energy is hovering around us right now.

So, Jackie, what I want to say to you is this:

You mattered, my friend. To me and to countless others—your life mattered. It still does. It always will. You made a difference. You led by example...and you blew us all away—every single day. Your inward and outward beauty dazzled us and your words and wisdom inspired us. You were a remarkable mother to Grant and Sophie, and wife to John and I know your legacy will live on through all that you shared with them and with us.

I don't believe any of that stops here. I won't believe this is goodbye. I am certain we will each connect with your energy when we need it most or even when we are not expecting it.

Personally, I'll look for you when I'm snowshoeing on my birthday, savoring the Indian food we both adored, swearing over a bad soccer call, and certainly in that first, delicious bite of that perfectly ripe tomato.

As I look out at all of you right now, I want to take a moment to appreciate the loving energy that is actually palpable here today.

We are all connected by our collective grief, but also by the love and respect we have for Jackie, John, Sophie, Grant, and even sweet Rocky.

Our hearts are hurting for all that we have lost, but our spirits are soaring with all that we've gained just being in Jackie's orbit.

It is my hope to honor Jackie's legacy by continuing to spread her "secret sauce." By tapping into our own "currency of empathy," we can make a difference by connecting and comforting one another—not only today while we are grieving, but moving forward into our everyday lives.

As Jackie taught us in her profound life's work, "Empathy is the missing link because it helps us be brave, work together, and move through change."

Let's make her proud. ●

Sharon Sobol Jordan

A brass band began to play, all of a sudden, right outside the amphitheater as the large Chautauqua audience listened, enthralled, to what Jackie had to say. Unfazed, she completed her talk on that warm August morning, and then brought Cleveland Police Commander Brandon Kutz to the stage to answer questions with her about empathy and policing. The Commander remarked to the capacity crowd, "I do a lot of public speaking, but I've never been so good that a band started playing while I was talking!" Remembering this moment at the City Club this October, he added: "A brass band should follow Jackie around everywhere she goes. When Jackie talks, that's what people hear."

I am Sharon Sobol Jordan. Jackie and I met over 15 years ago, and I think we both knew we had something special from the start. A mutual friend referred Jackie to me for an important project, and I hired her on the spot. At our first working session, Jackie and I both were excited—talking fast, hands flying—as the white-board filled with our ideas. In the midst of this, I turned to her and said, "I'm so glad that I picked you!" Without missing a beat, she turned to me and replied, "What makes *you* think you picked *me*?"

Jackie and I would go on to work on many exciting and innovative projects together. But I came to know her best as a friend. Over the past three years, we kept each other company, walking and talking in the woods every Sunday. We each would bring our "lists"—all the thoughts, ideas, and questions that didn't fit anyplace else during our week. We loved spending time together in it, figuring it all out as we went.

I miss keeping company with my friend, and I am grateful for all that she left behind.

Jackie lived a big life—a life of meaning, continuous learning, and growth—and she lived it out loud. We all were drawn to her and quickly disarmed by her sharp wit, easy laugh, abundant energy, entrepreneurial mind, and empathetic soul. She just sparkled!

When she started a conversation saying, "I need to tell you about a Jackie Unleashed moment," I knew I was in for a great story!

She modeled for us how to live life as a whole person. Her work, life, and love were fully integrated, particularly during these last few years, as her cancer journey seemed to unlock in her a whole new level of insight, creativity, power, and expression.

And she shared it all with us. She was so generous with her writing, speaking, podcasting, and posting. Telling her story as it was unfolding, she fascinated, delighted, challenged, and taught us so much, while at the same time—broke our hearts.

Why did she do it? We know that she was called to widely share her well-articulated "Currency of Empathy" approach. Jackie taught us that empathy is the ability to understand the feelings of another and have an appropriate emotional response. That growing her own superpower of empathy started—and always centered on—Sophie and Grant. That empathy is essential in both work and life, and particularly important in leadership. That empathy is the antidote to fear and that the opposite of fear is love, the ultimate expression of empathy and our humanity.

We know she was driven to co-create an inspired future. Jackie often quoted Madeleine L'Engle, who wrote, "A Wrinkle in Time," saying all true art is "channeling cosmos into chaos." This meant to Jackie that, "No matter what work you do, you can think of it as channeling a bit of heaven into life on earth. You will always be aligned with your mission in life if you do that," she told us.

Over the past three years, Jackie came to believe that her "job here is to go through hard things and articulate what needs to change about the system—*particularly, the health-*

care system—so that it won't be so hard anymore for others."

We know that she was extraordinarily heroic—while at the same time, a wife, mother, daughter, sister, and friend. She did an interview with a well-known podcaster just five months before she died where she described herself as "energy and love wrapped up in skin and bones." She told him that, at the moments she felt fear, she put her fear into words—written or spoken—because she found that the fear had less power when she got it out of her head. Jackie realized that she did not have to live in "big fear" of the future if she could focus only on what was happening in the present moment. "I share it with someone who can sit with it," she said, and "realize that this will pass. This feeling is not permanent and I will get beyond it." After the conversation, he titled the podcast, "The Bravest Person I Know—Jackie Acho."

In the end, I believe she did it all because she wanted to leave something meaningful and lasting behind, mostly for John, Sophie, and Grant. As she so eloquently put it, "Cancer has a way of chiseling away at a person, removing what doesn't really matter, leaving behind what does." And what mattered most to Jackie was spending precious time with her husband and kids, and others that allowed her to be authentic, including her beloved dog, Rocky.

Sophie and Grant, while I haven't spent much time with you, I feel like I know you so well. You were regular topics of detailed conversation on our weekly walks. Your mom loved and adored you so much. She so admired the people that you are and the inspired futures that you are creating. You centered her in ways that no one else could.

And John, of course, the Jackie we knew and loved would not have been possible without you. Another regular agenda item for our weekly walks. Having walked the path you are now on, there is so much I would like to say to you. But in this moment, I think Jackie said it best. In a blog post we wrote together, she described asking and hearing from me the story about before and after the death of my late husband Pat. I was so touched by how she wrote about that experience—she really got it. But re-reading it this week, I realized that she also wrote it for you, John. In her words, "Understanding Sharon's love for Pat also helped [me] understand what John carries, and how that love lives on with every memory, story, and feeling. Years don't diminish any of it...big loss is the price of big love."

In closing, Jackie and I often would talk of people that inspired us—particularly women.

One of those was Dolly Parton. The stories told by her lyrics brought Jackie a bit of comfort towards the end. In particular was the song, "If I Had Wings." Here's some of how it goes:

Oh, I've had my share of sorrow. Walked alone—alone down the road. I could have used a new tomorrow. If I had wings—I'd make it so. One cannot predict the future. One cannot undo the past. But we can make the present useful. Build the future that will last. If I had wings—I'd fly away. From all of my troubles—all of my wounds. And I would fly—'til I found freedom. If I had wings— If I had wings.

Thank you, my friend. Your lessons and your love continue to guide and inspire me and so many others. You live on in our hearts. ●

John LeMay

Good afternoon and thank you so much for being here — I know Jackie is rejoicing in seeing us all together.

Thank you to Kathryn, Rhonda, Susan, and Sharon for your wonderful remembrances.

Before I continue, I need to provide a warning — unfortunately the over/under on me keeping it together up here is about three minutes so this may be a team effort with Sophie, Grant, and [Rev.] Jeanne [Leinbach] ready to carry on as needed.

This won't surprise you, but Jackie provided some ground rules for this service — also not surprising is that rule number one was very empathetic, "Don't let it be too long — people shouldn't need to pee before it ends." We will do our best to meet her request.

First, I want to say thank you from the bottom of my heart and on behalf of Sophie and Grant. You all provided a powerful, loving, thoughtful counterweight to all the cruel sadness, grief, and pain that this journey entailed. You were all the good in the world on those days when all we could see was the bad. You allowed us to know we were cared for and loved in the moments Jackie and our family needed it most. We can never thank you enough.

You did all kinds of things — taking walks, traveling, cooking, supporting our children, walking the dog, sending flowers and kind notes and most importantly, just being present with Jackie and us through the journey. Thank you to all of Sophie and Grant's friends who so warmly and thoughtfully supported them through this journey, showing a level of maturity and empathy that was extraordinary—all your parents should be so proud.

Jackie was diagnosed almost three years ago. That has meant a long period during which we were supported by all of you. I'd like to mention a few people that made extraordinary efforts to support us

- Susan Colby – Thank you for the calls, the notes, the gifts—you knew just what to say and do, given your own journeys with cancer. Your travel from San Francisco to Istanbul was extraordinary.

- Sharon Sobol Jordan – Your Sunday walks with Jackie at the South Chagrin Reservation were such a highlight of her week—she always came back energized and with a brighter view of the world. She was nourished intellectually and emotionally, and of course we are grateful for your travel to Istanbul. Your visits during hospice care were a gift and I'm sure not easy given your own experience with cancer touching a loved one.

- Carnella Peck – You dropped everything to stay at our home and support Grant through the time we were in Turkey. You told us it was a blessing for you. And mind you, Carnella was living with a second semester high school senior who perhaps had a more robust social life than necessary. She even took on the after-prom sleepover—a duty no adult wants!

- Lisa and David Levine – You provided beautifully prepared meals, gifts, humor, gardening, and a swim, and were present in just the right way.

- Rhonda George Laurencelle – You provided great support to Jackie and your experience with cancer allowed you to connect with her in just the right way. It was also wonderful that you and your kids found a way to visit us in Istanbul.

- Jeanne Leinbach – You sat with me at the hospital while Jackie's initial surgery stretched to six then seven hours. You traveled to Istanbul and then also drove Jackie to Chicago for treatment and had a beautiful visit with

Jackie a few days before her passing. You were able to meet her where she was at every step of the journey.

- And finally, Kathryn Edelman – What didn't you do? She was with us on the terrible day in February 2020 when we learned of Jackie's diagnosis—immediately providing guidance on medical care given your personal experience with loved ones having ovarian cancer. She cooked her heart out for us—accommodating Jackie's many dietary restrictions and making incredible things that nourished her body and soul. The countless conversations where you met Jackie just where she was—sometimes sad, sometimes mad, sometimes depressed—just being with her through the journey which is incredibly difficult. You embody one of Jackie's favorite words, empathy, in every possible way.

- I could mention so many of you – Akua Saunders providing reiki treatment and prayer, Steff Hofner with the encouraging calls and frequent cards and gifts, Hallie Stewart with meals and looking after Grant, Heather Weingart organizing the meal train, Shelby Hersh with house call haircuts. Others that organized the Onaway school bus "drive by," put up Christmas lights, planned a surprise birthday party for Grant. My colleagues at Blue Point and portfolio company leadership who put up with my unreliable schedule, participation, and sometimes temperament. And of course, our families including Jackie's mother Barb and brother Mike, the extended Acho and Kittinger families, and my siblings who traveled to stay with Grant and when I reached out for help, responded, "It's an honor and privilege to help—you can't ask too much."

We are so grateful to all of you and can't thank you enough. A blessing of this journey is we got a front row seat to all the love and caring in the world.

The second thought I wanted to share may be a bit cliché, but I thought important. I wanted to share a moment from Jackie's journey that will hopefully help us all remember; nothing is guaranteed, and the small stuff really is the small stuff. We were reminded of this when during hospice, Jackie had to give a final hug to Grant before he returned to Villanova and Sophie before she returned to Spain. It was one of the saddest moments of the journey and made me reflect on the idea that the number of hugs we get is not guaranteed—they are a blessing to be savored and treasured. So perhaps one gift from Jackie's passing is a poignant reminder that the rich moments of love and connectedness that happen every day will at some point end. So maybe tuck that away and think about it each time you get that hug or other special moment—be in that moment and be grateful.

One last point before Sophie and Grant speak. I am generally an optimist—I try to find the good in most things—this journey has provided my ultimate challenge in that regard. It has been much easier to focus on the glass half empty part for the last three years. I've been told that over time one's grief about loss can evolve to gratitude for what you were given. In this case, for me, it was 25 years of something really, special. For our kids, 18 and 20 years. For some of you it may have been a short while, while for some of you it was much longer. Whatever time we did have with Jackie, we have so much to be grateful for—and today is a time to focus on all that good as it is a blessing that we can all celebrate. ●

Grant LeMay

As much as we may try, it is really hard to say that today is a celebration. Celebration connotes in my mind, feelings of joy and happiness. We're celebrating an amazing woman, but I think everyone here today feels the grief that comes with a celebration of this nature.

I expected to feel sad, to feel the hole in my heart that will follow me for the rest of my life. What I did not expect is the overwhelming feeling of pride that I have today. Proud as hell of my mom, who fought cancer as hard as she possibly could, and was truly the epitome of strength and bravery throughout every trial and tribulation the last three years brought. Proud of her for never being afraid to fight for her dreams, getting a PhD, writing two books, working in male-dominated fields and thriving, raising a family, and being a woman and mom I could look up to every day.

I'm proud of my sister, for surviving and thriving in college and then doing the same thing about 4,000 miles away from home, all the while her mom was dying. I'm proud of my dad, for being a pillar of stability in times when it felt impossible, and always putting his family before himself.

Our family will never be the same, but we wouldn't have survived without him, and I cannot overstate that enough. I'm proud of everyone for being here today, for recognizing that Jackie Acho was an amazing woman.

Many of you brought meals, gifts, flowers, talked to me when I needed it, hugged me when I was crying, and many of you have helped our family more than you can ever know. So thank you, thank you to everyone here today, for taking part in this journey, we truly could not have done it without you. ●

Sophie LeMay

My mom's beautiful friends, my brother, and my dad are tough acts to follow, and I only have a few things to add. She often told Grant and me that we surrounded ourselves with good people, and based on this room, I'd say we were led by example.

I first want to say that my parents' love is one of the greatest any of us have seen. I don't think my words will do much justice, so here are three of my favorite lines from the 100 reasons my Dad wrote up to share with my Mom when he proposed, all written on graph paper like a true finance man.

Number 2: The way you lay down on your carpet when you come home from traveling,

Number 45: You splash all over the bathroom when you wash your face, and

Number 100: You read People magazine.

For time's sake, I'll let those stand alone to support how clear their love was to everyone who saw it.

Secondly, though it's been said before, John LeMay is nothing short of a superhero. He's spent three years carrying the weight of impossible news after impossible news, flying across the world for six months, and has never in my life forgotten to switch my laundry to the dryer when I needed the favor. He did it all more gently and selflessly then you can imagine. This is another one where I can't quite put my gratitude and awe into words, so I'll leave it there.

Thirdly, we'll cover my mom's insane list of achievements and her infinite impact on people, but as her kid, those things didn't become part of my view of her until the last few years.

Instead, she was the best grocery shopper. She taught me to always pick produce from the back of the shelf and to help bag if the cashier was working solo. She hated clothes shopping, but taught me the value of staple pieces and gold jewelry, and never once made me question my body or my beauty.

Her unmatched persistence and brain carried me through my own health issues for years, and because of that, the two of us didn't quite get to have all the fun we wanted. Strangely enough, the last few months were the first time in my adult life that neither of us were trying to find health answers and fixes. We talked every day, about the signs she'd decided to send me, her time in Spain, the books she was reading and how boring it was to wait to die. She was one of my very best friends in the world and I'll miss her for too long to think about.

I finally cannot thank all of you enough. You have boosted us over and over when we couldn't quite go it alone and that's something I'll be here to repay for the rest of my life.

John LeMay

So, who was Jackie? A few things come to mind:

She had a unique set of talents to find in one person.

- **She had a rare intellect** with a special ability to see the world in large sweeping arcs and ideas and never got lost in the details. She loved to integrate big ideas and find a unique insight and then apply it. There is no better example than her work on empathy being applied to the Cleveland police—she could talk about empathy as a complex world-changing concept and in the next moment lead teams in helping police officers feel more engaged and better able to do their job.

- **She was a special communicator,** both as a speaker and writer.
  - Jackie loved public speaking and was at her best when the lights shined brightest. She had many speaking engagements including a TEDx talk, speaking at the Chautauqua Institution, and most recently as the 2022 Commencement speaker at John Carroll University.
  - Jackie was an excellent performer. She loved being on the stage, TV, or a podcast. But of all her great performances, the absolute best was the heroic performance she gave when having some of the hardest conversations you can have (telling your kids you have cancer). She was incredibly strong and thoughtful along every step. First letting them know something was not right, then sharing she had cancer, then cancer has come back, then the doctor has recommended hospice. She was always realistic but optimistic, gave enough information for them join us on the journey but not have it

take over their lives. And toward the end, she started an open dialog about facing death with dignity and grace. She shared she was not afraid of dying, had accomplished a lot, wished she could do more but had no regrets, would just miss watching them grow up but was confident she would do so, just from a different vantage point. She had all these conversations knowing the odds of surviving this cancer were very low.

- I always thought she was a great writer, but her cancer journey revealed a special, thoughtful, creative, and inspiring way of communicating. I remember sitting with her while she was on pain meds, getting an infusion with an IV in her arm and she said, "I just wrote a blog post—can you take a look?" That was the post sharing her difficult prognosis and our planned trip to Turkey—I thought it was extraordinary and after I read it sitting with her, through tears I asked how she did that. She said, "I write these in my head over time and then just type them out." I couldn't believe it.

• She also had some unexpected talents, belonging in the category of "these things don't go together." The PhD chemist from MIT and high school band geek was also a ringer in golf and billiards—taking down her husband when she felt the need.

She was also a person with strong passions.
- Cooking was an extraordinary passion and talent—she was the ultimate foodie. As many of you know, she had a severe cookbook addiction that was hard to manage—I think we have about 200 in our kitchen. I always found it remarkable that she could remember a meal from 10 years earlier and decide she was going to recreate it and then do so beautifully. When she was subject to a huge array of dietary restrictions, she took pride in her ability to "hack" a recipe—subbing out all the things she could not eat. She saw cooking as art and a way to take care of others—it was truly a love language for her.

- Music—we both loved to go see live music and I have fond memories of dancing at concerts in Chicago and here at Jacobs Pavilion at Nautica, House of Blues and Cain Park.

One of Jackie's dreams was to own the stage as a singer and if you ever saw her do "Proud Mary," the slow way, at karaoke, you would have seen she could really give Tina Turner a run for her money. The only problem was she couldn't sing. As you'd expect she committed to addressing this by taking singing lessons—she was even able to convince Karel Paukert, the extremely accomplished organist and choirmaster at St. Paul's Episcopal Church, to help her. Jackie was very excited for her first lesson and came to the choir room at St. Paul's. She settled in and Karel asked her to do a bit of singing so he could determine their starting point. Jackie sang a bit and Karel paused for a few minutes and then came to her, putting his hand on her shoulder, and in his distinctive Czech accent said, "Jackie, it is not time for singing lessons." Jackie, of course, then said, "Karel, I'm 45, when will be the time?!" So Jackie's dreams ended there but in a happy ironic twist, Sophie developed into a beautiful singer and Jackie was able to experience some of her dream through Sophie's beautiful performances.

But beyond her talents and passions, who was she really?
- **She had an infectious energy and enthusiasm** for people and things she cared about. When Jackie was excited about something, she was a force to be reckoned with. Her joy for life transmitted wherever she took her smile and ready laughter.

- **She was a wonderful partner in every way.** We were pretty close to perfectly aligned on all the things that really mattered. She was a wonderful thought partner and sounding board, a perfect co-parent and dinner companion. We were blessed with 25 years together. As Sophie noted, when I proposed to Jackie I wrote up a list of the reasons why I loved her, and the list only grew over our time together.

- **As a mother, she was equally extraordinary**, helping build an incredible foundation for our kids. We have been so richly blessed by Sophie and Grant and I attribute so much of who they are today to Jackie's efforts when they were quite young. Jackie stepped away from her career at McKinsey and Co. when she didn't feel that she could support the kids in the right way. A huge sacrifice and change to her life but she started her own business and capped her work at a few days a week so she could fully engage with the kids and enable me to continue with my career. She was at the center of helping the kids navigate whatever challenge arose and helping them grow and I am so grateful.

- **She saw people through a unique lens.** She was always ready to meet people where they were, to truly listen and understand. She didn't judge people based on their background or material trappings—if they had a good heart, she would embrace them. She was a great listener—she really could be present—really understanding what someone needed to share.

- **One way to summarize who Jackie was is to talk about how she handled her cancer diagnosis and treatment.** She attacked it like all her other passions—she was all in and determined to come up with a new path to help herself and others. I've never seen a more resilient person as she took on a bewildering array of often painful treatments and did so with incredible spirit. She was convinced if she had enough time, she really could have figured it out and I believe her. As many of you saw from reading her posts and blogs, she was passionate about rethinking cancer care in the most fundamental of ways. She railed against the common incrementalism and wrote with courage, passion, and insight about how things might be done better. (*That writing is published in this book titled, "Cancer Culture: Fixing the Landscape by Infusing Empathy."*) She hoped her writing will inspire a meaningful evolution in cancer care so that others in her position might have a very different experience.

- This quote from her, which I wrote down because it landed with me, summarizes who she was: "I can deal with the dying part but what really bothers me is the sadness and grief I will leave behind and that I will miss out on all the loving I want to do. There is so much left for me to do to try to help people. I wanted this cancer to have more meaning—I wanted to solve this problem for others." I found it remarkable that the "dying part" was well down on her list of concerns—well below worries about leaving others sad, not doing all the loving she wanted and not cracking the code on her super hard cancer.

Today is our moment to be grateful for the way Jackie brightened our lives, even if only for 54 years. We will always feel a bit cheated that she was taken from us at a young age but there is much to celebrate on this sad day. She leaves behind a wonderful and positive legacy through her work, her relationships, and her children.

One of Jackie's greatest hopes was that her work on empathy would change lives and in some small way, the world. She would love to know that all of you take some of her ideas with you and maybe share them with someone in your life. Perhaps the greatest final gift we could give her is extending her work a touch further into the world. If you enjoy her books, please write a review, and maybe gift it to someone that might enjoy it. Getting engagement on her books was one of her greatest joys and it will be one of her many legacies.

So, in closing I want to thank you all again for being here today and all your wonderful support.

Above all, we give thanks for the life of a woman we are so proud to call wife, mother, daughter, sister, and friend. The unique, the complex, the extraordinary, and irreplaceable Jackie whose beauty, both inside and outside, will never be extinguished from our minds.

I believe, that in some way, we will be together again, so all I will say is "bye for now" and rest in peace to my beautiful soulmate. ○

www.ingramcontent.com/pod-product-compliance
Lightning Source LLC
Chambersburg PA
CBHW030514080526
44586CB00011B/184